Mastering MICROSOFT PROJECT

A Comprehensive Guide from A to Z for Project Managers

Kiet Huynh

Table of Contents

Introduction 6
PART I Getting Started with Microsoft Project 8
   1.1 Understanding Project Management Concepts 8
      1.1.1. Introduction to Project Planning 8
      1.1.2. Key Project Management Terminologies 10
   1.2 Overview of Microsoft Project Interface 14
      1.2.1. Ribbon Interface Overview 14
      1.2.2. Workspace Customization Options 19
   1.3. Setting Up Your First Project 29
      1.3.1. Creating a New Project 29
      1.3.2. Project Information and Settings 39
PART II Navigating the Project Workspace 47
   2.1 Exploring the Ribbon Interface 47
      2.1.1. Tabs and Commands Overview 47
      2.1.2. Customizing the Ribbon 51
   2.2 Customizing the Quick Access Toolbar 56
      2.2.1. Adding and Removing Commands 56
      2.2.2. Quick Access Toolbar Settings 61
   2.3 Utilizing Views and Tables 66
      2.3.1. Understanding Different Views 66
      2.3.2. Customizing Views and Tables 70
      2.3.3. Using Filters and Groupings 73
PART III Creating and Managing Tasks 78
   3.1 Adding Tasks to Your Project 78
      3.1.1. Task Entry Methods 78
      3.1.2. Setting Task Properties 86

3.2 Organizing Tasks into Phases and Milestones 93
3.2.1. Creating Task Outlines 93
3.2.2. Defining Project Phases and Milestones 98
3.3 Linking and Unlinking Tasks 105
3.3.1. Task Dependencies Overview 105
3.3.2. Linking and Unlinking Tasks 108
3.3.3. Types of Task Relationships 112

PART IV Scheduling and Timeline Management 118
4.1 Understanding Task Dependencies 118
4.1.1. Types of Task Dependencies 118
4.1.1. Task Dependency Constraints 119
4.2 Adjusting Task Durations and Deadlines 123
4.2.1. Modifying Task Durations 123
4.2.2. Setting Task Deadlines 129
4.3 Managing Critical Paths 135
4.3.1. Identifying Critical Tasks 135
4.3.2. Optimizing Critical Path 140

PART V Resource Allocation and Management 146
5.1 Adding Resources to Your Project 146
5.1.1. Resource Types and Categories 146
5.1.2. Adding Resources to Resource Pool 149
5.2 Assigning Resources to Tasks 156
5.2.1. Resource Assignments Overview 156
5.2.2. Assigning Resources to Tasks 160
5.3 Tracking Resource Workloads 168
5.3.1. Resource Workload Analysis 168
5.3.2. Resource Leveling Techniques 171

PART VI Budgeting and Cost Management 177

TABLE OF CONTENTS

- 6.1 Estimating Project Costs 177
  - 6.1.1. Cost Estimation Techniques 177
  - 6.1.2. Cost Baseline and Contingency Planning 180
- 6.2 Tracking Expenses and Budgets 184
  - 6.2.1. Expense Tracking Methods 184
  - 6.2.2. Budget vs. Actual Analysis 188
- 6.3 Analyzing Cost Variances 193
  - 6.3.1. Cost Variance Calculation 193
  - 6.3.2. Cost Performance Index (CPI) Analysis 197

PART VII Reporting and Analysis **203**
- 7.1 Generating Project Reports 203
  - 7.1.1. Built-in Report Templates 203
  - 7.1.2. Custom Report Creation 217
- 7.2 Customizing Reports and Dashboards 221
  - 7.2.1. Report Customization Options 221
  - 7.2.2. Creating Dashboard Views 224
- 7.3 Analyzing Project Performance 233
  - 7.3.1. Key Performance Indicators (KPIs) 233
  - 7.3.2. Earned Value Management (EVM) Analysis 239

PART VIII Collaboration and Integration **243**
- 8.1 Sharing Projects with Team Members 243
  - 8.1.1. Collaborative Project Setup 243
  - 8.1.2. Sharing Options and Permissions 248
- 8.2 Integrating with Microsoft Office Suite 256
  - 8.2.1. Importing and Exporting Data 256
  - 8.2.2. Integration with Excel, Outlook, and SharePoint 259
- 8.3 Syncing with Project Management Tools 267
  - 8.3.1. Third-party Tool Integration 267

TABLE OF CONTENTS

8.3.2. Syncing with Agile and Kanban Tools 270

Conclusion 275

Introduction

Welcome to *"Mastering Microsoft Project: A Comprehensive Guide from A to Z for Project Managers."* In today's fast-paced and complex business environment, effective project management is essential for the success of any organization. With the increasing demand for timely delivery, cost efficiency, and quality assurance, project managers are continuously seeking tools and techniques to streamline their processes and enhance their project outcomes.

Microsoft Project stands as one of the most powerful and widely used project management tools available today. With its robust features and user-friendly interface, Microsoft Project empowers project managers to plan, execute, and monitor projects with precision and efficiency. However, harnessing the full potential of this tool requires comprehensive understanding and proficiency.

In this guide, we will take you on a journey from the fundamentals to the advanced features of Microsoft Project, providing you with the knowledge and skills necessary to become a proficient user. Whether you are a seasoned project manager looking to enhance your skills or a newcomer seeking to master project management software, this guide is designed to cater to your needs.

Throughout the following chapters, we will delve into various aspects of Microsoft Project, starting with the basics such as project creation and task scheduling. We will then progress to more advanced topics including resource management, cost tracking, and reporting. Each chapter will be accompanied by practical examples, tips, and best practices to reinforce your learning and facilitate real-world application.

By the end of this guide, you will not only be proficient in using Microsoft Project but also equipped with the insights and strategies to effectively manage projects of any scale or complexity. Whether you are managing a small team or overseeing large-scale projects, the *principles and techniques covered in this guide will empower you to deliver successful outcomes consistently.*

So, without further ado, let us embark on this journey to mastering Microsoft Project and unlocking the full potential of your project management endeavors. Whether you're a novice or an experienced practitioner, there's something valuable here for everyone. Let's dive in!

PART I
Getting Started with Microsoft Project

1.1 Understanding Project Management Concepts

1.1.1. Introduction to Project Planning

Project planning is the cornerstone of successful project management. It involves the systematic organization and delineation of project objectives, tasks, resources, timelines, and deliverables to achieve project goals efficiently and effectively. In this section, we'll delve deeper into the fundamental concepts of project planning and explore the essential steps involved.

The Importance of Project Planning:

Project planning lays the foundation for project success by providing a roadmap for project execution and control. It enables project managers to anticipate potential challenges, allocate resources strategically, mitigate risks, and ensure alignment with stakeholders' expectations. Effective project planning enhances communication, collaboration, and decision-making throughout the project lifecycle.

Key Components of Project Planning:

1. Defining Project Objectives: Clearly defining project objectives is essential for setting the direction and scope of the project. Objectives should be specific, measurable, achievable, relevant, and time-bound (SMART), providing a clear understanding of what the project aims to accomplish.

2. Creating Work Breakdown Structure (WBS): The WBS breaks down the project scope into manageable tasks, subtasks, and deliverables, facilitating a hierarchical structure for organizing and tracking project activities. It serves as a visual representation of the project's scope and enables effective task allocation and resource management.

3. Estimating Time and Resources: Accurate estimation of time, effort, and resources required for each task is crucial for developing realistic project schedules and budgets. Techniques such as expert judgment, analogous estimation, parametric estimation, and three-point estimation help in predicting task durations and resource needs.

4. Developing Project Schedule: The project schedule outlines the sequence of tasks, dependencies, durations, and milestones required to complete the project within the specified timeframe. Tools such as Gantt charts, network diagrams, and critical path analysis assist in visualizing and managing the project schedule effectively.

5. Identifying and Managing Risks: Risk identification involves identifying potential threats and opportunities that may impact the project's success. Risk assessment, analysis, and response planning help in proactively addressing risks and minimizing their impact on project outcomes.

6. Defining Communication and Stakeholder Engagement: Effective communication is essential for keeping stakeholders informed, engaged, and aligned with project goals and progress. Establishing a communication plan, defining communication channels, and engaging stakeholders throughout the project lifecycle foster collaboration and support.

7. Establishing Quality Management Processes: Quality management encompasses processes and activities to ensure that project deliverables meet predefined quality standards and customer requirements. Quality planning, assurance, and control mechanisms help in identifying, preventing, and addressing quality issues throughout the project.

8. Creating Project Documentation: Documentation serves as a repository of project information, including project plans, schedules, budgets, risk registers, and status reports. Clear and comprehensive documentation ensures transparency, accountability, and knowledge transfer within the project team and stakeholders.

Best Practices for Effective Project Planning:

1. Engage Stakeholders Early: Involve key stakeholders in the project planning process from the outset to gain their buy-in, insights, and support. Collaborative stakeholder engagement fosters alignment, commitment, and ownership of project outcomes.

2. Iterative Planning Approach: Adopt an iterative planning approach that allows for flexibility and adaptation to changing project requirements and dynamics. Continuously review and refine the project plan based on new information, lessons learned, and stakeholder feedback.

3. Use of Project Management Tools: Leverage project management tools and software, such as Microsoft Project, to streamline the planning process, automate repetitive tasks, and enhance collaboration and communication among project team members.

4. Regular Monitoring and Control: Establish monitoring and control mechanisms to track project progress, identify deviations from the plan, and take corrective actions as needed. Regular progress reviews, status updates, and performance metrics enable timely decision-making and course corrections.

5. Document Lessons Learned: Document lessons learned throughout the project planning process to capture insights, best practices, and areas for improvement. Reviewing and sharing lessons learned with the project team and stakeholders contribute to continuous learning and process improvement.

Conclusion:

Project planning is a critical phase in the project management lifecycle, laying the groundwork for project success. By understanding the key concepts and best practices of project planning, project managers can effectively navigate the complexities of project execution, mitigate risks, and deliver value to stakeholders. In the subsequent sections, we will explore the practical application of project planning principles using Microsoft Project, empowering project managers to plan, execute, and control projects with confidence and proficiency.

1.1.2. Key Project Management Terminologies

In the realm of project management, a robust understanding of key terminologies is paramount to effectively communicate, plan, execute, and monitor projects. This section aims to elucidate the essential terminologies commonly used in project management and their significance in facilitating project success.

1. Project Scope: The project scope defines the boundaries, objectives, deliverables, and requirements of a project. It outlines what is included and excluded from the project, providing clarity and alignment among stakeholders regarding project expectations and outcomes.

2. Work Breakdown Structure (WBS): The WBS is a hierarchical decomposition of the project scope into smaller, more manageable work packages or tasks. It serves as a foundational tool for organizing, planning, and tracking project activities, enabling effective resource allocation and task assignment.

3. Project Milestone: A project milestone represents a significant event or achievement within the project timeline, marking key stages of progress or completion. Milestones provide checkpoints for monitoring project advancement and serve as motivational markers for the project team.

4. Critical Path: The critical path is the longest sequence of dependent tasks in a project that determines the minimum duration required to complete the project. Tasks on the critical path have zero slack or float, meaning any delay in these tasks will directly impact the project's overall timeline.

5. Task Dependency: Task dependency refers to the logical relationships between tasks in a project, dictating the sequence and precedence of task execution. Common types of task dependencies include finish-to-start, start-to-start, finish-to-finish, and start-to-finish relationships.

6. Resource Allocation: Resource allocation involves assigning available resources, including personnel, equipment, and materials, to specific project tasks or activities.

Effective resource allocation ensures optimal utilization of resources and helps prevent overallocation or underutilization of resources.

7. Stakeholder Management: Stakeholder management encompasses the identification, analysis, and engagement of individuals or groups with vested interests or influence in the project. It involves fostering positive relationships, addressing stakeholders' concerns, and ensuring alignment with project objectives and outcomes.

8. Risk Management: Risk management involves identifying, assessing, and mitigating potential threats or opportunities that may impact the project's success. It includes risk identification, risk analysis, risk response planning, and risk monitoring and control throughout the project lifecycle.

9. Project Constraints: Project constraints are factors that limit the project's ability to achieve its objectives within the specified constraints of time, cost, and scope. Common project constraints include budgetary limitations, resource constraints, and regulatory requirements.

10. Baseline: A project baseline is a reference point or snapshot of the project's initial scope, schedule, and budget against which actual performance is measured and compared. Baselines provide a benchmark for tracking project progress and assessing deviations from the original plan.

11. Change Management: Change management involves the systematic approach to managing changes to project scope, schedule, and resources throughout the project lifecycle. It includes processes for change identification, evaluation, approval, and implementation to minimize disruptions and maintain project integrity.

12. Communication Plan: A communication plan outlines the strategies, channels, and frequency of communication to effectively disseminate project information to stakeholders. It ensures clear, timely, and relevant communication among project team members and stakeholders to promote collaboration and alignment.

Conclusion:

Mastering key project management terminologies is essential for project managers to effectively communicate, plan, and execute projects. By understanding these terminologies and their significance, project managers can navigate the complexities of project management with confidence and proficiency. In the subsequent sections, we will explore practical applications of these concepts using Microsoft Project, empowering project managers to harness its capabilities for successful project delivery.

1.2 Overview of Microsoft Project Interface

1.2.1. Ribbon Interface Overview

Structure of the Ribbon Interface

The Ribbon interface comprises tabs, groups, and commands, meticulously organized to streamline project management tasks. Let's dissect each of these components:

1. Tabs: Tabs are the primary navigation elements of the Ribbon. Each tab represents a distinct set of commands related to specific project management aspects. In Microsoft Project, the default tabs include tasks, resources, project, view, format, and others. These tabs encapsulate related functionalities, simplifying the user's workflow.

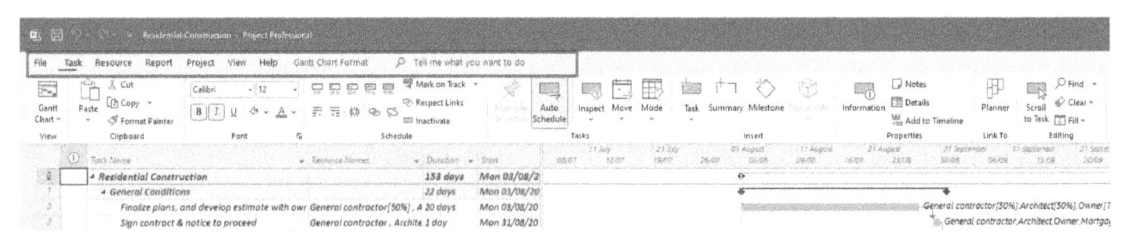

2. Groups: Within each tab, commands are further categorized into groups based on their functionalities. For instance, in the "Tasks" tab, you may find groups such as "Task," "Schedule," "Properties," etc. Grouping commands logically enhances user experience by presenting them in contextually relevant clusters.

3. Commands: Commands are the individual tools or functions available within each group. These commands enable users to perform specific actions or operations related to project management. Examples of commands include "Add New Task," "Assign Resource," "Change Task Duration," and so forth.

PART I: GETTING STARTED WITH MICROSOFT PROJECT

Navigating the Ribbon

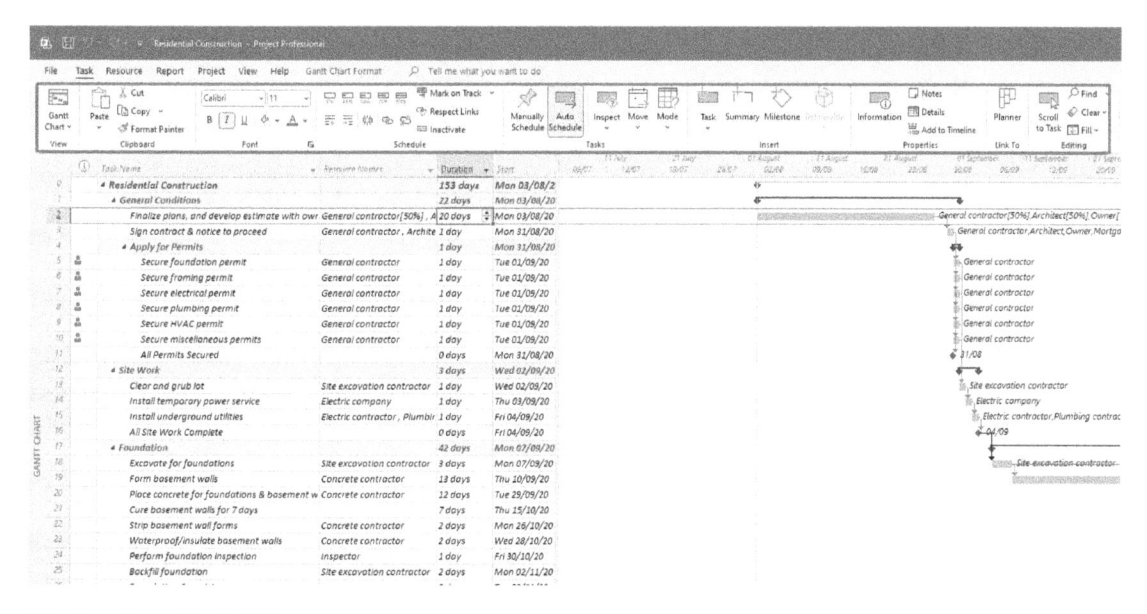

Navigating the Ribbon is intuitive, allowing users to swiftly access desired commands. Here's a brief guide on how to navigate the Ribbon effectively:

1. Tab Selection: To switch between different tabs, simply click on the tab name. Each tab corresponds to a specific aspect of project management, offering a tailored set of commands.

2. Group Navigation: Within each tab, navigate through different groups by clicking on the group names. This action reveals a cluster of related commands associated with the selected group.

3. Command Execution: Execute commands by clicking on the respective command buttons within the groups. Alternatively, some commands may feature drop-down menus or dialog boxes for additional options and settings.

Page 15 | 276

4. Keyboard Shortcuts: For power users, mastering keyboard shortcuts can expedite task execution. Most commands within the Ribbon interface have associated keyboard shortcuts for quick access. Learning and utilizing these shortcuts can significantly enhance productivity.

Customizing the Ribbon

One of the standout features of the Ribbon interface is its flexibility for customization. Users can personalize the Ribbon according to their preferences and workflow requirements. Here's how you can customize the Ribbon:

1. Customizing Tabs: Microsoft Project allows users to add, remove, or rearrange tabs to tailor the Ribbon layout. This enables users to prioritize frequently used functionalities and hide irrelevant tabs, thereby optimizing workspace efficiency.

2. Modifying Groups and Commands: Within each tab, users can customize groups by adding, removing, or reordering them. Similarly, individual commands can be added to custom groups or removed from the Ribbon altogether. This granular level of customization empowers users to create a personalized environment aligned with their specific needs.

3. Quick Access Toolbar: In addition to the Ribbon, users can leverage the Quick Access Toolbar to access frequently used commands effortlessly. This toolbar resides above the Ribbon and can be customized with preferred commands for quick access, further enhancing user convenience.

4. Keyboard Shortcuts Customization: Advanced users can customize keyboard shortcuts to streamline their workflow further. Microsoft Project allows users to assign or modify keyboard shortcuts for specific commands, facilitating rapid task execution.

Microsoft Project offers customization options to tailor the Ribbon according to your preferences and workflow requirements. Here's how you can customize the Ribbon:

Customizing Tabs:

To add, remove, or rearrange tabs, right-click on the Ribbon and select "Customize the Ribbon." From there, you can customize the layout to prioritize frequently used functionalities.

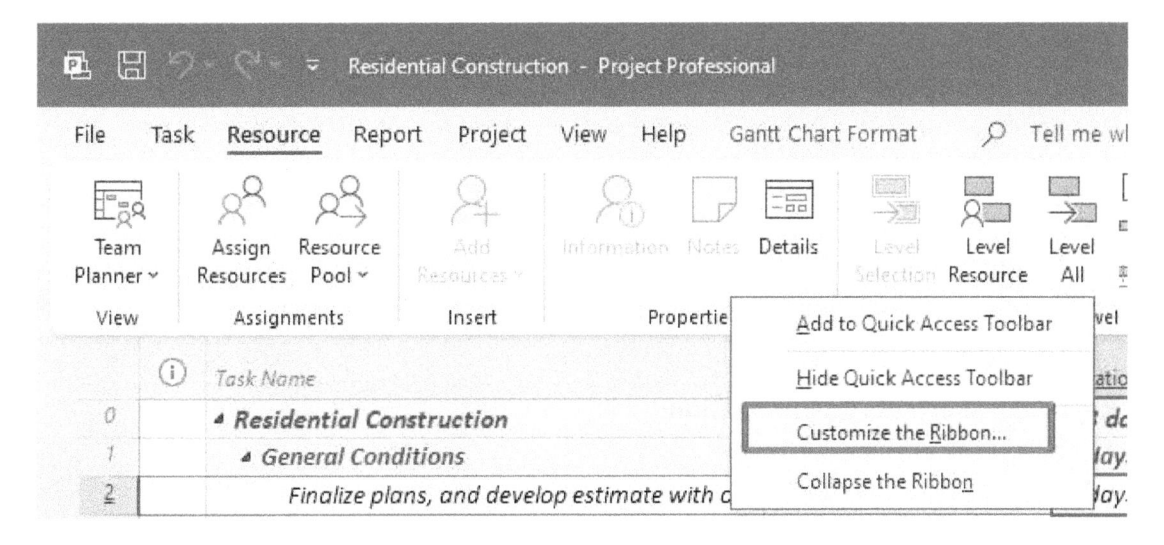

Modifying Groups and Commands:

Within each tab, right-click on the Ribbon and choose "Customize the Ribbon." Here, you can add, remove, or reorder groups and commands to create a personalized workspace.

Quick Access Toolbar:

Customize the Quick Access Toolbar located above the Ribbon by clicking on the dropdown arrow and selecting "More Commands." Add frequently used commands to the toolbar for quick access.

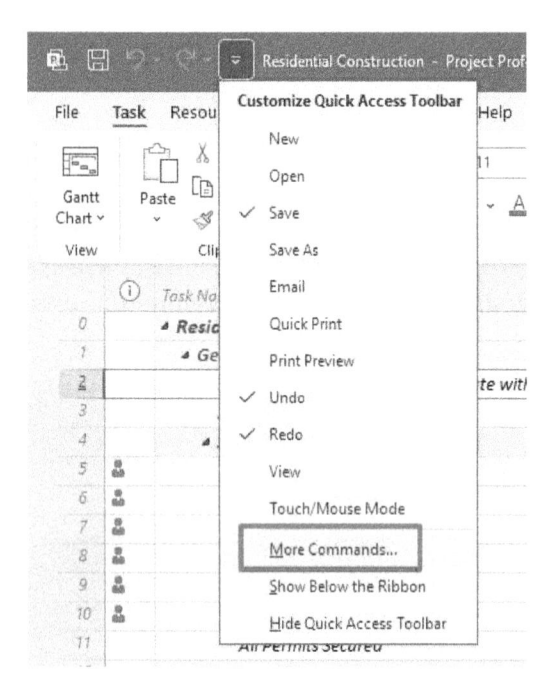

Keyboard Shortcuts Customization:

To customize keyboard shortcuts, go to File > Options > Customize Ribbon. Here, you can assign or modify keyboard shortcuts for specific commands, further streamlining your workflow.

By following these step-by-step instructions, you can navigate and customize the Ribbon interface in Microsoft Project with ease, optimizing your project management workflow.

Conclusion

In conclusion, the Ribbon interface is a cornerstone of Microsoft Project, serving as a centralized hub for project management operations. Its structured layout, comprising tabs, groups, and commands, simplifies navigation and enhances user experience. By understanding the Ribbon's structure, navigating its components, and leveraging customization options, project managers can optimize their workflow and achieve greater efficiency in managing projects using Microsoft Project.

1.2.2. Workspace Customization Options

Workspace customization in Microsoft Project is essential for tailoring the software to meet the specific needs of your project and your team. By customizing the workspace, you can streamline processes, increase efficiency, and ensure that the interface displays the information most relevant to your project management tasks. In this section, we'll delve into the various customization options available in Microsoft Project and how you can leverage them to optimize your project management experience.

Customizing the Ribbon

The Ribbon interface in Microsoft Project provides access to various commands and functions organized into tabs and groups. While the default Ribbon configuration may suit many users, customizing it can enhance productivity by placing frequently used commands within easy reach.

To customize the Ribbon:

1. *Click on the File tab:* This opens the Backstage view.

2. *Select Options:* This opens the Project Options dialog box.

3. *Choose Customize Ribbon:* Here, you'll see a list of tabs on the right side representing the Ribbon.

4. *Modify Tabs and Groups:* You can customize existing tabs and groups or create new ones by selecting commands from the list on the left and adding them to the desired tab or group on the right.

5. *Rename Tabs or Groups:* To make the Ribbon more intuitive, you can rename tabs or groups by right-clicking on them and selecting Rename.

PART I: GETTING STARTED WITH MICROSOFT PROJECT

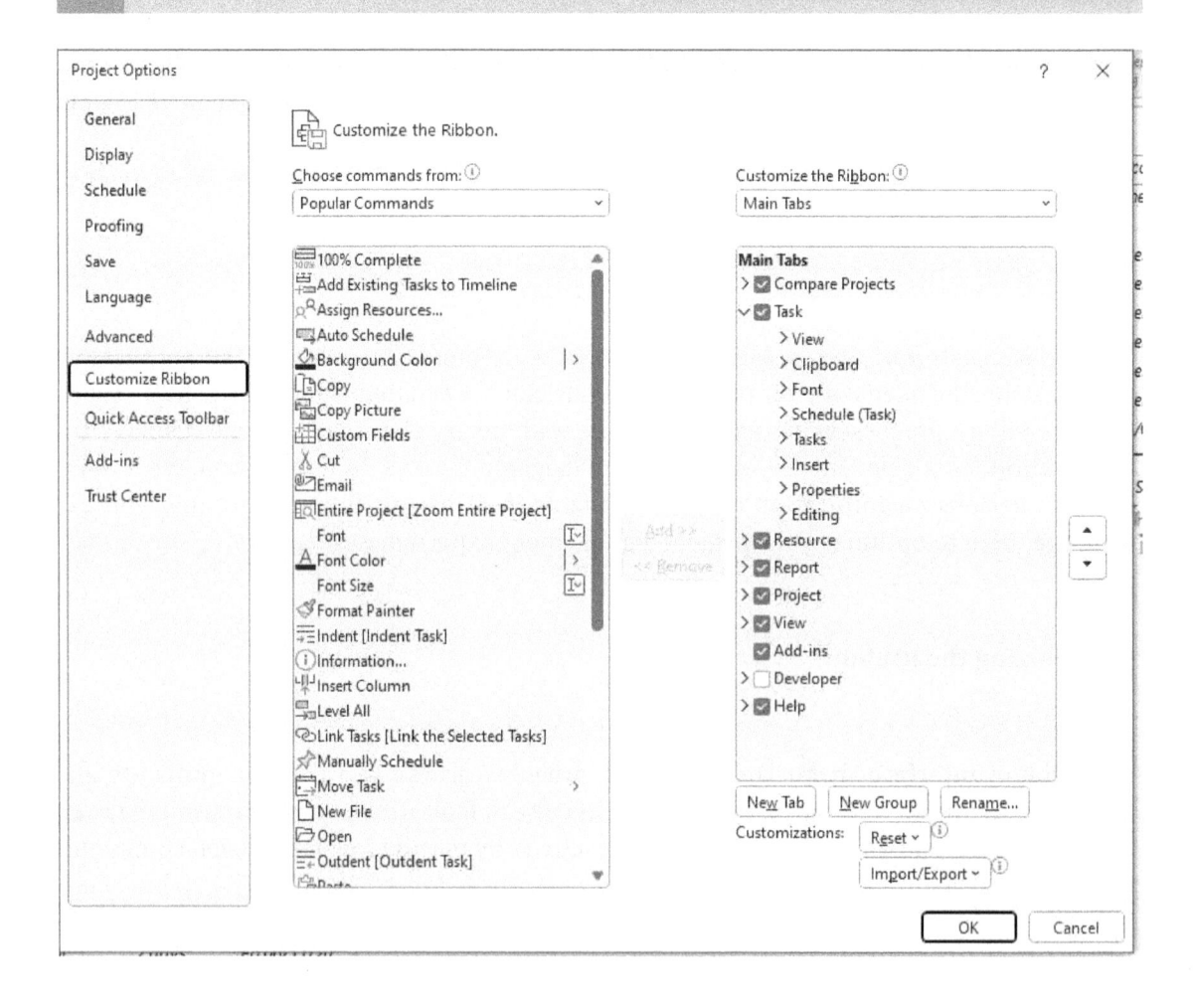

By customizing the Ribbon, you can ensure that the most frequently used commands are easily accessible, saving time and improving workflow efficiency.

Tailoring Views

Microsoft Project offers various views to visualize project data, such as Gantt Chart, Task Usage, Resource Sheet, and more. Customizing these views allows you to focus on specific aspects of your project, hide irrelevant information, and present data in a format that best suits your needs.

To customize views:

1. Navigate to the View tab: Here, you'll find a variety of view options.

2. Select the desired view: Choose the view you want to customize from the View tab.

3. Modify the view: You can adjust the view settings, such as adding or removing columns, applying filters, grouping tasks or resources, and adjusting the timescale.

4. Save the customized view: Once you've tailored the view to your liking, you can save it for future use by clicking on the View tab, selecting the More Views dropdown menu, and choosing Save View.

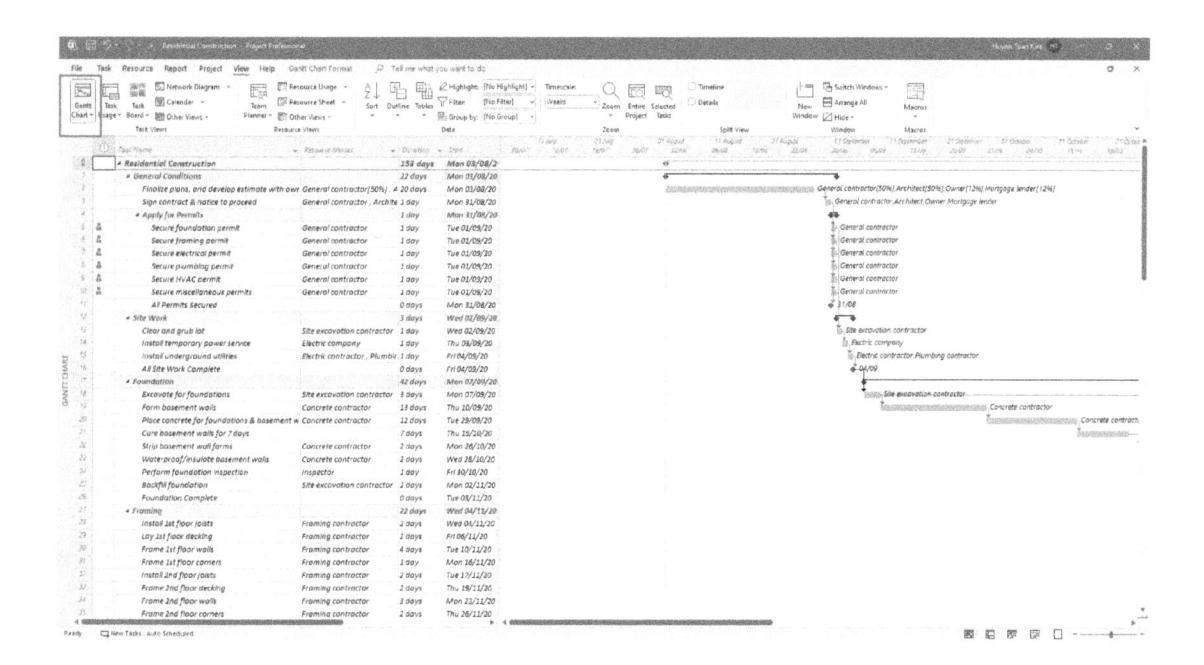

PART I: GETTING STARTED WITH MICROSOFT PROJECT

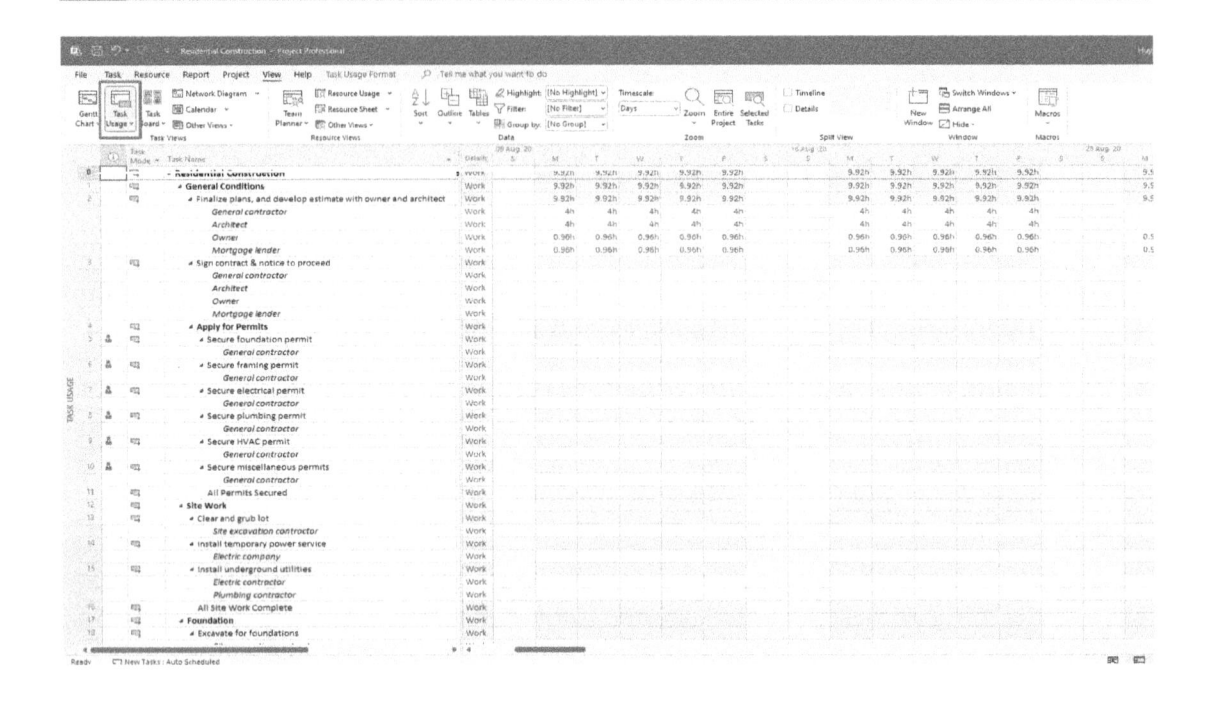

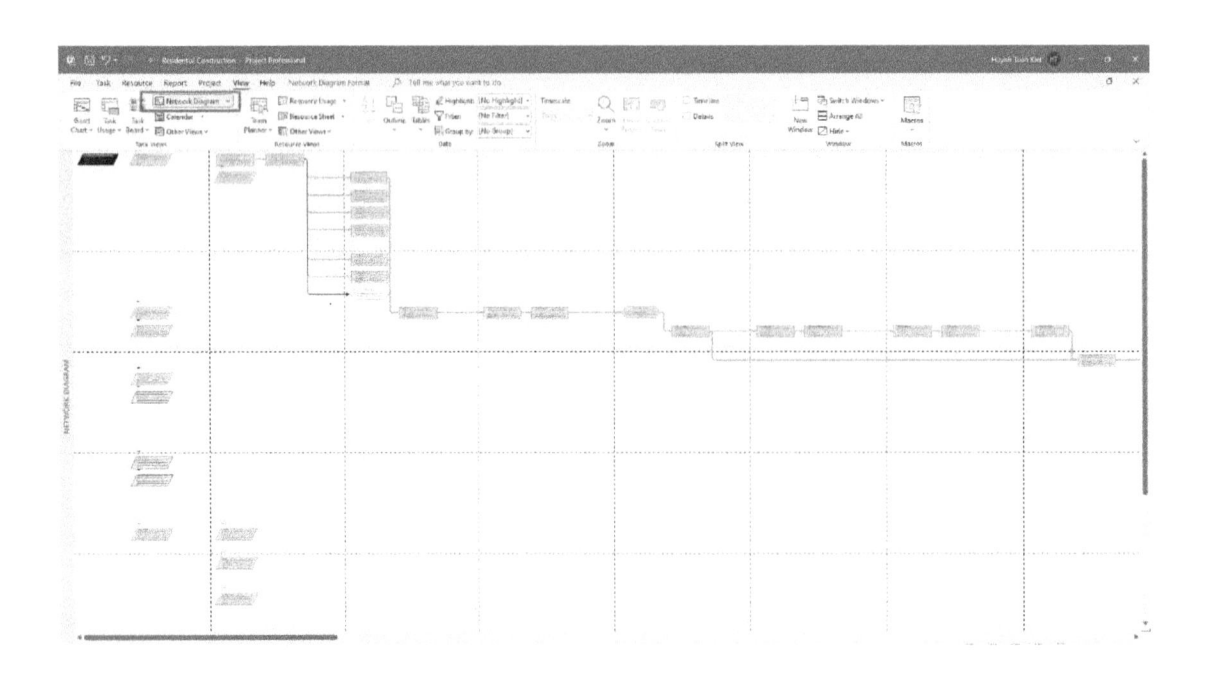

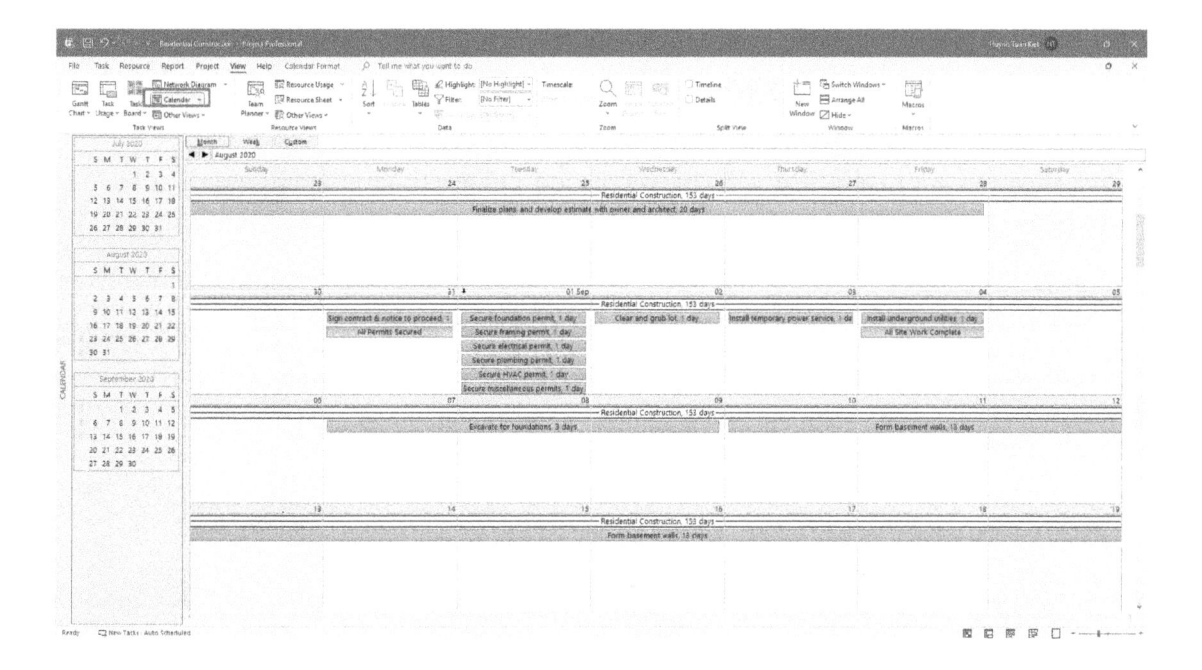

Customizing views allows you to focus on the information that matters most to you, improving clarity and aiding decision-making.

Personalizing Quick Access Toolbar

The Quick Access Toolbar (QAT) provides quick access to commonly used commands, regardless of which tab is currently selected in the Ribbon. Personalizing the QAT allows you to add frequently used commands for easy access.

To personalize the Quick Access Toolbar:

1. Click on the dropdown arrow at the end of the Quick Access Toolbar, located above the Ribbon.

2. Choose More Commands: This opens the Project Options dialog box with the Quick Access Toolbar tab selected.

3. Select commands to add: From the list on the left, choose the commands you want to add to the Quick Access Toolbar and click Add.

4. Modify the order: Use the up and down arrows to rearrange the order of commands on the Quick Access Toolbar.

5. Customize icon display: You can choose to display icons only, text only, or both icons and text for added clarity.

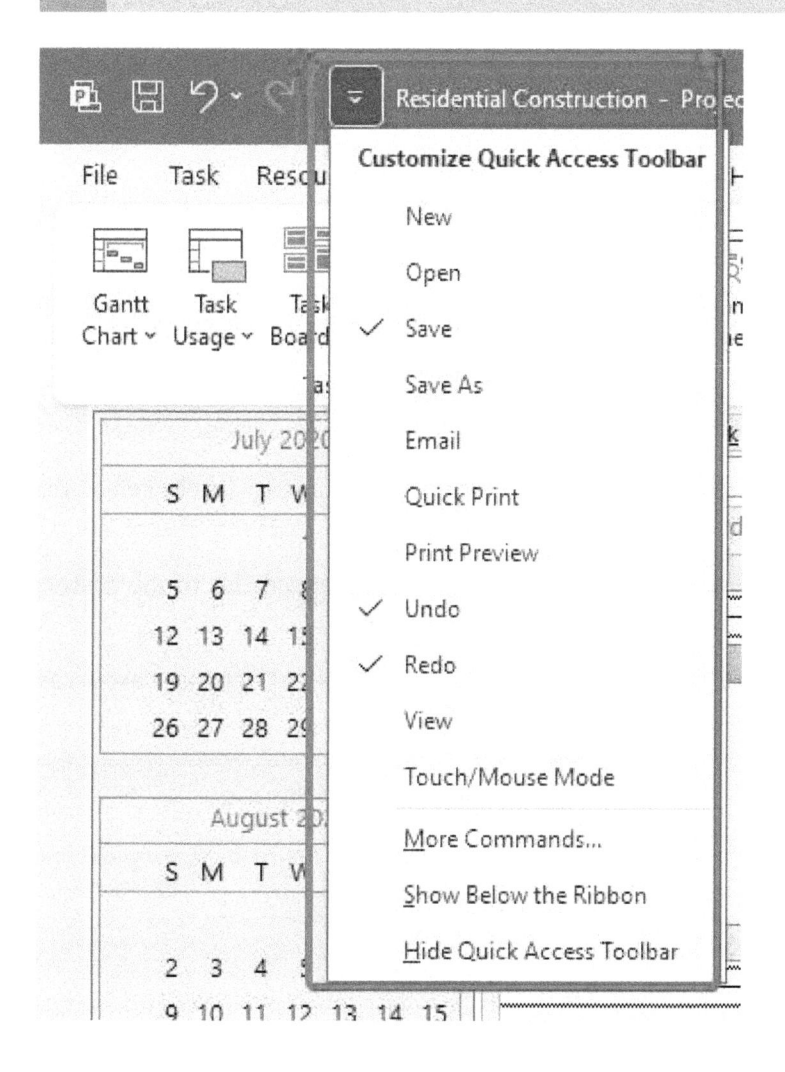

Personalizing the Quick Access Toolbar ensures that essential commands are always within reach, regardless of which tab is active in the Ribbon.

Creating Custom Fields

Custom fields allow you to add project-specific information that is not covered by the default fields in Microsoft Project. By creating custom fields, you can track additional data relevant to your project, such as project codes, customer information, or unique task attributes.

To create custom fields:

1. Navigate to the Project tab: Here, you'll find the Custom Fields option in the Properties group.

2. Select Custom Fields: This opens the Custom Fields dialog box.

3. Choose the field type: Depending on the type of data you want to track, select the appropriate field type, such as Text, Number, Date, or Flag.

4. Define field properties: Specify the name, data type, and other properties of the custom field.

5. Apply the custom field: Once created, you can apply the custom field to tasks, resources, or assignments by adding it to the appropriate table or form.

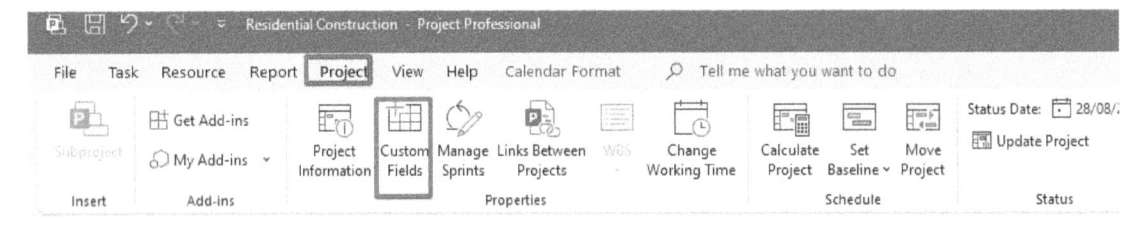

Creating custom fields allows you to tailor Microsoft Project to the specific requirements of your project, enhancing data tracking and analysis capabilities.

Utilizing Templates

Templates in Microsoft Project provide predefined structures and settings for common project types, saving time and effort in project setup. By utilizing templates, you can ensure consistency across projects and leverage best practices in project management.

To use templates:

1. Click on the File tab: This opens the Backstage view.

2. Select New: Here, you'll find a variety of templates categorized by project type.

3. Choose a template: Browse through the available templates and select the one that best matches your project requirements.

4. Customize as needed: Once the template is applied, you can customize it further to align with your specific project goals and preferences.

5. Save customized template: If you've made significant customizations to the template, you can save it for future use by clicking on the File tab, selecting Save As, and choosing the Project Template (.mpt) file format.

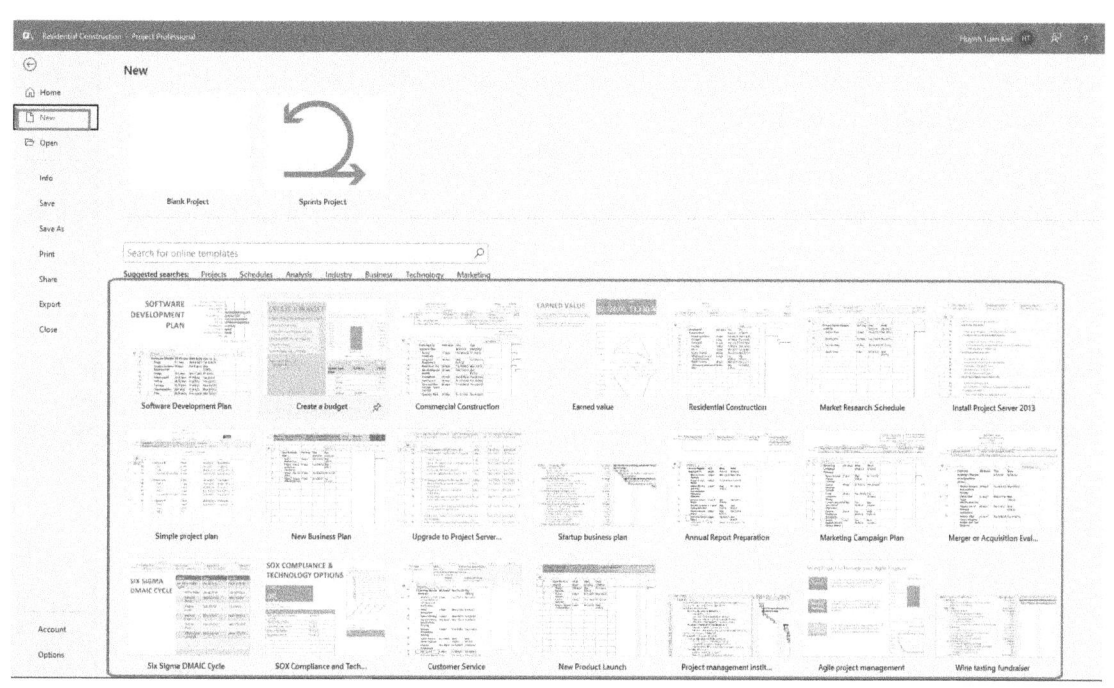

By leveraging templates, you can jumpstart your project planning process with predefined structures and settings, accelerating project initiation and ensuring consistency across projects.

Integrating with Other Applications

Microsoft Project offers integration capabilities with other Microsoft Office applications, such as Excel, Outlook, and SharePoint. Integrating Project with these applications allows for seamless data exchange, improved collaboration, and enhanced productivity.

To integrate with other applications:

1. Export data to Excel: You can export project data to Excel for further analysis or reporting by selecting the desired data range, clicking on the Copy button, and pasting it into an Excel spreadsheet.

2. Synchronize tasks with Outlook: You can synchronize project tasks with Outlook to manage deadlines, appointments, and reminders more effectively by clicking on the Task tab and selecting Sync to Outlook.

3. Collaborate with SharePoint: You can share project files and collaborate with team members using SharePoint by uploading project files to a SharePoint site and granting access to authorized users.

Integrating Microsoft Project with other applications enhances cross-functional collaboration, streamlines data management, and improves overall project efficiency.

Conclusion

Customizing the workspace in Microsoft Project is essential for optimizing project management processes and maximizing productivity. By tailoring the Ribbon, views, Quick Access Toolbar, custom fields, templates, and integration with other applications, you can create a personalized project management environment that aligns with your specific needs and preferences. Experiment with different customization options to find the configuration that works best for you and your team, and continuously refine it as your project evolves. With a customized workspace, you can efficiently plan, execute, and track your projects with Microsoft Project, driving successful project outcomes.

1.3. Setting Up Your First Project

1.3.1. Creating a New Project

Once you have created a new project in Microsoft Project, the next crucial step is to define its fundamental details and settings. These details not only provide a roadmap for your project but also serve as the foundation upon which you will build and manage your project's schedule, resources, and tasks. In this section, we will explore the various aspects of project information and settings in Microsoft Project, guiding you through the process of setting up your first project effectively.

Project Information

Before delving into the specifics of your project plan, it's essential to establish its basic information. This includes defining the project's start date, finish date, and other essential details that provide context for your project's timeline and scope. To set up project information in Microsoft Project, follow these steps:

1. Access Project Information: Navigate to the "Project" tab on the Ribbon interface at the top of the Microsoft Project window. Within the "Properties" group, click on the "Project Information" button. Alternatively, you can double-click on the project name in the Gantt Chart view to access project properties.

2. General Tab: In the "Project Information" dialog box that appears, you will find several tabs containing different sets of project details. Start with the "General" tab, where you can input basic information such as the project title, start date, and finish date. Additionally, you can specify whether the project is manually scheduled or automatically scheduled, depending on your preference and project requirements.

3. Schedule From: One critical decision to make is whether to schedule the project from the project start date or a specific date. This selection determines how Microsoft Project calculates task durations and scheduling constraints. Choose the appropriate option based on your project's needs.

4. Status Date: The status date is used to indicate the date up to which the project's progress is measured. It's particularly useful for tracking project status and generating reports. Ensure that the status date reflects the current state of the project.

5. Default Start Time and End Time: Define the default start and end times for tasks within your project. This setting allows Microsoft Project to schedule tasks with these default timings unless otherwise specified.

6. Calendar: Assign a base calendar to your project, which defines the standard working hours, holidays, and non-working days for project tasks. You can select from predefined calendars or create custom calendars tailored to your project's schedule.

7. Options: Click on the "Options" button to access additional project settings, including calculation options, working time, and scheduling defaults. Review and adjust these settings according to your project management practices and organizational standards.

8. Advanced Tab: Explore the "Advanced" tab to configure advanced project properties such as currency, project priority, and project file properties. These details provide further context and customization options for your project.

9. Ok: Once you have input all the necessary project information and settings, click "Ok" to apply the changes and close the "Project Information" dialog box.

By defining comprehensive project information and settings, you establish a solid foundation for your project plan and enable Microsoft Project to accurately schedule tasks, allocate resources, and track progress throughout the project lifecycle.

Task Information

In addition to setting up project-level information, it's crucial to define detailed information for individual tasks within your project. Task information encompasses various aspects, including task duration, dependencies, constraints, resources, and more. Managing task information effectively is essential for creating a well-structured and realistic project schedule. Here's how to configure task information in Microsoft Project:

1. Task Entry: Begin by entering tasks into your project plan either directly into the Gantt Chart view or the Task Sheet view. Specify the task name, duration, start date, and other relevant details as you create each task.

2. Task Mode: Microsoft Project offers three task modes: Auto Scheduled, Manually Scheduled, and Inactive. The default mode is typically Auto Scheduled, where Microsoft Project automatically schedules tasks based on dependencies and constraints. You can change the task mode as needed by selecting the desired mode from the Task Mode column in the Gantt Chart view.

3. Duration: Define the duration of each task, indicating the amount of work required to complete it. You can specify durations in various units such as hours, days, weeks, or months, depending on the granularity of your project schedule.

4. Dependencies: Establish task dependencies to define the sequence in which tasks must be completed. Dependencies create logical relationships between tasks, ensuring that certain tasks cannot start or finish until their predecessors are complete. To set task dependencies, use the "Predecessors" column in the Gantt Chart view to specify the task IDs of preceding tasks.

5. Constraints: Task constraints dictate when a task can start or finish based on specific dates or conditions. Common constraints include "Start No Earlier Than," "Start No Later Than," "Finish No Earlier Than," and "Finish No Later Than." You can apply constraints to tasks using the "Constraint Type" and "Constraint Date" columns in the Gantt Chart view.

6. Resources: Assign resources to tasks to indicate who will perform the work. Resources can include individual team members, equipment, or other assets required to complete the task. Use the "Resource Names" column in the Gantt Chart view to assign resources to tasks.

7. Task Notes: Provide additional context or instructions for tasks by adding task notes. Task notes allow you to communicate important details or requirements directly within the project plan. You can access and edit task notes by double-clicking on a task and navigating to the "Notes" tab in the Task Information dialog box.

8. Task Types: Microsoft Project supports three task types: Fixed Units, Fixed Work, and Fixed Duration. Each task type behaves differently in terms of task duration, work, and resource allocation. Select the appropriate task type based on the nature of your tasks and the constraints involved.

9. Task Constraints vs. Deadlines: Distinguish between task constraints and deadlines within your project plan. While constraints restrict the scheduling flexibility of tasks, deadlines serve as target dates for task completion without imposing scheduling restrictions. Use deadlines judiciously to communicate project milestones and critical dates.

10. Task Information Dialog Box: For more detailed task configuration, double-click on a task in the Gantt Chart view to open the Task Information dialog box. Here, you can access and modify task properties, including task details, resource assignments, constraints, and more.

By carefully managing task information, you create a structured and realistic project schedule that aligns with your project goals and constraints. Microsoft Project provides robust tools and features to facilitate task management and ensure project success.

In this section, we'll walk through setting up project information and settings in Microsoft Project step by step, using a hypothetical construction project as an example.

Example: Construction of a Residential Building

Let's imagine we're managing the construction of a residential building. We'll start by setting up the project information and settings in Microsoft Project.

Step 1: Access Project Information

- Open Microsoft Project and create a new project.

- Navigate to the "Project" tab on the Ribbon interface.

- Click on the "Project Information" button in the "Properties" group.

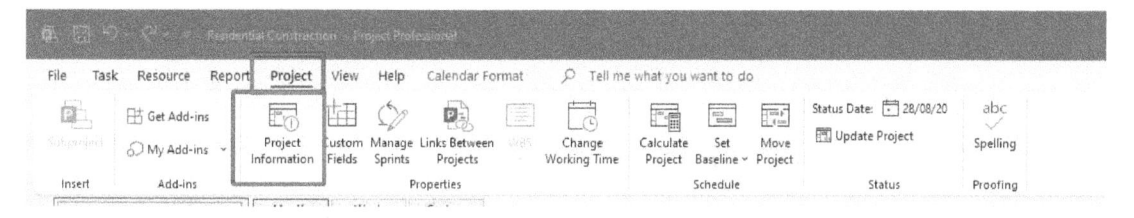

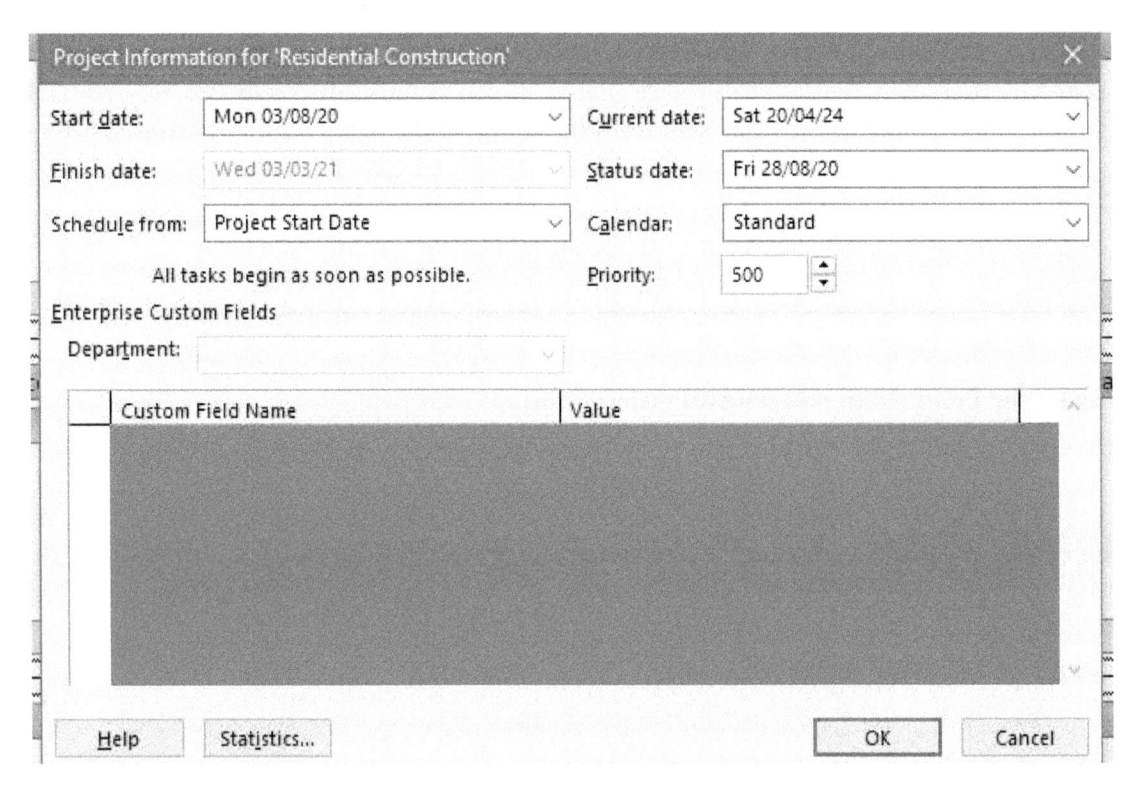

Step 2: General Tab

- In the "General" tab of the "Project Information" dialog box:

  - Enter the project title: "Residential Building Construction."

  - Set the start date: April 1, 2024.

  - Set the finish date: December 31, 2024.

  - Choose "Schedule from Start Date" to schedule tasks from the project start date.

  - Leave the status date as the current date.

  - Define the default start time and end time as 8:00 AM and 5:00 PM, respectively.

  - Assign the standard calendar to the project, which includes working hours from Monday to Friday, 8:00 AM to 5:00 PM, with weekends off.

Step 3: Advanced Tab

- Navigate to the "Advanced" tab of the "Project Option" dialog box:

  - Set the project currency to USD (United States Dollar).

  - Assign a priority level to the project (e.g., High).

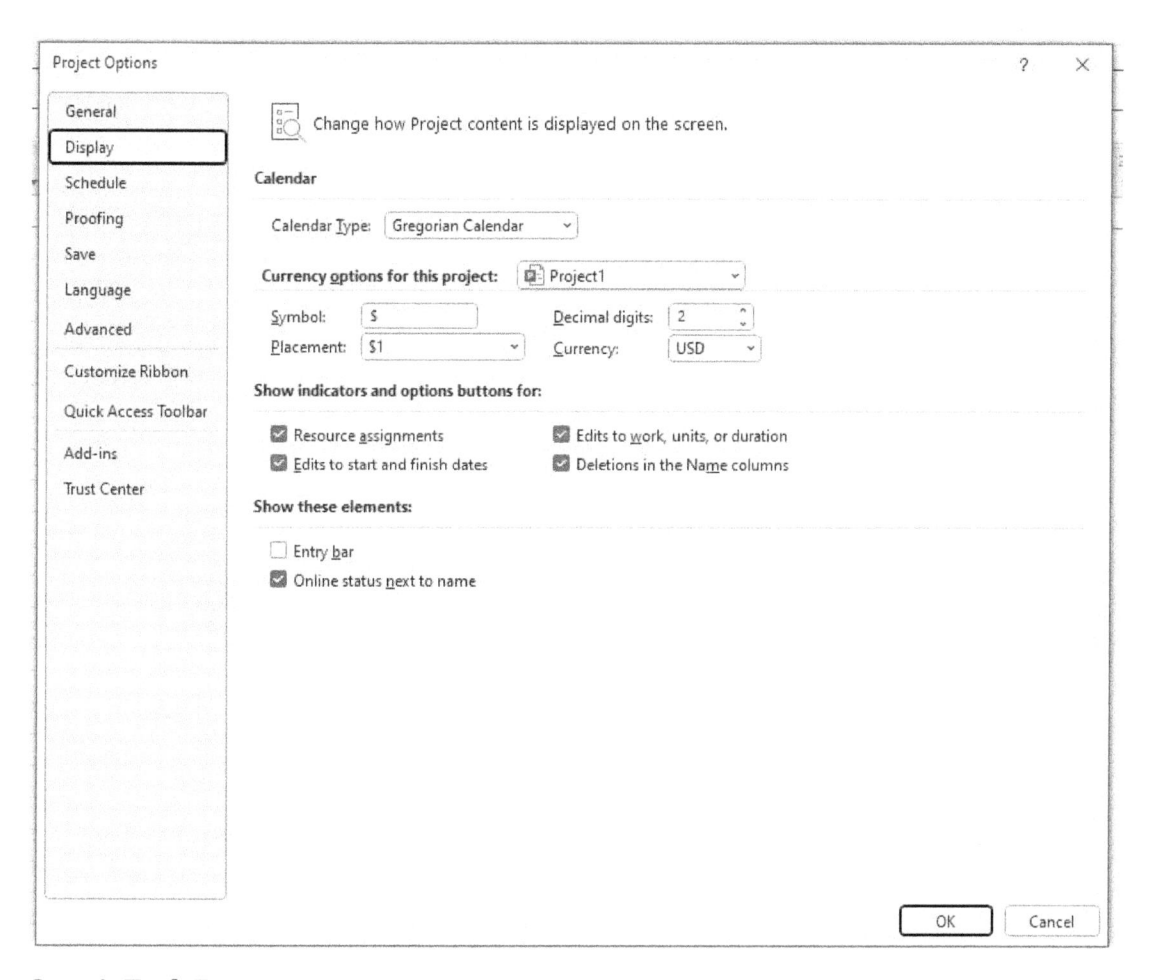

Step 4: Task Entry

- Switch to the Gantt Chart view.

- Start entering tasks for the construction project, such as "Site Preparation," "Foundation Construction," "Building Framing," "Interior Work," and "Final Inspections."

- Specify the duration of each task based on project estimates or historical data.

- Define task dependencies by linking tasks sequentially. For example, "Foundation Construction" cannot start until "Site Preparation" is complete.

- Assign resources to tasks, such as construction workers, equipment, and materials.

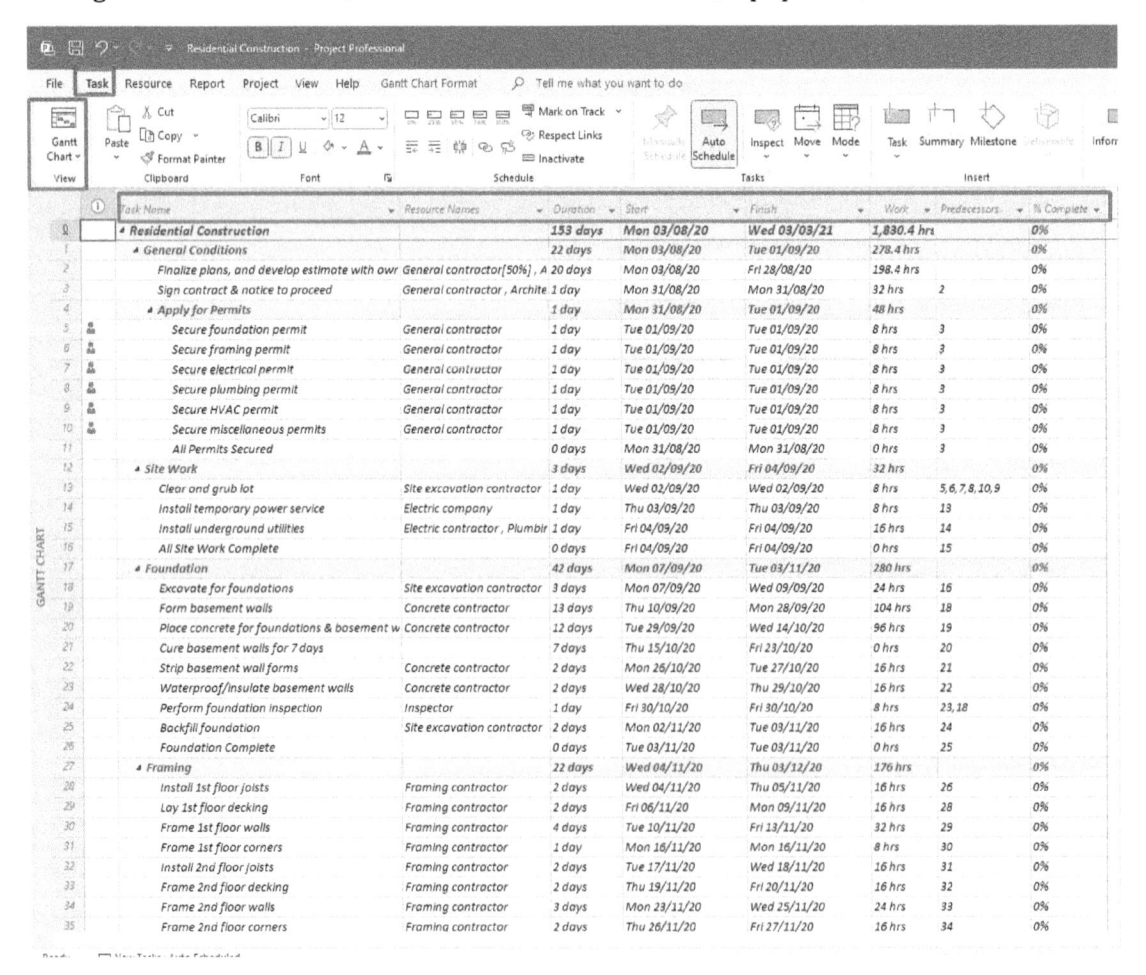

Step 5: Task Constraints and Deadlines

- Apply constraints to tasks where necessary. For instance, if there's a specific date by which the foundation must be completed due to weather constraints, set a "Finish No Later Than" constraint.

- Set deadlines for critical milestones, such as the completion of the building framing. These deadlines serve as targets but do not impose scheduling constraints.

Step 6: Task Information Dialog Box

- Double-click on a task in the Gantt Chart view to open the Task Information dialog box.

- Navigate through the tabs to access and modify task properties, including task details, resources, constraints, and notes.

- Review and adjust task information as needed to ensure clarity and accuracy.

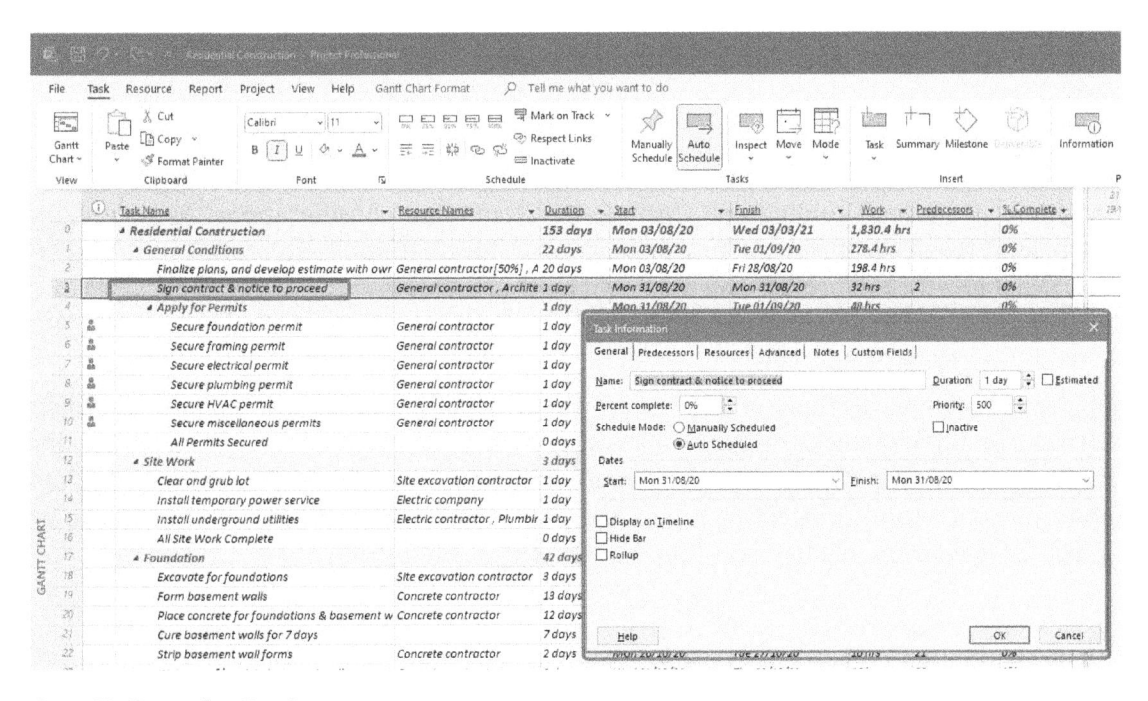

Step 7: Save the Project

- Once you've set up project information and task details, save the project file to preserve your work.

By following these steps, you've effectively set up project information and settings for the construction of a residential building in Microsoft Project. This foundation provides a clear roadmap for project execution and facilitates effective project management throughout the construction process.

Summary

Setting up your first project in Microsoft Project involves defining essential project information and configuring task details to create a comprehensive project plan. By establishing project start dates, scheduling preferences, and other settings, you provide a framework for effective project management. Additionally, defining task durations, dependencies, resources, and constraints enables you to create a realistic project schedule that reflects the scope and objectives of your project.

In this section, we explored the process of setting up project information and task details in Microsoft Project, guiding you through key steps and considerations. By leveraging Microsoft Project's features and functionality, you can create well-structured project plans that facilitate efficient project execution and management.

In the subsequent sections of this guide, we will delve deeper into advanced project management techniques, resource allocation strategies, scheduling optimization, and more. By mastering Microsoft Project, you will enhance your project management skills and drive successful project outcomes. Stay tuned for further insights and guidance on maximizing your use of Microsoft Project.

1.3.2. Project Information and Settings

Setting up your project in Microsoft Project involves defining crucial details and configuring settings that will govern how your project progresses and how information is presented. In this section, we delve deeper into the project information and settings, equipping you with the knowledge to initiate your project effectively.

Before diving into the intricacies of task scheduling and resource allocation, it's imperative to establish fundamental project information. Microsoft Project provides a dedicated space for entering essential details about your project, aiding in its identification and categorization. Let's explore the key components of project information:

Project Title and Description

Begin by specifying a clear and concise title for your project. This title should encapsulate the essence of your endeavor, enabling stakeholders to quickly grasp its purpose. Additionally, provide a brief description that outlines the project's objectives, scope, and deliverables. This description serves as a reference point for team members and stakeholders, fostering alignment and clarity.

Project Start Date

Identifying the project's start date is pivotal in establishing temporal boundaries. Whether it's the commencement of planning activities or the initiation of execution, pinpointing the start date sets the project timeline in motion. Microsoft Project allows you to designate the exact date when the project activities are slated to begin, facilitating accurate scheduling and resource allocation.

Project Duration and End Date

Alongside the start date, ascertain the anticipated duration of your project. This duration encompasses the entire span from initiation to completion, encompassing all tasks and milestones. Based on this duration and the start date, Microsoft Project calculates the project's end date, providing a holistic view of the timeline. Understanding the project's duration is indispensable for strategic planning and resource management.

Project Calendar

Every project operates within a specific timeframe dictated by its calendar. Microsoft Project offers various calendar options, including standard calendars and custom calendars tailored to unique project requirements. Specify the working hours, non-working days, and holidays pertinent to your project to accurately reflect its temporal constraints. By aligning the project calendar with organizational schedules, you ensure coherence and consistency in scheduling activities.

[] Configuring Project Settings

In addition to defining project-specific information, configuring settings within Microsoft Project empowers you to tailor the software to suit your project's nuances. These settings govern various aspects of project management, ranging from task dependencies to resource availability. Let's explore the pivotal project settings that warrant attention:

Task Dependencies

Task dependencies elucidate the sequential relationships between project activities, delineating the order in which tasks must be executed. Within Microsoft Project, you can specify dependencies using different types, such as finish-to-start, start-to-start, finish-to-finish, and start-to-finish. By accurately defining task dependencies, you establish the logical flow of work and mitigate scheduling conflicts.

Resource Availability

Efficient resource management hinges on understanding resource availability and allocation. Microsoft Project enables you to input resource calendars, specifying the working hours and availability of each resource. By aligning resource availability with project demands, you prevent overallocation and ensure optimal utilization of resources. Additionally, you can define resource availability in terms of percentages or specific working hours, granting flexibility in resource allocation.

Task Constraints

Task constraints delineate the constraints or limitations that influence task scheduling. Whether it's a fixed start date, a mandatory finish date, or a specific duration, constraints shape the execution timeline of tasks. Microsoft Project offers various types of task constraints, including Start No Earlier Than (SNET), Start No Later Than (SNLT), Finish No Earlier Than (FNET), and Finish No Later Than (FNLT). By judiciously applying task constraints, you accommodate project constraints while preserving scheduling flexibility.

Project Baselines

Baselining serves as a snapshot of the project's initial plan, capturing key metrics such as schedule, cost, and scope. Microsoft Project allows you to establish baselines at different stages of the project, enabling comparative analysis and performance tracking. By setting baselines, you create a benchmark against which actual progress can be measured, facilitating variance analysis and proactive decision-making.

For example:

Project Title and Description

Title: Residential Construction Project

Description: The Residential Construction Project aims to build a single-family home in the suburban area of [insert location]. The project encompasses all phases of construction, from initial planning and permitting to final inspections and handover. The completed residence will adhere to local building codes and reflect the highest standards of quality and craftsmanship.

Steps:

Tab Location: File tab -> Info

Open Microsoft Project and create a new project.

In the project information section, enter "Residential Construction Project" as the title.

Provide a brief description of the project, highlighting its objectives, scope, and deliverables.

Project Start Date

Start Date: April 1, 2024

The project officially begins on April 1, 2024, marking the initiation of planning and preparatory activities.

Steps:

Tab Location: Project tab -> Properties

Navigate to the project information section.

Locate the field for the start date and input "April 1, 2024" as the start date of the project.

Project Duration and End Date

Duration: 12 months

End Date: March 31, 2025

The project is slated to span 12 months, culminating in the completion and handover of the residential property by March 31, 2025.

Steps:

Tab Location: Project tab -> Properties

Calculate the project duration (in months) based on the planned timeline.

Input the project duration as "12 months" in the appropriate field.

Microsoft Project will automatically calculate the end date based on the start date and duration.

Project Calendar

Calendar: Standard Workweek Calendar

- **Working Hours:** Monday to Friday, 8:00 AM to 5:00 PM

- **Non-Working Days:** Saturday, Sunday

- **Holidays:** Independence Day (July 4), Thanksgiving (Fourth Thursday in November), Christmas (December 25), New Year's Day (January 1), Labor Day (First Monday in September)

Steps:

Tab Location: Project tab -> Properties

Click on "Change Working Time" in the Properties group.

Access the project calendar settings.

Choose the standard workweek calendar template.

Adjust the working hours to reflect Monday to Friday, 8:00 AM to 5:00 PM.

Designate Saturdays and Sundays as non-working days.

Add holidays such as Independence Day, Thanksgiving, Christmas, New Year's Day, and Labor Day to the calendar.

Configuring Project Settings

Task Dependencies

1. Foundation Preparation: Must precede all other construction tasks.

2. Frame Construction: Cannot begin until foundation is complete.

3. Roofing Installation: Dependent on completion of frame construction.

4. Interior Finishing: Sequentially follows roofing installation.

Steps:

Tab Location: Task tab -> Schedule

Select the tasks you want to link.

Click on "Link Tasks" in the Schedule group.

Choose the type of relationship (Finish to Start, Start to Start, etc.) from the dropdown menu.

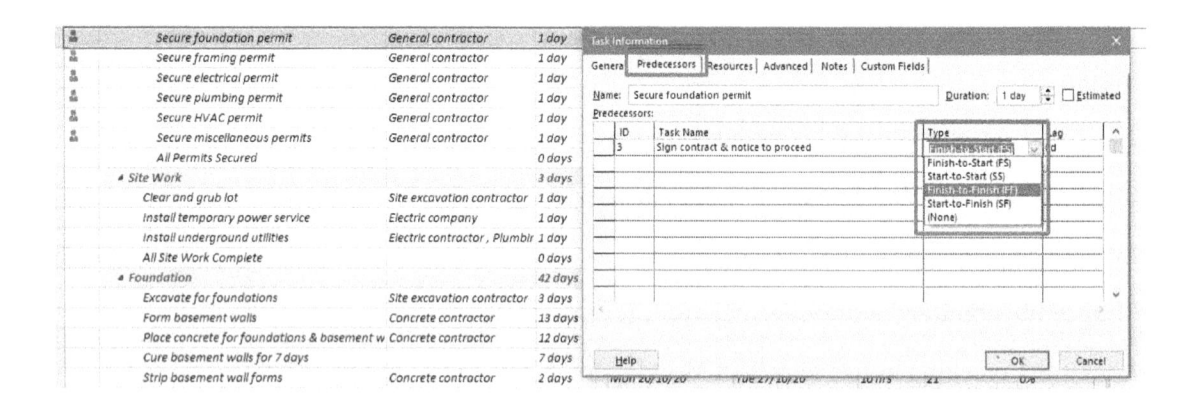

Resource Availability

- **Construction Crew:** Available Monday to Friday, 8:00 AM to 5:00 PM

- **Architectural Consultant:** Available for design consultations on weekdays, flexible hours.

- **Building Inspector:** Available for inspections as scheduled, typically during weekdays.

Steps:

Tab Location: Resource tab -> Change Working Time

Select the resource whose calendar you want to modify.

Click on "Change Working Time" in the Properties group.

Adjust the working hours and non-working days for the selected resource.

Task Constraints

1. Start No Earlier Than (SNET):

- **Land Acquisition:** Cannot begin before April 1, 2024.

- **Permit Approval:** Dependent on completion of land acquisition.

2. Finish No Later Than (FNLT):

- **Project Completion:** Must be finished by March 31, 2025.

Steps:

Tab Location: Task tab -> Properties

Select the task you want to add a constraint to.

Click on "Information" in the Properties group.

Choose the desired constraint type from the dropdown menu under the Advanced tab.

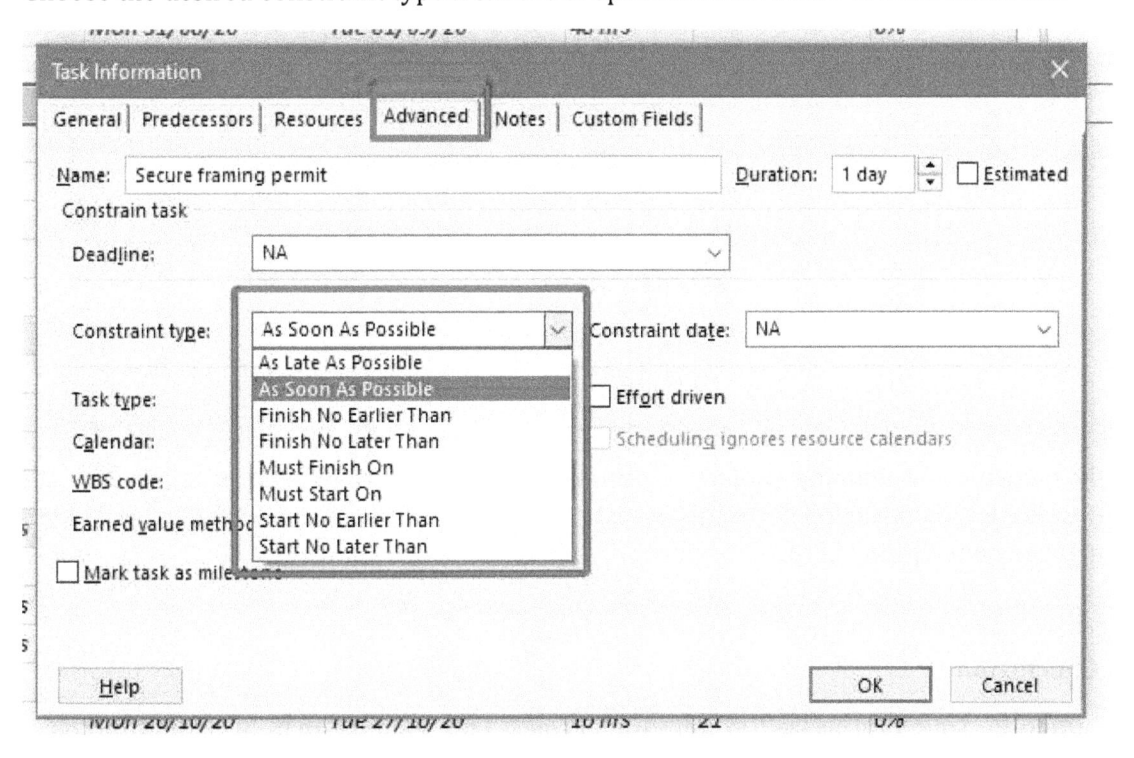

Project Baselines

1. Schedule Baseline: Captures the initial timeline for project tasks and milestones.

2. Cost Baseline: Documents the projected budget allocation for the residential construction project.

Steps:

Tab Location: Project tab -> Schedule

Click on "Set Baseline" in the Schedule group.

Choose the type of baseline you want to set (schedule, cost, etc.).

Confirm the baseline setting by clicking "OK" in the dialog box.

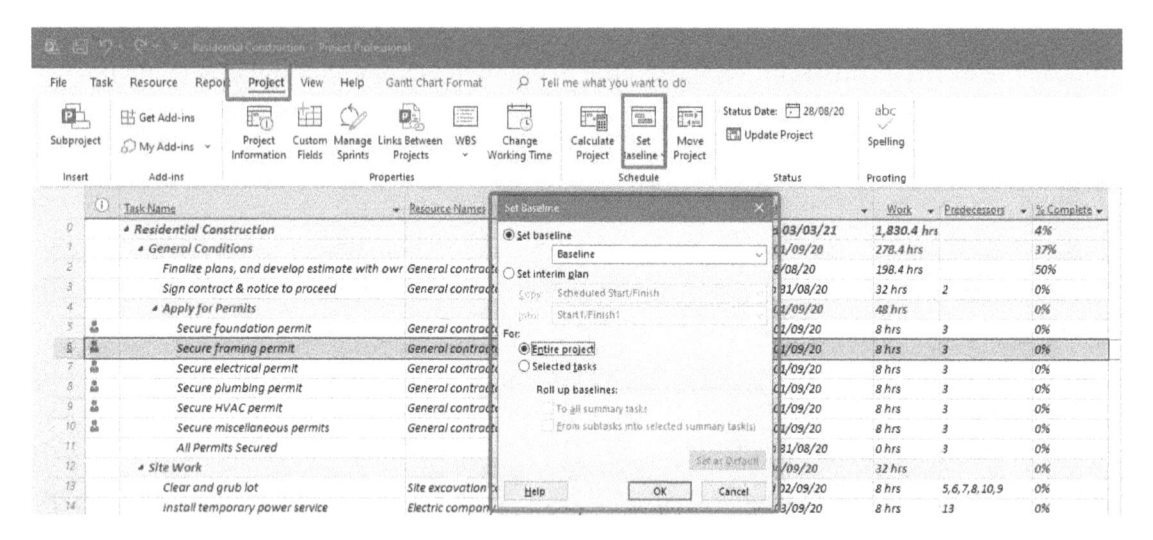

By meticulously defining project information and configuring settings tailored to the Residential Construction Project, you establish a solid foundation for effective project management within Microsoft Project.

Conclusion

Setting up your first project in Microsoft Project entails more than just inputting basic information—it involves laying the groundwork for effective project management. By meticulously defining project details and configuring settings, you establish a robust framework that guides project execution and facilitates informed decision-making. Embrace the power of Microsoft Project to streamline your project initiation process and embark on a path to project mastery.

PART II
Navigating the Project Workspace

2.1 Exploring the Ribbon Interface

2.1.1. Tabs and Commands Overview

The Ribbon Interface in Microsoft Project is a dynamic tool that organizes commands into a series of tabs at the top of the program window. Each tab relates to specific tasks or functions, making it easier for project managers to find and execute commands efficiently. In this section, we will delve deeper into understanding the structure of the Ribbon Interface, exploring its various tabs and commands.

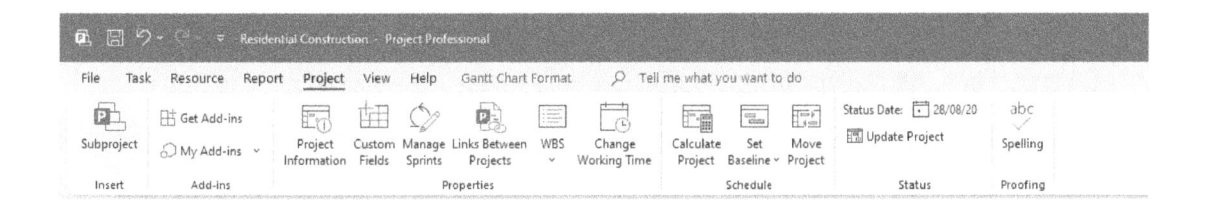

The Ribbon Interface comprises several tabs, each containing a collection of commands relevant to a particular aspect of project management. Let's examine the primary tabs and their corresponding commands:

1. File Tab: The File tab is your gateway to managing projects, setting options, and accessing various functionalities related to file management. Here, you can create, open, save, and print projects. Additionally, you can customize Project options, manage accounts, and access help and support.

   - New: Create a new project from scratch or choose from various project templates.

   - Open: Open existing projects stored on your computer or network.

   - Save & Save As: Save your project with its current state or save it with a different name/location.

   - Print: Print project information, reports, or views.

   - Options: Customize Project settings and preferences.

   - Account: Manage your Microsoft account and subscriptions.

   - Help: Access Project help and support resources.

2. Home Tab: The Home tab contains essential commands for managing tasks, resources, and formatting project elements.

   - Clipboard: Cut, copy, and paste project elements such as tasks, resources, and text.

   - Font & Paragraph: Modify text formatting and alignment within project views.

   - Editing: Find and replace project information, as well as undo and redo actions.

   - Views: Switch between different project views to analyze and manage project data effectively.

   - Zoom: Adjust the zoom level to focus on specific project details.

   - Sort & Filter: Arrange and filter project data based on specific criteria.

   - Schedule: Manage task scheduling options and constraints.

   - Insert: Add new tasks, resources, or columns to your project.

3. Task Tab: The Task tab provides commands specifically tailored for managing project tasks and task-related operations.

  - Clipboard: Cut, copy, and paste tasks within the project or between different projects.

  - Properties: Define task properties such as task type, constraints, and deadlines.

  - Editing: Modify task details, durations, and dependencies.

  - Schedule: Adjust task scheduling settings, including start and finish dates.

  - Insert: Insert new tasks or subtasks into the project plan.

  - Assignments: Assign resources to tasks and manage resource allocations.

4. Resource Tab: The Resource tab focuses on resource management tasks, allowing you to allocate, assign, and analyze resource usage within your project.

  - Clipboard: Copy, cut, and paste resource information within the project or across different projects.

  - Properties: Define resource properties such as resource type, availability, and cost rates.

  - Assignments: Assign resources to tasks and adjust resource allocations.

  - View: Switch between different resource views to analyze and manage resource data effectively.

  - Level: Manage resource overallocation and resolve resource conflicts.

  - Team: Collaborate with project team members and manage resource assignments.

5. Project Tab: The Project tab encompasses commands for managing project settings, options, and overall project properties.

  - Properties: Define project properties such as start date, finish date, and project status.

- Project Information: View and modify general project information, including project name and file location.

- Schedule: Configure project scheduling options, including calendar settings and working hours.

- Project Options: Customize Project settings and preferences to align with project requirements.

- Reports: Generate and customize project reports to communicate project status and progress effectively.

6. View Tab: The View tab offers commands for customizing project views, allowing you to tailor the display of project information according to your preferences.

- Task Views: Switch between different task views such as Gantt Chart, Task Sheet, and Network Diagram.

- Resource Views: Access various resource views like Resource Sheet, Resource Usage, and Team Planner.

- Other Views: Explore additional project views such as Calendar, Timeline, and Network Diagram.

- Split View: Split the project window to view multiple project views simultaneously.

- Data: Customize the display of project data by adding or removing columns, rows, and fields.

- Window: Manage project windows and arrange multiple project views for efficient analysis.

7. Format Tab: The Format tab provides commands for formatting project elements such as tasks, resources, and timeline views.

- Bar Styles: Customize the appearance of task bars in the Gantt Chart view.

- Text Styles: Define text formatting styles for different project elements.

- Gridlines: Configure gridline settings to improve the readability of project views.

- Zoom: Adjust the zoom level to focus on specific details within project views.

- Sheet Options: Customize the display of project sheets, including task and resource sheets.

- Timeline: Format the timeline view to highlight key project milestones and deadlines.

8. Developer Tab: The Developer tab is designed for advanced users who want to customize Project functionality using macros and Visual Basic for Applications (VBA).

- Macros: Record, run, and manage macros to automate repetitive tasks in Project.

- Visual Basic: Access the Visual Basic Editor to write, edit, and debug VBA code for Project automation.

- Add-Ins: Manage add-ins and extensions to extend Project's capabilities and integrate with other applications.

- XML: Import and export project data using XML files for interoperability with other software systems.

By familiarizing yourself with the tabs and commands within the Ribbon Interface, you can streamline your project management workflows and leverage the full power of Microsoft Project to plan, execute, and track your projects effectively. Experiment with different commands and explore the extensive capabilities offered by Project to optimize your project management practices.

2.1.2. Customizing the Ribbon

Customizing the Ribbon in Microsoft Project is a powerful feature that allows users to tailor the interface to their specific needs and preferences. By adding or removing tabs, groups, and commands, project managers can streamline their workflow and access the tools they use most frequently with ease. In this section, we will delve deeper into the process of customizing the Ribbon, exploring various options and functionalities available.

Understanding Ribbon Customization

The Ribbon in Microsoft Project is organized into tabs, each containing groups of related commands. While the default Ribbon configuration covers most basic project management tasks, customizing it can enhance productivity by providing quick access to specialized functions. To customize the Ribbon, users can follow these steps:

1. Accessing Ribbon Customization: To begin customizing the Ribbon, navigate to the File tab and select "Options." In the Project Options dialog box, click on "Customize Ribbon."

2. Adding Tabs and Groups: Users can add new tabs and groups to the Ribbon to accommodate specific tasks or workflows. Click on the "New Tab" or "New Group" button to create custom tabs or groups, respectively. Assigning meaningful labels to these elements ensures clarity and ease of use.

3. Adding Commands: After creating custom tabs and groups, users can populate them with commands relevant to their project management activities. From the list of available commands, select the desired ones and add them to the appropriate groups. Users can also create custom commands or macros to extend functionality further.

4. Removing Tabs, Groups, and Commands: In addition to adding elements, users can remove unnecessary tabs, groups, or commands from the Ribbon to declutter the interface. Simply select the item to be removed and click on the "Remove" button.

5. Organizing Commands: Organizing commands within groups allows for intuitive navigation and efficient access. Users can rearrange commands within groups by selecting them and using the arrow buttons to move them up, down, left, or right.

6. Resetting Ribbon Customization: If users wish to revert to the default Ribbon configuration, they can do so by clicking on the "Reset" button located at the bottom of the Customize Ribbon dialog box. This action restores the Ribbon to its original state, undoing any customizations made.

Practical Applications of Ribbon Customization

Customizing the Ribbon in Microsoft Project offers numerous benefits for project managers seeking to optimize their workflow. Here are some practical applications of Ribbon customization:

1. Tailoring the Interface to Specific Projects: Different projects may require access to distinct sets of tools and commands. By customizing the Ribbon, project managers can create task-specific tabs and groups, ensuring that essential functions are readily available.

2. Streamlining Common Tasks: Project managers often perform repetitive tasks as part of their daily routines. Customizing the Ribbon allows them to assemble frequently used commands into dedicated groups, reducing the time and effort required to access essential functions.

3. Enhancing User Productivity: A well-organized Ribbon promotes user productivity by eliminating clutter and presenting relevant commands in a logical manner. Customizing the Ribbon according to individual preferences enables project managers to work more efficiently and effectively.

4. Integrating Third-Party Add-Ins: Microsoft Project supports the integration of third-party add-ins, which can extend the software's functionality. Customizing the Ribbon enables users to incorporate commands from add-ins into their workspace, seamlessly integrating external tools into their project management environment.

Best Practices for Ribbon Customization

While customizing the Ribbon offers considerable flexibility, it is essential to adhere to best practices to ensure an optimal user experience. Here are some recommendations for effective Ribbon customization:

1. Keep it Simple: Avoid overloading the Ribbon with unnecessary tabs, groups, or commands. A clutter-free interface enhances usability and reduces cognitive load for users.

2. Prioritize Frequently Used Commands: Place commonly used commands in prominent locations within the Ribbon to expedite task execution. Consider grouping related commands together to facilitate intuitive navigation.

3. Seek Feedback: Solicit feedback from team members or colleagues regarding Ribbon customization. Their input can provide valuable insights into workflow requirements and help refine the interface for maximum efficiency.

4. Regular Review and Refinement: As project requirements evolve, periodically review and refine the Ribbon customization to align with changing needs. Remove obsolete commands and adjust the layout as necessary to maintain relevance and effectiveness.

Conclusion

Customizing the Ribbon in Microsoft Project empowers project managers to tailor the interface to their unique requirements, optimizing efficiency and productivity. By adding, removing, and organizing tabs, groups, and commands, users can create a personalized workspace that facilitates seamless project management. By following best practices and regularly reviewing customization settings, project managers can harness the full potential of the Ribbon to streamline workflows and achieve project success.

2.2 Customizing the Quick Access Toolbar

2.2.1. Adding and Removing Commands

The Quick Access Toolbar (QAT) in Microsoft Project is a versatile feature that allows users to access frequently used commands with ease, streamlining their workflow and enhancing productivity. In this section, we will delve deeper into customizing the Quick Access Toolbar to tailor it to your specific needs.

Adding and Removing Commands

Adding Commands to the Quick Access Toolbar:

Microsoft Project offers a plethora of commands that you can add to the Quick Access Toolbar, enabling quick access to functions you use frequently. Follow these simple steps to add commands to the QAT:

1. Accessing the Customize Dialog Box:

   - Click on the down arrow at the end of the Quick Access Toolbar.

   - Select "More Commands" from the dropdown menu. This action opens the Project Options dialog box with the Customize tab selected.

2. Choosing Commands:

   - In the Customize tab, you'll find two columns: "Choose commands from" on the left and "Customize Quick Access Toolbar" on the right.

   - From the "Choose commands from" dropdown menu, select the category containing the command you want to add. For example, if you wish to add a command related to task management, select "All Commands."

- Scroll through the list of commands and click on the one you want to add to the QAT.

3. Adding Commands:

   - After selecting the desired command, click the "Add" button positioned between the two columns. This action moves the selected command to the "Customize Quick Access Toolbar" column on the right.

   - Repeat this process for each command you wish to add.

4. Organizing Commands:

   - Commands are added to the QAT in the order they are selected. To rearrange them, select a command in the "Customize Quick Access Toolbar" column and use the up and down arrows on the right to reposition it.

5. Finalizing Changes:

   - Once you've added and organized all desired commands, click "OK" to save your changes and exit the Customize dialog box.

Removing Commands from the Quick Access Toolbar:

If you find that you no longer need certain commands on the Quick Access Toolbar or wish to declutter it, you can remove them effortlessly. Here's how:

1. Accessing the Customize Dialog Box:

   - Follow the same steps mentioned above to access the Customize dialog box.

2. Removing Commands:

- In the "Customize Quick Access Toolbar" column on the right, you'll see a list of commands currently added to the QAT.

- Select the command you want to remove from the QAT.

3. Removing Commands:

- After selecting the command you wish to remove, click the "Remove" button positioned between the two columns. This action removes the selected command from the QAT.

- Repeat this process for each command you want to remove.

4. Finalizing Changes:

- Once you've removed all desired commands, click "OK" to save your changes and exit the Customize dialog box.

Best Practices for Customizing the Quick Access Toolbar:

- *Prioritize Frequently Used Commands:* Reserve space on the QAT for commands you use most frequently to maximize efficiency.

- *Keep It Concise:* Avoid cluttering the QAT with too many commands to maintain a clean and intuitive interface.

- *Regularly Review and Adjust:* As your workflow evolves, periodically review the commands on the QAT and make adjustments accordingly to ensure optimal productivity.

Best Practices for Customizing the Quick Access Toolbar:

Customizing the Quick Access Toolbar (QAT) in Microsoft Project is not just about adding your favorite commands; it's also about optimizing your workflow for maximum efficiency. Here are some best practices to consider when customizing the QAT:

1. Prioritize Frequently Used Commands:

- Identify the commands you use most frequently during your project management tasks. These could include commands for creating new tasks, adjusting durations, assigning resources, or updating progress.

- Prioritize adding these high-use commands to the QAT to ensure they are always easily accessible with just a single click.

Example: If you find yourself regularly adjusting task durations, adding the "Increase Duration" and "Decrease Duration" commands to the QAT can save you valuable time.

2. Keep It Concise:

- While the QAT offers ample space for customization, avoid overcrowding it with too many commands. A cluttered toolbar can become overwhelming and defeat the purpose of quick access.

- Limit the number of commands on the QAT to those that are truly essential for your daily tasks.

Example: Instead of adding every possible command related to resource management, focus on including only the most frequently used ones, such as "Assign Resources" and "Level Resources."

3. Group Commands by Functionality:

- Organize the commands on the QAT based on their functionality or relevance to specific project management tasks.

- Grouping related commands together can make it easier to locate the desired function quickly, further streamlining your workflow.

Example: Group commands related to task management, such as creating, deleting, and indenting tasks, in one section of the QAT, while placing resource-related commands, such as assigning resources and resolving resource overallocations, in another section.

4. Regularly Review and Adjust:

- Project management needs evolve over time, and so should your customized QAT.

- Periodically review the commands on the QAT and assess their relevance and usage. Remove any commands that have become obsolete or are rarely used, and consider adding new commands that have become essential to your workflow.

Example: If you adopt a new project management methodology that requires frequent use of a specific command, such as "Mark as Milestone," consider adding it to the QAT to facilitate its quick access.

5. Consider Collaborative Needs:

- If you're working on a project with a team, consider customizing the QAT to align with the common tasks and processes shared among team members.

- Ensure that the commands on the QAT are intuitive and familiar to all team members to promote consistency and collaboration.

Example: If your team frequently reviews project schedules together, consider adding commands such as "Zoom In" and "Zoom Out" to the QAT to facilitate easy navigation during group discussions.

By customizing the Quick Access Toolbar in Microsoft Project, you can tailor the interface to align with your unique workflow, saving time and effort in accessing essential commands. Whether you're managing tasks, resources, or schedules, the QAT empowers you to work more efficiently and effectively.

2.2.2. Quick Access Toolbar Settings

The Quick Access Toolbar (QAT) in Microsoft Project serves as a customizable toolbar located at the top-left corner of the application window. It provides easy access to frequently used commands, regardless of which tab is currently selected in the Ribbon interface. While the default QAT configuration includes commonly used commands such as Save, Undo, and Redo, Project allows users to personalize this toolbar according to their specific preferences and workflow requirements. This section delves into the various settings and customization options available for the Quick Access Toolbar in Microsoft Project.

Understanding Quick Access Toolbar Settings

Before delving into customization options, it's essential to understand the core settings and functionalities of the Quick Access Toolbar in Microsoft Project.

1. Default Commands:

By default, the Quick Access Toolbar includes commonly used commands such as Save, Undo, and Redo. These commands are universally essential for project management tasks and are readily accessible regardless of the active tab in the Ribbon interface.

2. Positioning:

The Quick Access Toolbar is positioned by default above the Ribbon interface, at the top-left corner of the application window. However, users have the flexibility to relocate it below the Ribbon for easier access, especially for those accustomed to other Microsoft Office applications where the QAT typically resides below the Ribbon.

3. Customization:

Microsoft Project allows users to customize the Quick Access Toolbar extensively. Users can add frequently used commands, remove existing ones, and even create custom groups to organize related commands efficiently. Customization options provide users with the flexibility to tailor the QAT to their unique workflow requirements, thereby enhancing productivity and efficiency.

Customizing the Quick Access Toolbar

Microsoft Project offers a plethora of customization options for the Quick Access Toolbar, empowering users to tailor it to their specific needs and preferences. Here's a comprehensive guide to customizing the QAT in Microsoft Project:

1. Adding Commands:

To add commands to the Quick Access Toolbar, follow these steps:

- Click on the down arrow located at the right end of the QAT.

- Select "More Commands" from the dropdown menu.

- In the "Project Options" dialog box that appears, navigate to the "Quick Access Toolbar" tab.

- From the "Choose commands from" dropdown menu, select the desired category of commands (e.g., Popular Commands, All Commands, Macros).

- Select the command you wish to add from the list on the left.

- Click the "Add" button to move the selected command to the list on the right.

- Click "OK" to apply the changes and close the dialog box.

2. Removing Commands:

To remove commands from the Quick Access Toolbar, follow these steps:

- Click on the down arrow located at the right end of the QAT.

- Select "More Commands" from the dropdown menu.

- In the "Project Options" dialog box, navigate to the "Quick Access Toolbar" tab.

- Select the command you wish to remove from the list on the right.

- Click the "Remove" button.

- Click "OK" to apply the changes and close the dialog box.

3. Rearranging Commands:

Users can rearrange the order of commands on the Quick Access Toolbar to prioritize frequently used commands. To rearrange commands, simply click and drag a command to the desired position on the toolbar.

4. Creating Custom Groups:

Microsoft Project allows users to create custom groups on the Quick Access Toolbar to organize related commands efficiently. To create a custom group, follow these steps:

- Click on the down arrow located at the right end of the QAT.

- Select "More Commands" from the dropdown menu.

- In the "Project Options" dialog box, navigate to the "Quick Access Toolbar" tab.

- Click the "New Group" button.

- Select the desired commands from the list on the left and add them to the newly created group.

- Click "OK" to apply the changes and close the dialog box.

5. Importing and Exporting Customizations:

Users can import and export Quick Access Toolbar customizations to ensure consistency across multiple instances of Microsoft Project or to share customizations with colleagues. To import or export customizations, navigate to the "Project Options" dialog box and select the "Quick Access Toolbar" tab. Then, use the "Import/Export" buttons to save or load customizations from a file.

Best Practices for Quick Access Toolbar Customization

While the Quick Access Toolbar offers extensive customization options, it's essential to adopt best practices to optimize its effectiveness:

1. Prioritize Frequently Used Commands:

Identify the commands you use most frequently in your project management tasks and prioritize them on the Quick Access Toolbar for easy access.

2. Organize Commands into Logical Groups:

Group related commands together to streamline workflow and enhance efficiency. Custom groups allow for better organization and quicker access to specific sets of commands.

3. Review and Refine Customizations Regularly:

Periodically review your Quick Access Toolbar customizations to ensure they align with your evolving workflow and project management needs. Refine the toolbar as necessary to maintain optimal efficiency.

4. Share Customizations with Team Members:

If working in a collaborative environment, consider sharing your Quick Access Toolbar customizations with team members to promote consistency and facilitate seamless collaboration.

Conclusion

The Quick Access Toolbar in Microsoft Project serves as a versatile tool for enhancing productivity and streamlining workflow. By leveraging its extensive customization options, project managers can tailor the QAT to their specific needs and preferences, thereby optimizing efficiency and effectiveness in project management tasks. Understanding the various settings and customization options empowers users to make the most out of the Quick Access Toolbar, ultimately contributing to successful project execution and delivery.

2.3 Utilizing Views and Tables

2.3.1. Understanding Different Views

Views and tables are fundamental components of Microsoft Project that allow project managers to visualize and organize project data effectively. Understanding the various views available and how to customize them to suit specific project needs is essential for maximizing productivity and gaining insights into project progress. In this section, we will delve into the different views offered by Microsoft Project and explore strategies for utilizing them efficiently.

Microsoft Project provides a diverse range of views, each tailored to address specific aspects of project planning, tracking, and reporting. These views offer unique perspectives on project data, enabling project managers to analyze information comprehensively. Understanding the purpose and functionality of each view is crucial for selecting the most appropriate one for a given task. Let's explore some of the key views available in Microsoft Project:

1. Gantt Chart View: The Gantt Chart view is perhaps the most commonly used view in Microsoft Project. It displays tasks as bars along a timescale, providing a visual representation of task durations, dependencies, and progress. The Gantt Chart view allows project managers to easily identify task relationships, critical paths, and overall project timelines.

PART II: NAVIGATING THE PROJECT WORKSPACE

2. Task Usage View: In the Task Usage view, tasks are listed vertically, and resource assignments are displayed horizontally. This view offers insights into resource allocation and workload distribution across tasks. Project managers can analyze resource utilization, identify overallocated resources, and make adjustments to optimize resource assignments.

PART II: NAVIGATING THE PROJECT WORKSPACE

3. Resource Sheet View: The Resource Sheet view presents project resources in a tabular format, allowing project managers to manage resource-related information efficiently. It provides essential details such as resource names, types, rates, and availability. Project managers can add, edit, or remove resources directly from this view, streamlining resource management processes.

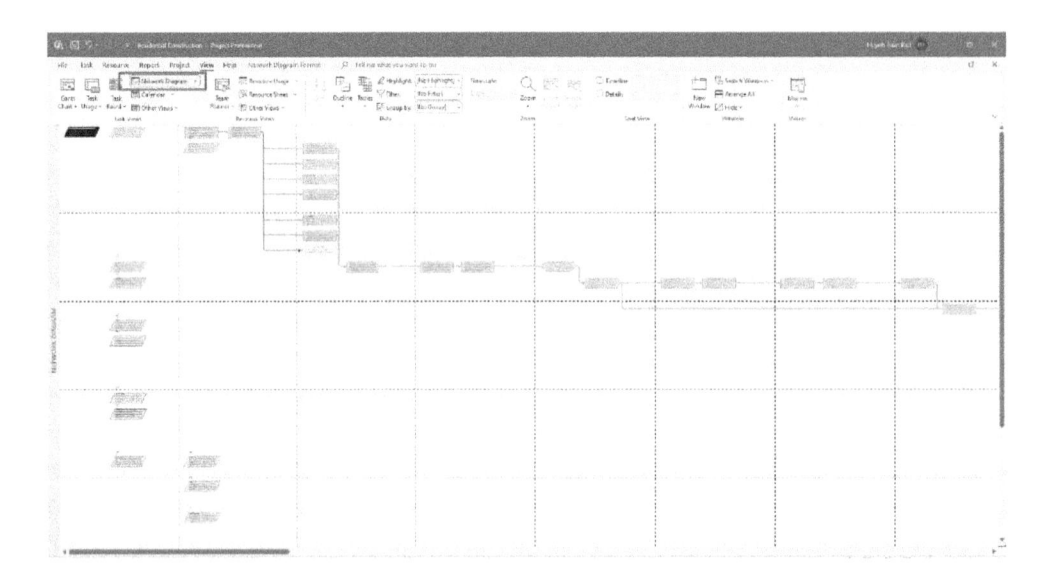

4. Calendar View: The Calendar view displays project tasks and milestones on a calendar grid, making it easier to visualize project schedules and deadlines. Project managers can identify task durations, overlaps, and scheduling conflicts more intuitively. Additionally, the Calendar view allows users to adjust working hours, non-working days, and holidays to reflect project-specific calendars accurately.

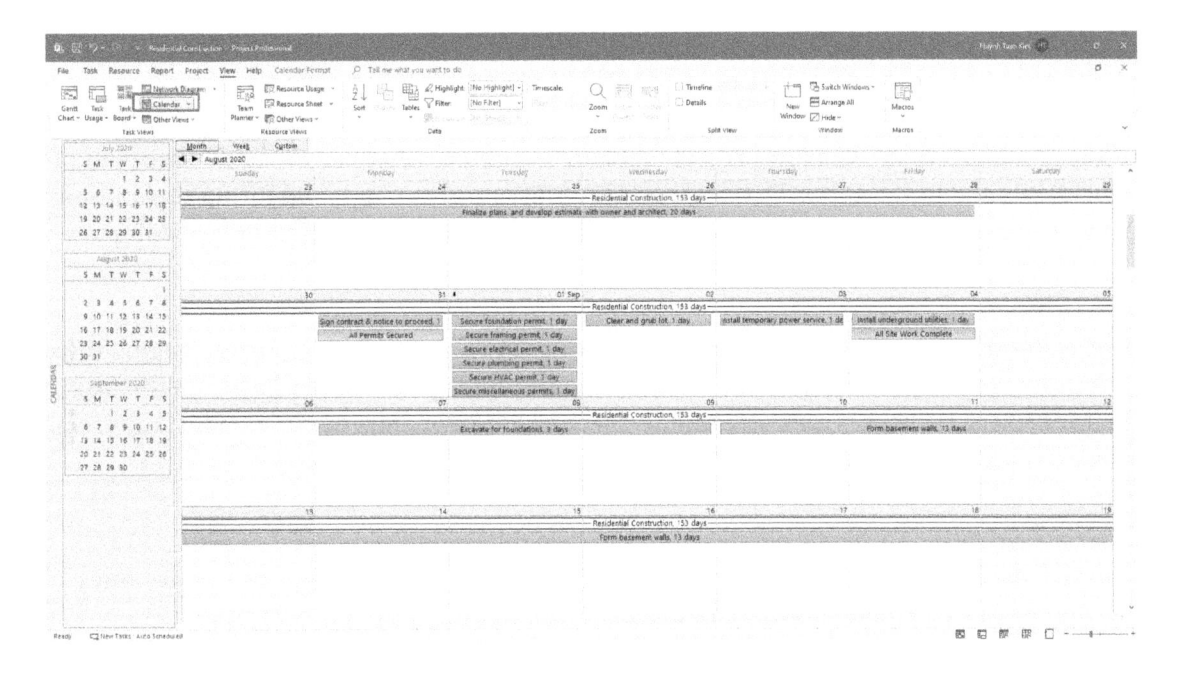

5. Network Diagram View: The Network Diagram view illustrates task dependencies using nodes and arrows, offering a visual representation of project workflows and critical paths. Project managers can analyze the sequence of tasks, identify bottlenecks, and assess the impact of delays on project timelines. The Network Diagram view facilitates comprehensive planning and optimization of project schedules.

6. Timeline View: Introduced in recent versions of Microsoft Project, the Timeline view provides a high-level overview of key milestones and tasks. Project managers can customize the timeline by selecting relevant tasks and milestones to include, adjusting their duration and formatting. The Timeline view is particularly useful for creating presentations and sharing project status updates with stakeholders.

7. Reports View: Microsoft Project offers a variety of predefined reports that consolidate project data into informative summaries. These reports cover various aspects of project management, including task progress, resource allocation, and cost analysis. Project managers can generate, customize, and export reports to communicate project performance effectively.

8. Custom Views: In addition to the predefined views provided by Microsoft Project, users can create custom views tailored to their specific requirements. Custom views allow project managers to display project data in a manner that aligns with their unique workflows and preferences. By defining custom filters, groupings, and formatting options, users can create personalized views that enhance productivity and decision-making.

Understanding the strengths and limitations of each view is essential for leveraging them effectively in project management. By selecting the appropriate views based on the task at hand, project managers can streamline their workflows, improve communication, and drive project success.

In the next subsection, we will explore strategies for customizing views and tables to further enhance productivity and data analysis capabilities in Microsoft Project.

2.3.2. Customizing Views and Tables

Customizing views and tables in Microsoft Project is a pivotal aspect of tailoring the software to meet the specific needs of your project and team. By customizing views and tables, you can streamline the display of information, focus on critical data, and enhance overall project management efficiency. This section delves into the various customization options available within Microsoft Project to empower project managers to optimize their workspace effectively.

Customizing Views

Views in Microsoft Project offer different perspectives of project data, allowing project managers to visualize information in various formats. Customizing views enables users to modify existing views or create new ones tailored to their project requirements. Here's how you can customize views in Microsoft Project:

Modifying Existing Views:

- *Selecting the View:* Navigate to the "View" tab on the Ribbon and choose the desired view from the "Task Views" or "Resource Views" group.

- *Adjusting View Settings:* Click on the "View Settings" button to modify the settings of the selected view, such as filtering tasks, adjusting timescales, or customizing columns.

- *Saving Changes:* After adjusting the settings, click "OK" to apply the modifications to the current view.

Creating New Views:

- *Accessing View Organizer:* Go to the "View" tab, click on the "Other Views" dropdown menu, and select "More Views" to access the View Organizer.

- *Adding a New View:* In the View Organizer dialog box, click "New" and specify the name and type of the new view (e.g., Gantt Chart, Task Sheet, Resource Sheet).

- *Customizing View Fields:* Define which fields are displayed in the view by selecting the "Details" button and choosing the desired fields from the Field Picker.

- *Setting Filters and Groupings:* Configure filters and groupings to organize and display data according to specific criteria.

- *Saving the Custom View:* Once the customization is complete, click "OK" to save the new view.

Customizing Tables

Tables in Microsoft Project determine the columns and data displayed within a view. Customizing tables allows project managers to tailor the presentation of information to suit their project management needs. Follow these steps to customize tables effectively:

Editing Existing Tables:

- *Selecting the Table:* Navigate to the "View" tab and click on the "Tables" dropdown menu to choose the desired table.

- *Modifying Table Columns:* Click on the "Table" dropdown menu again and select "More Tables" to access the Table Organizer. From there, select the table you want to modify and click "Edit" to adjust the columns.

- *Adding or Removing Columns:* In the "Column Definition" dialog box, add or remove columns by selecting them from the Available Columns list and using the arrow buttons to move them to the Displayed Columns list or vice versa.

- *Reordering Columns:* Change the order of columns by selecting a column in the "Displayed Columns" list and using the up and down arrow buttons to adjust its position.

- *Customizing Column Properties:* Click on the "Field Settings" button to customize the properties of individual columns, such as renaming, formatting, or setting specific display options.

- *Saving Changes:* Once the desired modifications are made, click "OK" to save the changes to the table.

Creating New Tables:

- *Accessing Table Organizer:* Follow the same steps as editing existing tables to access the Table Organizer.

- *Adding a New Table:* In the Table Organizer dialog box, click "New" and specify the name and type of the new table.

- *Defining Table Columns:* Customize the columns of the new table by selecting the "Column Definition" button and adding or removing columns as required.

- *Setting Column Properties:* Adjust the properties of each column using the "Field Settings" button to ensure the table displays the desired information accurately.

- *Saving the Custom Table:* Once the customization is complete, click "OK" to save the new table.

Conclusion

Customizing views and tables in Microsoft Project is indispensable for project managers aiming to maximize productivity and efficiency in project management. By tailoring views to display relevant data and customizing tables to present information in a clear and concise manner, project managers can effectively monitor progress, track resources, and make informed decisions throughout the project lifecycle. Mastering the art of customization empowers project managers to harness the full potential of Microsoft Project, turning it into a powerful tool for project planning, execution, and control.

2.3.3. Using Filters and Groupings

Filters and groupings are powerful tools in Microsoft Project that allow project managers to organize and analyze project data more effectively. By applying filters, you can focus on specific tasks, resources, or other project elements based on criteria such as dates, priorities, or resources. Grouping, on the other hand, enables you to categorize and summarize project information for better clarity and understanding. In this section, we will delve into the intricacies of using filters and groupings in Microsoft Project to enhance project management efficiency.

Utilizing Filters

Filters in Microsoft Project enable you to narrow down the information displayed in your project plan based on specific criteria. This feature is invaluable when dealing with large or complex projects, allowing you to focus on pertinent details. Here's how to effectively utilize filters:

1. Applying Filters:

   - To apply a filter, navigate to the "View" tab on the ribbon and click on the "Filter" dropdown menu.

- Select the desired filter criteria from the predefined options, such as "Incomplete Tasks" or "Critical Tasks."

- Alternatively, you can create custom filters by clicking on the "More Filters" option and specifying your criteria.

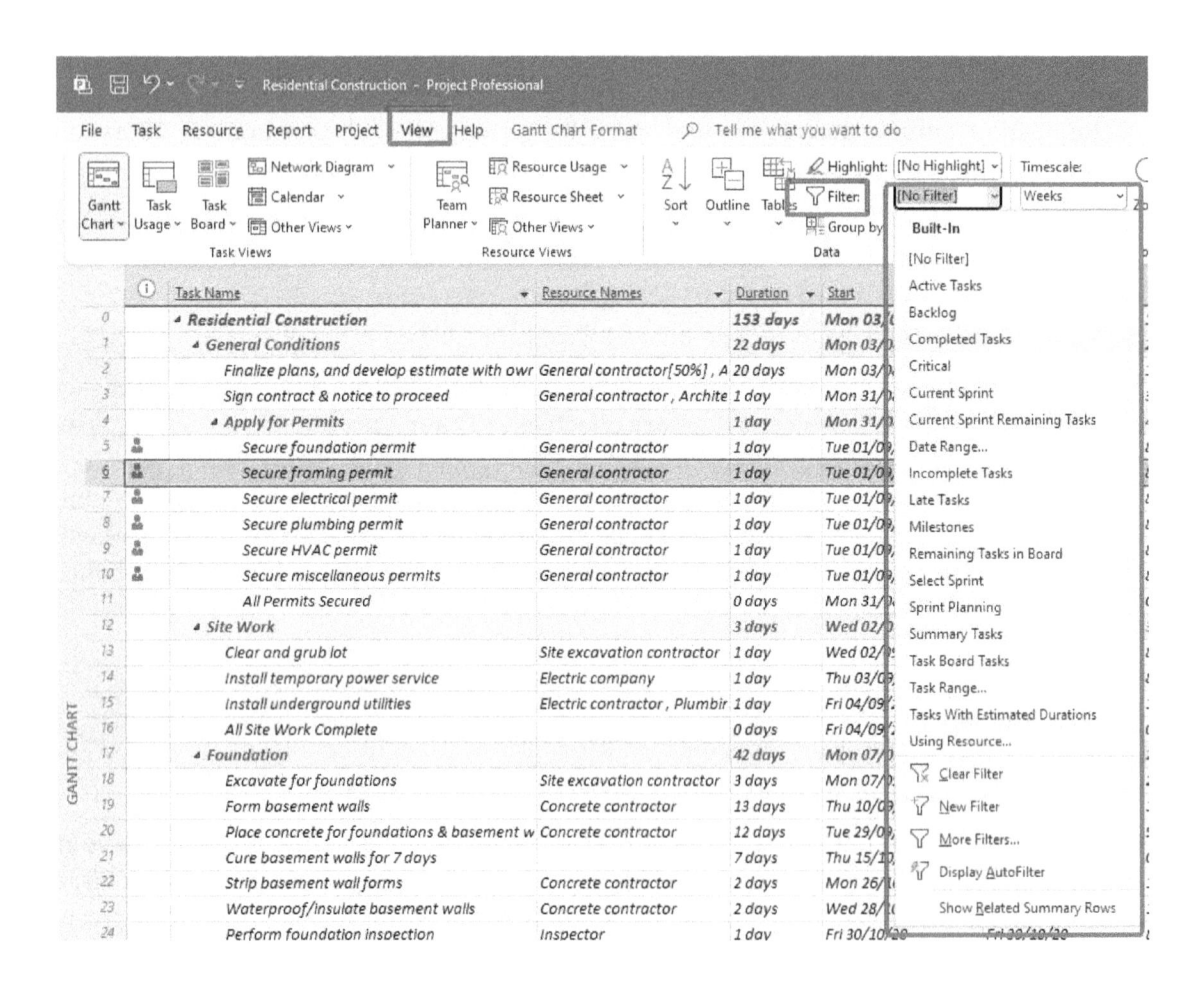

2. Customizing Filters:

- Microsoft Project offers extensive customization options for filters, allowing you to tailor them to your project's specific requirements.

- You can modify existing filters or create new ones by selecting the "More Filters" option and configuring the criteria using logical operators such as "equals," "contains," or "greater than."

3. Saving Filters:

   - Once you've created a custom filter, you can save it for future use by clicking on the "Save Filter" button and providing a name for the filter.

   - Saved filters appear in the "Filter" dropdown menu for easy access, allowing you to quickly apply them whenever needed.

4. Combining Filters:

   - Microsoft Project enables you to apply multiple filters simultaneously to refine your project data further.

   - To combine filters, simply apply one filter and then apply another, or use the "More Filters" option to specify multiple criteria.

5. Clearing Filters:

   - If you want to revert to displaying all project data, you can easily clear any applied filters by selecting the "All Tasks" or "All Resources" option from the "Filter" dropdown menu.

Using Groupings

Groupings in Microsoft Project facilitate the organization and analysis of project data by categorizing related items together. This feature is particularly useful for summarizing information and identifying patterns within your project plan. Here's how to leverage groupings effectively:

1. Grouping Tasks:

- To group tasks based on specific criteria, such as task type or resource assignment, navigate to the "View" tab and click on the "Group By" dropdown menu.

   - Choose the desired grouping criteria, such as "Task Type" or "Resource Name," to categorize tasks accordingly.

2. Customizing Groupings:

   - Microsoft Project offers flexibility in customizing groupings to suit your preferences.

   - You can adjust the order of groupings by dragging and dropping them within the "Group By" dropdown menu or create custom groupings by selecting the "More Groups" option.

3. Expanding and Collapsing Groups:

   - Once you've applied groupings, you can expand or collapse groups to view or hide underlying details.

   - Click on the arrow icon next to a group header to expand or collapse the group as needed, providing a concise overview of project data.

4. Summarizing Data:

   - Groupings enable you to generate summary information for each group, such as total duration or resource workload.

   - Microsoft Project automatically calculates summary values based on the underlying tasks or resources within each group, providing valuable insights into project metrics.

5. Printing Grouped Data:

   - When printing project reports, you can choose to include grouped data for a structured presentation of project information.

   - Ensure that the desired groupings are applied before generating the report to reflect the desired organization of data.

Conclusion

Filters and groupings are indispensable features in Microsoft Project for streamlining project management processes and enhancing data analysis capabilities. By leveraging filters, you can focus on specific aspects of your project plan, while groupings enable you to organize and summarize information for clearer insights. Mastering the use of filters and groupings empowers project managers to efficiently navigate and manipulate project data, ultimately contributing to the success of their projects.

PART III
Creating and Managing Tasks

3.1 Adding Tasks to Your Project

3.1.1. Task Entry Methods

In Microsoft Project, adding tasks to your project can be accomplished through various methods, each suited to different project management styles, preferences, and project complexity levels. Understanding these task entry methods equips project managers with the flexibility to choose the most efficient approach for their specific projects. In this section, we will explore the different task entry methods available in Microsoft Project and discuss their respective advantages and best-use scenarios.

Manual Task Entry

Manual task entry involves directly inputting task details into Microsoft Project without utilizing any automated features. This method offers the highest level of control and flexibility, allowing project managers to meticulously define each task according to project requirements. To manually add tasks:

1. Select a Task Entry Point: Navigate to the Gantt Chart view or Task Sheet view in Microsoft Project.

2. Click on the Task Name Cell: Choose the cell where you want to insert the new task.

3. Enter Task Details: Input the task name, start date, duration, and any other relevant information directly into the selected cell.

4. Press Enter: Once you've entered the task details, press Enter to confirm and move to the next task entry or cell.

Manual task entry is ideal for projects with a limited number of tasks or when precise control over task details is paramount. However, it may become time-consuming and error-prone for larger or more complex projects.

Task Creation Wizard

The Task Creation Wizard in Microsoft Project offers a guided approach to adding tasks, assisting users in systematically inputting task details. This method is particularly beneficial for users who prefer a structured workflow or are less familiar with project management terminology. To use the Task Creation Wizard:

1. Navigate to the Task Tab: Go to the Task tab on the ribbon at the top of the Microsoft Project interface.

2. Click on "Task Wizard": Locate the Task Wizard button and click on it to launch the Task Creation Wizard.

3. Follow the Prompts: The Task Creation Wizard will prompt you to enter task details step-by-step, such as task name, start date, duration, dependencies, and resources.

4. Review and Confirm: Once you've entered all the necessary details, review the summary provided by the Task Creation Wizard and confirm to add the tasks to your project.

The Task Creation Wizard streamlines the task entry process, reducing the likelihood of overlooking essential details and ensuring consistency across tasks. It is particularly useful for novice users or when quickly creating a project plan.

Importing Tasks from External Sources

Microsoft Project allows users to import tasks from external sources such as Excel spreadsheets, SharePoint lists, or other project management software. This method enables seamless integration of existing task lists or project plans into Microsoft Project, saving time and effort in manual data entry. To import tasks from external sources:

1. Prepare the External Data: Organize the task data in the external source, ensuring it is formatted correctly and compatible with Microsoft Project.

2. Navigate to the Import Wizard: In Microsoft Project, go to the File tab, select "Import," and choose the appropriate import option based on the source of your task data (e.g., Excel, SharePoint).

3. Follow the Import Steps: The Import Wizard will guide you through the process of mapping fields, selecting data to import, and configuring import settings.

4. Review and Confirm: Once the import process is complete, review the imported tasks in Microsoft Project to ensure accuracy and make any necessary adjustments.

Importing tasks from external sources is invaluable when transitioning from another project management tool or consolidating task data from multiple sources. It facilitates smooth data transfer and minimizes the risk of data entry errors.

Copy and Paste

Copying and pasting tasks within or between Microsoft Project files is a quick and efficient method for adding tasks, especially when dealing with repetitive or similar tasks. This method allows project managers to leverage existing task structures and templates, saving time and maintaining consistency across projects. To copy and paste tasks:

1. Select the Tasks to Copy: In the Gantt Chart view or Task Sheet view, select the tasks you want to copy by clicking on their task bars or selecting them from the task list.

2. Copy the Tasks: Right-click on the selected tasks and choose the "Copy" option from the context menu, or use the keyboard shortcut (Ctrl + C).

3. Navigate to the Paste Location: Move the cursor to the location where you want to paste the copied tasks within the same project or a different project file.

4. Paste the Tasks: Right-click in the desired location and select the "Paste" option from the context menu, or use the keyboard shortcut (Ctrl + V).

Copying and pasting tasks is particularly useful for creating project templates, replicating recurring task sequences, or transferring task structures between related projects. It promotes consistency and accelerates the project planning process.

Task Import from Outlook or SharePoint Tasks List

Microsoft Project offers integration with Outlook and SharePoint, allowing users to import tasks directly from Outlook tasks or SharePoint tasks lists. This integration streamlines task management by centralizing task data and facilitating collaboration among team members. To import tasks from Outlook or SharePoint:

1. Navigate to the Import Wizard: In Microsoft Project, go to the File tab, select "Import," and choose the option to import tasks from Outlook or SharePoint.

2. Authenticate and Connect: Follow the prompts to authenticate your Outlook or SharePoint account and establish a connection between Microsoft Project and the respective platform.

3. Select Tasks to Import: Choose the specific tasks or task lists you want to import into Microsoft Project.

4. Map Fields (if necessary): If there are differences in field names or formats between Outlook/SharePoint and Microsoft Project, map the fields accordingly to ensure accurate import.

5. Review and Confirm: Once the import process is complete, review the imported tasks in Microsoft Project to verify their details and make any necessary adjustments.

Importing tasks from Outlook or SharePoint enhances task visibility and collaboration by integrating task management with familiar productivity tools. It simplifies the process of assigning and tracking tasks across different platforms, promoting efficient project execution.

Task Import from Project Templates

Microsoft Project allows users to create and utilize project templates, which serve as predefined project structures containing tasks, resources, and other project elements. Importing tasks from project templates enables project managers to leverage standardized project frameworks and accelerate project planning. To import tasks from project templates:

1. Create or Select a Project Template: Start by creating a project template with the desired task structure and settings, or select an existing project template from the templates library.

2. Open Your Project: Launch Microsoft Project and open the project file where you want to import tasks from the project template.

3. Navigate to the Import Wizard: Go to the File tab, select "Import," and choose the option to import tasks from a project template.

4. Select the Template: Browse and select the project template you want to import tasks from.

5. Review and Confirm: Preview the tasks and other project elements included in the template, and confirm to import them into your project.

Importing tasks from project templates promotes consistency and standardization across projects by utilizing established project structures and best practices. It simplifies project setup and ensures adherence to organizational guidelines.

Task Creation via Email

Microsoft Project enables task creation directly from emails by leveraging its integration with Outlook. This feature facilitates seamless task assignment and tracking by converting emails into actionable tasks within Microsoft Project. To create tasks via email:

1. Open Outlook: Launch Microsoft Outlook and navigate to the email containing the task information you want to convert into a project task.

2. Select the Task: Highlight the relevant email or emails that contain the task details.

3. Convert to Task: Right-click on the selected email(s) and choose the option to "Create Task" or "Create Microsoft Project Task" from the context menu.

4. Configure Task Details: Specify the task name, start date, due date, priority, and any other relevant information for the task.

5. Save and Send: Once you've entered the task details, save the task within Outlook and optionally send it to the assigned resource(s) for action.

Creating tasks via email enhances communication and collaboration by seamlessly integrating task management with email workflows. It simplifies task assignment and ensures that actionable items from email correspondence are promptly addressed within the project context.

Task Creation via Voice Commands (Integration with Virtual Assistants)

With the advancement of technology, Microsoft Project offers integration with virtual assistants such as Cortana or third-party voice-enabled applications, enabling users to create tasks using voice commands. This hands-free task entry method enhances productivity by allowing users to capture task information verbally, without the need for manual input. To create tasks via voice commands:

1. Activate Voice Assistant: Invoke the voice assistant feature on your device by saying the wake word or pressing the designated activation button.

2. Issue Task Creation Command: Clearly state the task details, including the task name, start date, duration, and any other relevant information, using natural language.

3. Confirm Task Creation: Review the task details provided by the voice assistant and confirm to create the task in Microsoft Project.

4. Review and Edit (if necessary): After the task is created, review its details within Microsoft Project and make any necessary adjustments or additions.

Task creation via voice commands offers a convenient and efficient way to capture task information on-the-go or when hands are occupied. It streamlines task entry and reduces the need for manual data input, enhancing user productivity.

Task Creation via Mobile App

Microsoft Project's mobile app extends task creation capabilities to mobile devices, enabling users to create tasks anytime, anywhere, directly from their smartphones or tablets. This mobile task entry method empowers project managers to stay connected to their projects and capture task information on the fly. To create tasks via the mobile app:

1. Download and Install the Mobile App: Install the Microsoft Project mobile app on your iOS or Android device from the respective app store.

2. Log In: Launch the app and log in with your Microsoft Project account credentials to access your projects.

3. Navigate to Task Creation: Navigate to the task creation section within the app, typically located in the project dashboard or task management interface.

4. Enter Task Details: Input the task name, start date, duration, and any other necessary information using the mobile app's interface.

5. Save and Sync: Save the newly created task within the mobile app, ensuring that it syncs seamlessly with your Microsoft Project account and project file.

Task creation via the mobile app enhances project accessibility and flexibility by enabling project managers to manage tasks from anywhere with an internet connection. It facilitates real-time task updates and enhances collaboration among team members, even when they're on the move.

3.1.2. Setting Task Properties

Once you have added tasks to your project in Microsoft Project, the next step is to define and set their properties. Task properties encompass a range of attributes that provide crucial information about each task, including its duration, start and finish dates, resource assignments, constraints, and dependencies. Mastering the settings of task properties enables project managers to accurately plan, schedule, and monitor the progress of their projects. In this section, we will delve into the essential task properties and explore how to effectively configure them within Microsoft Project.

Task Duration

Task duration represents the amount of work required to complete a task. It can be expressed in various units such as hours, days, weeks, or months. Understanding and accurately estimating task durations are vital for creating realistic project schedules.

Microsoft Project offers flexible options for specifying task durations, including fixed durations, effort-driven tasks, and task types.

- *Fixed Duration:* In fixed duration tasks, the duration remains constant regardless of changes in resource assignments or work effort. This type of task is suitable for activities that require a specific amount of time to complete, such as waiting for a delivery or a curing process.

- *Effort-Driven Tasks:* Effort-driven tasks automatically adjust their duration based on the number of resources assigned to them. When additional resources are added, the total work effort is distributed among the resources, potentially reducing the task duration. Conversely, removing resources may extend the duration to accommodate the reduced workforce.

- *Task Types:* Microsoft Project offers different task types, such as Fixed Units, Fixed Duration, and Fixed Work. Each task type behaves differently in terms of duration, work, and resource allocation. Understanding these task types allows project managers to model task behavior accurately.

Task Constraints

Task constraints define the limitations or restrictions on when a task can start or finish. Constraints can be imposed by external factors such as project deadlines, resource availability, or dependencies on preceding tasks. While constraints provide valuable guidance, excessive constraints can restrict schedule flexibility and increase the risk of schedule conflicts. It is essential to use constraints judiciously and consider alternative scheduling options whenever possible.

- *Types of Constraints:* Microsoft Project offers various types of constraints, including Finish No Earlier Than (FNET), Finish No Later Than (FNLT), Start No Earlier Than (SNET), Start No Later Than (SNLT), Must Finish On (MFO), Must Start On (MSO), As Late As Possible

(ALAP), and As Soon As Possible (ASAP). Each type of constraint influences the scheduling of tasks differently.

- *Constraint Prioritization:* When multiple constraints are applied to a task, Microsoft Project prioritizes them based on their hierarchy. Understanding the order of constraint prioritization helps project managers ensure that tasks are scheduled according to the intended constraints.

1. Finish No Earlier Than (FNET): Specifies the earliest date or time when a task can finish. The task cannot finish before this specified date.

2. Finish No Later Than (FNLT): Sets the latest allowable finish date or time for a task. The task must be completed by this specified date.

3. Start No Earlier Than (SNET): Defines the earliest allowable start date or time for a task. The task cannot begin before this specified date.

4. Start No Later Than (SNLT): Specifies the latest allowable start date or time for a task. The task must start by this specified date.

5. Must Finish On (MFO): Mandates that a task must be completed on a specific date. The task is constrained to finish exactly on the specified date.

6. Must Start On (MSO): Requires a task to start on a particular date. The task is constrained to begin precisely on the specified date.

7. As Late As Possible (ALAP): Allows the task to start as late as possible without delaying the project finish date. It provides flexibility in scheduling by delaying the start of the task as much as possible.

8. As Soon As Possible (ASAP): Directs the task to start as soon as possible. It schedules the task to begin immediately, considering dependencies and resource availability.

Understanding the implications of each constraint type helps project managers ensure that tasks are scheduled appropriately and that project deadlines are met without unnecessary constraints hindering flexibility.

Task Dependencies

Task dependencies establish the relationships between different tasks in a project. These relationships define the sequence in which tasks must be executed to achieve project objectives. Microsoft Project supports various types of task dependencies, including finish-to-start (FS), start-to-start (SS), finish-to-finish (FF), and start-to-finish (SF). By accurately defining task dependencies, project managers can ensure smooth project progression and avoid scheduling conflicts.

- *Dependency Types:* Each type of task dependency governs how the start or finish of one task affects the start or finish of its successor. Understanding the characteristics of each dependency type is essential for creating realistic and efficient project schedules.

- *Lead and Lag Time:* Lead time allows for acceleration in the successor task, enabling overlap between tasks, while lag time introduces a delay between tasks. Mastering the use of lead and lag time enhances schedule flexibility and optimizes project timelines.

1. Finish-to-Start (FS): The successor task cannot start until the predecessor task finishes. This is the most common type of dependency.

2. Start-to-Start (SS): The successor task cannot start until the predecessor task starts. Both tasks occur simultaneously but may have different durations.

3. Finish-to-Finish (FF): The successor task cannot finish until the predecessor task finishes. Both tasks end simultaneously but may have different start times.

4. Start-to-Finish (SF): The successor task cannot finish until the predecessor task starts. This type is less common and often used to model scenarios where two tasks are related in a unique way.

Each type of dependency offers specific advantages and is used to model different relationships between tasks within a project. By accurately defining task dependencies, project managers can ensure that tasks are sequenced logically and that the project progresses smoothly toward completion.

Task Resources

Task resources represent the individuals, equipment, or materials required to complete a task. Assigning resources to tasks allows project managers to allocate work efficiently and monitor resource utilization. Microsoft Project offers robust resource management capabilities, including resource allocation, leveling, and tracking. By effectively managing task resources, project managers can optimize workforce productivity and ensure project success.

- *Resource Allocation:* Assigning appropriate resources to tasks ensures that the necessary skills and capacities are available to complete the work on schedule. Microsoft Project provides tools for resource assignment, including resource calendars, availability profiles, and resource leveling.

- *Resource Leveling:* Resource leveling optimizes resource utilization by resolving overallocation and balancing workloads across resources. By smoothing resource assignments, project managers can avoid resource bottlenecks and prevent project delays.

- *Resource Tracking:* Monitoring resource performance allows project managers to identify potential issues such as underutilization or overallocation promptly. Microsoft Project offers features for tracking resource progress, including resource usage views, histograms, and reports.

Task Notes and Attachments

Task notes and attachments provide additional information and documentation related to individual tasks. Notes can include details such as task descriptions, instructions, or references to external resources. Attachments enable project managers to associate relevant files or documents directly with tasks, enhancing communication and collaboration within the project team. By leveraging task notes and attachments, project managers can ensure clarity and accessibility of task information throughout the project lifecycle.

- *Task Notes:* Adding descriptive notes to tasks helps clarify their purpose, requirements, or dependencies. Task notes serve as a valuable reference for team members and stakeholders, facilitating better understanding and communication.

- *Task Attachments:* Attaching files or documents to tasks allows project managers to consolidate relevant information in a centralized location. Attachments can include specifications, drawings, reports, or any other materials essential for task execution. By providing easy access to supporting documents, task attachments streamline collaboration and decision-making.

Conclusion

Setting task properties is a fundamental aspect of project management in Microsoft Project. By accurately defining task durations, constraints, dependencies, resources, and supplementary information, project managers can create comprehensive and actionable project plans. Mastering the configuration of task properties enables project managers to optimize project schedules, allocate resources effectively, and mitigate risks. With Microsoft Project's robust features and capabilities, project managers can streamline project management processes and drive project success from initiation to completion.

3.2 Organizing Tasks into Phases and Milestones

3.2.1. Creating Task Outlines

In project management, creating a well-organized task outline is paramount to ensure clarity, efficiency, and effective communication within the project team. Task outlines serve as the backbone of your project plan, providing a hierarchical structure that breaks down the project into manageable components. This section will delve into the significance of task outlines, methods for creating them, and best practices for maintaining them throughout the project lifecycle.

Importance of Task Outlines

Task outlines, also known as work breakdown structures (WBS), offer several benefits to project managers and team members:

1. Clarity and Structure: By breaking down the project into smaller, digestible tasks, a task outline provides clarity on project scope and deliverables. It delineates the sequence of activities required to accomplish project objectives, offering a structured roadmap for project execution.

2. Granular Planning: Task outlines allow for granular planning by organizing project work into manageable components. This facilitates better estimation of resources, time, and costs associated with each task, leading to more accurate project scheduling and budgeting.

3. Communication and Collaboration: A well-defined task outline enhances communication and collaboration among project stakeholders. It provides a common language for discussing project details, facilitating effective coordination and alignment of efforts across the team.

4. Progress Tracking: Task outlines serve as a reference for tracking progress throughout the project lifecycle. By breaking the project into smaller milestones and tasks, it becomes easier to monitor progress, identify bottlenecks, and take corrective actions as needed.

Methods for Creating Task Outlines

Creating a task outline involves decomposing the project scope into smaller, manageable tasks in a hierarchical manner. Several methods can be employed to develop a comprehensive task outline:

1. Top-Down Approach: In this method, the project manager starts by identifying the major deliverables or project phases and then decomposes them into sub-phases or tasks. This approach provides a high-level view of the project's structure before drilling down into finer details.

2. Bottom-Up Approach: Conversely, the bottom-up approach begins with identifying individual tasks or work packages and then aggregating them to form higher-level deliverables or phases. This method allows for a more detailed analysis of tasks from the ground up.

3. Mind Mapping: Mind mapping is a visual technique that involves brainstorming ideas and organizing them in a hierarchical, interconnected format. Project managers can use mind mapping tools to capture project tasks, dependencies, and relationships in a visually appealing and intuitive manner.

4. Work Packages Identification: Work packages are discrete units of work that can be assigned to a specific team member or group. Breaking down the project scope into work packages helps in identifying individual tasks and organizing them into a structured outline.

5. Use of Templates: Project management software often provides pre-defined templates for creating task outlines based on industry best practices. These templates offer a starting point for structuring project work and can be customized to suit the specific needs of the project.

Best Practices for Maintaining Task Outlines

Once created, task outlines require regular maintenance and updates to ensure their relevance and accuracy throughout the project lifecycle. Here are some best practices for maintaining task outlines:

1. Regular Review and Revision: Schedule periodic reviews of the task outline to incorporate any changes in project scope, requirements, or priorities. Update the outline accordingly to reflect the current status of the project.

2. Document Changes: Document any changes or updates made to the task outline, including the rationale behind the modifications and the impact on project deliverables, schedule, and resources. This helps in maintaining a clear audit trail of project revisions.

3. Version Control: Implement version control mechanisms to track different iterations of the task outline. Maintain a master copy of the outline and use versioning to manage revisions and ensure that all stakeholders are working with the latest version.

4. Alignment with Project Objectives: Ensure that the task outline remains aligned with the project objectives and goals. Regularly assess whether the outlined tasks contribute towards achieving project success and make adjustments as necessary.

5. Engage Stakeholders: Involve relevant stakeholders, such as team members, clients, and sponsors, in the review and validation of the task outline. Solicit feedback and incorporate suggestions to improve the comprehensiveness and accuracy of the outline.

6. Training and Documentation: Provide training to project team members on how to use and interpret the task outline effectively. Develop documentation that outlines the purpose, structure, and guidelines for maintaining the task outline throughout the project.

By adhering to these best practices, project managers can ensure that the task outline remains a valuable tool for planning, executing, and monitoring project activities effectively.

Conclusion

Creating and maintaining a well-organized task outline is essential for successful project management. Task outlines provide a structured framework for breaking down the project scope, planning project activities, and tracking progress towards project goals. By following the methods and best practices outlined in this section, project managers can develop comprehensive task outlines that serve as invaluable guides for project execution and control.

Let's consider a hypothetical project to develop a mobile application for a ride-sharing service. We'll create a task outline using the top-down approach.

Project: Mobile App Development for Ride-Sharing Service

1. Project Initiation

  - 1.1 Define Project Scope

  - 1.2 Identify Stakeholders

  - 1.3 Conduct Market Research

2. Planning Phase

- 2.1 Gather Requirements

- 2.2 Develop Project Plan

    - 2.2.1 Define Project Objectives

    - 2.2.2 Create Work Breakdown Structure

- 2.3 Resource Allocation

- 2.4 Risk Assessment and Mitigation

3. Development Phase

- 3.1 Design User Interface

- 3.2 Backend Development

    - 3.2.1 Database Design

    - 3.2.2 Server Configuration

- 3.3 Frontend Development

- 3.4 Integration Testing

4. Testing Phase

- 4.1 Unit Testing

- 4.2 System Testing

- 4.3 User Acceptance Testing

- 4.4 Bug Fixing and Quality Assurance

5. Deployment Phase

- 5.1 App Deployment to App Stores

- 5.2 Marketing and Promotion

- 5.3 User Training and Support

6. Post-Deployment Activities

- 6.1 Monitor App Performance

- 6.2 Gather User Feedback

- 6.3 Continuous Improvement and Updates

This task outline provides a structured breakdown of the project activities from initiation to post-deployment. Each major phase is further broken down into specific tasks and subtasks, enabling project managers to plan, allocate resources, and track progress effectively. As the project progresses, tasks can be added, modified, or reorganized to adapt to changing requirements and priorities.

3.2.2. Defining Project Phases and Milestones

Defining project phases and milestones is a critical aspect of project planning and execution. Project phases represent a collection of related tasks that mark a significant stage or achievement in the project's lifecycle. On the other hand, milestones are specific points in time within a phase that signify the completion of a key deliverable or the achievement of an important goal. Effectively defining project phases and milestones helps project managers and team members track progress, manage dependencies, and ensure that the project stays on track towards its ultimate objectives.

Importance of Project Phases and Milestones

1. Structuring the Project: Breaking down a project into phases provides a structured approach to project management. It helps in organizing tasks, allocating resources, and managing dependencies more effectively.

2. Progress Tracking: Project phases and milestones serve as checkpoints for monitoring progress. They allow project managers to assess whether the project is advancing according to the schedule and if adjustments are needed to keep it on track.

3. Communication and Reporting: Clearly defined phases and milestones facilitate communication among project stakeholders. They provide a common language for discussing project progress, risks, and issues, thereby enhancing transparency and alignment among team members and stakeholders.

4. Risk Management: Identifying project phases and milestones enables project managers to anticipate and mitigate risks more effectively. By breaking the project into manageable segments, potential risks can be identified early and appropriate risk mitigation strategies can be implemented.

Guidelines for Defining Project Phases and Milestones

1. Understand Project Scope: Before defining project phases and milestones, it's essential to have a thorough understanding of the project scope, objectives, and deliverables. This clarity ensures that the phases and milestones are aligned with the project's goals and requirements.

2. Involve Key Stakeholders: Collaboration with key stakeholders, including clients, team members, and subject matter experts, is crucial in defining project phases and milestones. Their input helps in identifying critical tasks, dependencies, and key deliverables.

3. Use a Hierarchical Structure: Organize project phases in a hierarchical structure, with each phase representing a broader stage of the project. Break down each phase into smaller, more manageable tasks and activities.

4. Focus on Deliverables and Outcomes: Define milestones based on tangible deliverables or outcomes rather than intermediate tasks. Milestones should represent significant achievements or completions within each phase of the project.

5. Set Clear Criteria for Milestone Completion: Clearly define the criteria that indicate the completion of each milestone. This ensures that there is no ambiguity regarding when a milestone has been achieved and allows for accurate tracking of progress.

6. Consider Dependencies and Constraints: Take into account task dependencies, resource constraints, and external factors when defining project phases and milestones. Ensure that dependencies between tasks are properly identified and managed to prevent delays and bottlenecks.

7. Be Flexible and Iterative: Project phases and milestones should be flexible enough to accommodate changes and adjustments during the project lifecycle. Review and update them regularly based on evolving project requirements, feedback from stakeholders, and lessons learned from previous phases.

Examples of Project Phases and Milestones

1. Initiation Phase: This phase involves defining project objectives, establishing project governance, and obtaining approval to proceed. Milestones in this phase may include the completion of a project charter, stakeholder identification, and project kickoff meeting.

2. Planning Phase: During this phase, detailed project plans are developed, including scope, schedule, budget, and resource allocation. Milestones may include the completion of a project management plan, stakeholder communication plan, and risk management plan.

3. Execution Phase: This phase focuses on executing the project activities according to the project plan. Milestones may include the completion of key deliverables, such as the development of a prototype, the launch of a marketing campaign, or the implementation of a software system.

4. Monitoring and Controlling Phase: In this phase, project performance is monitored, and corrective actions are taken as needed to keep the project on track. Milestones may include regular progress reviews, variance analysis reports, and change control board meetings.

5. Closure Phase: The closure phase involves formally closing out the project, documenting lessons learned, and transitioning deliverables to the client or end-users. Milestones may include the completion of a final project report, customer acceptance, and project closure meeting.

Here are specific examples illustrating project phases and milestones for a hypothetical software development project:

Example: Software Development Project

1. Initiation Phase:

  - *Milestone 1:* Completion of Project Charter

   - Description: Formal document outlining project objectives, scope, stakeholders, and high-level requirements.

   - Criteria for Completion: Approval by project sponsor and key stakeholders.

2. Planning Phase:

  - *Milestone 2:* Finalization of Project Plan

   - Description: Detailed project plan including scope, schedule, budget, resource allocation, and risk management approach.

   - Criteria for Completion: Approval by project manager and project team.

3. Design Phase:

- *Milestone 3:* Completion of System Design Specification

- Description: Detailed technical specifications outlining system architecture, data models, and user interface designs.

- Criteria for Completion: Approval by development team and client.

4. Development Phase:

- *Milestone 4:* Alpha Release

- Description: Initial version of the software with core functionalities implemented.

- Criteria for Completion: Successful completion of alpha testing with identified bugs logged and prioritized.

- *Milestone 5:* Beta Release

- Description: Beta version of the software for wider testing and feedback from select users or stakeholders.

- Criteria for Completion: Completion of beta testing with major issues resolved and performance improvements implemented.

5. Testing Phase:

- *Milestone 6:* User Acceptance Testing (UAT) Sign-Off

- Description: Formal acceptance of the software by the client or end-users based on predefined acceptance criteria.

- Criteria for Completion: Successful completion of UAT with no critical defects outstanding.

6. Deployment Phase:

- *Milestone 7:* Production Deployment

- Description: Deployment of the final version of the software into the production environment.

- Criteria for Completion: Successful deployment with no disruption to business operations.

7. Post-Deployment Phase:

- *Milestone 8:* Post-Deployment Review

- Description: Review of the project's performance, lessons learned, and opportunities for improvement.

- Criteria for Completion: Completion of post-deployment review meeting with key stakeholders and documentation of lessons learned.

In this example, each project phase is accompanied by specific milestones that signify the completion of key deliverables or achievements. These milestones help track progress, manage dependencies, and ensure successful project completion.

Tools for Managing Project Phases and Milestones

Several project management tools and software applications can help in defining, tracking, and managing project phases and milestones. Microsoft Project, for example, provides features for creating project plans, defining tasks and milestones, setting dependencies, and generating progress reports. Other popular project management tools include Asana, Trello, and Jira, each offering unique features for managing project phases and milestones effectively.

- Microsoft Project: For creating and managing project plans, defining tasks, and tracking progress.

- Jira: For issue tracking, agile project management, and collaboration among development teams.

- Confluence: For documenting project requirements, design specifications, and meeting notes.

In conclusion, defining project phases and milestones is a fundamental aspect of project management that provides structure, clarity, and accountability throughout the project lifecycle. By following the guidelines outlined above and leveraging appropriate tools and techniques, project managers can effectively define, track, and manage project phases and milestones to ensure the successful delivery of project objectives.

3.3 Linking and Unlinking Tasks

3.3.1. Task Dependencies Overview

In project management, tasks rarely exist in isolation. They are often interdependent, meaning the completion of one task may rely on the completion of another. This interconnection between tasks is managed through task dependencies. Understanding how to link and unlink tasks, as well as comprehending the various types of task relationships, is fundamental to effective project planning and execution.

Task dependencies define the relationships between tasks in a project. They determine the sequence in which tasks should be executed, ensuring that the project progresses smoothly from start to finish. By establishing dependencies, project managers can create realistic schedules, identify critical paths, and manage project constraints effectively.

Types of Task Dependencies

There are four primary types of task dependencies:

1. Finish-to-Start (FS): This is the most common type of dependency, where the successor task cannot start until the predecessor task is complete. It represents a sequential relationship between tasks.

2. Start-to-Start (SS): In this type of dependency, the successor task cannot start until the predecessor task has started. Both tasks occur simultaneously but have different start dates.

3. Finish-to-Finish (FF): Here, the successor task cannot finish until the predecessor task has finished. Both tasks occur simultaneously but have different end dates.

4. Start-to-Finish (SF): This is the least common type of dependency, where the successor task cannot finish until the predecessor task has started. It represents a relationship where the completion of one task allows the other to finish.

Understanding these dependency types allows project managers to accurately model the relationships between tasks and determine the most efficient sequence for completing them.

Benefits of Task Dependencies

Implementing task dependencies offers several benefits to project management:

- *Sequence Management:* Dependencies help in establishing the order in which tasks should be executed, preventing conflicts and ensuring a logical flow of work.

- *Resource Allocation:* By understanding task dependencies, project managers can allocate resources more effectively, ensuring that resources are available when needed.

- *Critical Path Analysis:* Task dependencies play a crucial role in identifying the critical path of a project—the longest sequence of tasks that determines the minimum duration required to complete the project.

- *Risk Management:* Recognizing dependencies allows project managers to anticipate potential delays or bottlenecks and proactively mitigate risks.

Establishing Task Dependencies

In Microsoft Project, establishing task dependencies is straightforward. Here's how to do it:

1. Identify Predecessor and Successor Tasks: Determine which tasks are dependent on others and which tasks they depend on.

2. Select the Predecessor Task: In the Gantt Chart view, select the predecessor task—the task that must be completed before the successor task can begin.

3. Link Tasks: Click on the "Link Tasks" button or press "Ctrl" + "F2" to establish a finish-to-start dependency between the selected predecessor and the successor task.

4. Adjust Dependency Types: Depending on the nature of the relationship, you may need to adjust the dependency type. Right-click on the dependency line and choose the appropriate type from the context menu.

5. Review and Refine: Once dependencies are established, review the project schedule to ensure that it reflects the desired sequence of tasks. Make any necessary adjustments to refine the schedule.

By following these steps, project managers can effectively establish and manage task dependencies in Microsoft Project, facilitating smooth project execution and successful delivery.

Conclusion

Task dependencies are integral to project management, providing the framework for sequencing tasks, allocating resources, and managing project schedules. Understanding how to link and unlink tasks, as well as recognizing the various types of task relationships, empowers project managers to create realistic schedules, identify critical paths, and mitigate risks effectively. By leveraging the features of Microsoft Project, project managers can streamline the process of establishing and managing task dependencies, ultimately contributing to the successful delivery of projects.

3.3.2. Linking and Unlinking Tasks

Linking and unlinking tasks in Microsoft Project is a fundamental aspect of establishing task dependencies, which dictate the sequence in which tasks are performed within a project. By linking tasks, you create relationships that determine the start and finish dates of tasks based on the completion of preceding tasks. Conversely, unlinking tasks removes these dependencies, allowing for more flexibility in scheduling.

Linking Tasks:

Linking tasks in Microsoft Project is a straightforward process that can be accomplished using various methods, including the Gantt Chart view, Task Information dialog box, and Task Dependency dialog box.

Using the Gantt Chart View:

1. Navigate to the Gantt Chart View: Open your project in Microsoft Project and switch to the Gantt Chart view.

2. Select the Tasks to Link: Click on the first task you want to link, hold down the "Ctrl" key (Cmd key on Mac), and then click on the subsequent tasks you want to link. Alternatively, you can click and drag to select multiple tasks.

3. Link the Tasks: Once the tasks are selected, right-click on one of the selected tasks to open the context menu. From the menu, choose "Link Tasks." This action will establish dependencies between the selected tasks based on their sequence.

4. Review the Dependencies: After linking the tasks, review the Gantt Chart to ensure that the dependencies are accurately represented. You should see arrows indicating the flow of tasks based on their dependencies.

Using the Task Information Dialog Box:

1. Select the First Task: Click on the task you want to link from the Gantt Chart view to highlight it.

2. Open Task Information: Right-click on the selected task and choose "Task Information" from the context menu. Alternatively, you can double-click on the task to open the Task Information dialog box.

3. Navigate to the Predecessors Tab: In the Task Information dialog box, navigate to the "Predecessors" tab.

4. Add Predecessor Tasks: In the "Predecessors" tab, click on the empty cell under the "Task Name" column and type or select the name of the task that precedes the current task. You can add multiple predecessor tasks by separating them with commas.

5. Specify Dependency Type: In the "Type" column, specify the type of dependency relationship between the tasks (e.g., Finish-to-Start, Start-to-Start, Finish-to-Finish, Start-to-Finish).

6. Save Changes: Click "OK" to save the changes and establish the dependencies between the tasks.

Unlinking Tasks:

Unlinking tasks in Microsoft Project removes the dependency relationships between them, allowing for independent scheduling.

Using the Gantt Chart View:

1. Navigate to the Gantt Chart View: Open your project in Microsoft Project and switch to the Gantt Chart view.

2. Select the Linked Tasks: Click on one of the linked tasks to select it.

3. Unlink the Tasks: Right-click on the selected task to open the context menu, and then choose "Unlink Tasks." This action will remove the dependency relationships between the selected tasks.

4. Review the Changes: After unlinking the tasks, review the Gantt Chart to ensure that the tasks are no longer linked, indicated by the absence of arrows between them.

Using the Task Information Dialog Box:

1. Select the Task: Click on the task you want to unlink to highlight it in the Gantt Chart view.

2. Open Task Information: Right-click on the selected task and choose "Task Information" from the context menu. Alternatively, you can double-click on the task to open the Task Information dialog box.

3. Navigate to the Predecessors Tab: In the Task Information dialog box, navigate to the "Predecessors" tab.

4. Remove Predecessor Tasks: In the "Predecessors" tab, select the name(s) of the predecessor task(s) listed and press the "Delete" key on your keyboard to remove them.

5. Save Changes: Click "OK" to save the changes and remove the dependency relationships between the tasks.

Benefits of Linking and Unlinking Tasks:

Linking tasks in Microsoft Project offers several benefits:

1. Sequence Management: Linking tasks helps in defining the sequence in which tasks should be executed, ensuring a logical flow of work within the project.

2. Dependency Management: Task dependencies enable accurate scheduling by ensuring that tasks are completed in the correct order based on their relationships.

3. Critical Path Analysis: Linking tasks facilitates critical path analysis, allowing project managers to identify the longest path of tasks and determine the minimum project duration.

4. Flexibility: Unlinking tasks provides flexibility in scheduling by removing strict dependency relationships, allowing for adjustments without affecting other tasks.

5. Scenario Planning: By linking and unlinking tasks, project managers can conduct scenario planning to evaluate the impact of changes on project schedules and outcomes.

In conclusion, mastering the art of linking and unlinking tasks in Microsoft Project is essential for effective project management. By understanding how to establish and remove task dependencies, project managers can optimize scheduling, manage dependencies, and ensure project success.

3.3.3. Types of Task Relationships

In Microsoft Project, task relationships define the sequence in which tasks should be executed within a project. These relationships dictate the flow of work and ensure that tasks are completed in the correct order. Understanding the different types of task relationships available in Microsoft Project is crucial for effective project planning and scheduling. Let's explore the various types of task relationships:

1. Finish-to-Start (FS):

  - This is the most common type of task relationship.

  - It signifies that the successor task cannot start until the predecessor task finishes.

  - In simpler terms, Task B cannot begin until Task A is completed.

2. Start-to-Start (SS):

  - With this relationship, the successor task can start as soon as the predecessor task begins.

  - It allows for overlapping of tasks.

- For example, Task B can start at the same time as Task A.

3. Finish-to-Finish (FF):

- In this relationship, the successor task can only finish once the predecessor task is finished.

- It is useful when two tasks must end simultaneously or have a dependency on each other's completion.

- For instance, if Task B involves reviewing the results of Task A, Task B cannot end until Task A finishes.

4. Start-to-Finish (SF):

- This relationship is less common and often more complex.

- It means that the successor task cannot finish until the predecessor task starts.

- It is typically used in scenarios where the start of one task triggers the completion of another.

- An example could be a training session that cannot end until a certain task begins.

Certainly! Let's illustrate each type of task relationship with a specific example:

1. Finish-to-Start (FS):

Example: Building a House

- Task A: Pouring Foundation
- Task B: Framing Walls

In this scenario, Task B (Framing Walls) cannot start until Task A (Pouring Foundation) is completed. The pouring of the foundation is a prerequisite for framing the walls of the house.

2. Start-to-Start (SS):

Example: Research Project

- Task A: Literature Review
- Task B: Data Collection

For this research project, Task B (Data Collection) can start as soon as Task A (Literature Review) begins. Both tasks can overlap, allowing for a more efficient use of time.

3. Finish-to-Finish (FF):

Example: Software Testing

- Task A: Code Development
- Task B: Testing

In software development, Task B (Testing) cannot finish until Task A (Code Development) is complete. Testing is dependent on the completion of coding to ensure that the software functions as intended.

4. Start-to-Finish (SF):

Example: Event Planning

- Task A: Event Setup
- Task B: Event Cleanup

In event planning, Task B (Event Cleanup) cannot finish until Task A (Event Setup) starts. The cleanup process can only commence once the setup phase begins, ensuring a smooth transition from one phase to the next.

These examples demonstrate how different types of task relationships govern the sequencing of activities within a project, highlighting their importance in project management and scheduling.

Establishing Task Relationships in Microsoft Project:

Now that we've covered the different types of task relationships, let's delve into how you can establish these relationships within Microsoft Project:

1. Using the Gantt Chart:

  - The Gantt Chart view in Microsoft Project provides a visual representation of your project schedule.

  - To establish task relationships using the Gantt Chart, simply select the predecessor task, then select the successor task, and choose the appropriate relationship type from the Task tab.

2. Using the Task Information Dialog Box:

- Another method is to use the Task Information dialog box.

   - Double-click on the predecessor task to open the Task Information dialog box, go to the Predecessors tab, and add the successor task with the desired relationship type.

3. *Using Task Dependency Commands:*

   - Microsoft Project offers specific commands to establish task relationships quickly.

   - These commands can be found in the Schedule group on the Task tab.

   - You can choose from options like "Link Tasks" or "Unlink Tasks" to create or remove relationships between tasks.

Managing Task Relationships:

Once task relationships are established, it's essential to manage them effectively throughout the project lifecycle. Here are some tips for managing task relationships in Microsoft Project:

1. *Regularly Review and Update Dependencies:*

   - As the project progresses, task dependencies may need to be adjusted.

   - Regularly review and update task relationships to reflect any changes in project scope or timeline.

2. *Use Constraints Wisely:*

   - Constraints can be used to control the start or finish dates of tasks, but they can also impact task relationships.

   - Be cautious when applying constraints, as they can sometimes conflict with task dependencies and lead to scheduling issues.

3. Utilize Lag and Lead Time:

   - Lag and lead time can be added to task relationships to introduce delays or overlaps between tasks.

   - Use these options strategically to fine-tune the sequence of tasks and optimize project scheduling.

4. Monitor Critical Path:

   - The critical path in a project is the sequence of tasks that determines the project's overall duration.

   - Keep a close eye on tasks on the critical path and their relationships to ensure that any delays are promptly addressed to avoid project delays.

Conclusion:

Task relationships play a fundamental role in project management, shaping the flow and sequence of work within a project. By understanding the various types of task relationships and how to establish and manage them effectively in Microsoft Project, project managers can create realistic schedules and ensure project success. Regularly reviewing and updating task relationships, utilizing available tools and techniques, and monitoring critical paths are essential practices for effective task relationship management.

PART IV
Scheduling and Timeline Management

4.1 Understanding Task Dependencies

4.1.1. Types of Task Dependencies

"In the previous section, **'3.3.3. Types of Task Relationships**,' we extensively covered the various types of task dependencies, also known as task relationships. These dependencies play a fundamental role in shaping the sequencing and interdependencies of tasks within a project. Let's briefly recap the key types of task dependencies discussed:

1. Finish-to-Start (FS): This dependency indicates that the successor task cannot start until the predecessor task is completed. It represents the most common and straightforward relationship between tasks.

2. Start-to-Start (SS): In this relationship, the successor task cannot start until the predecessor task begins. It allows for overlapping activities and is useful when certain tasks can commence simultaneously.

3. Finish-to-Finish (FF): Here, the successor task cannot finish until the predecessor task is completed. This dependency ensures synchronization between related activities, as both tasks must conclude concurrently.

4. Start-to-Finish (SF): This less common relationship dictates that the successor task cannot finish until the predecessor task begins. It may lead to complex scheduling scenarios and is used sparingly.

By understanding these types of task dependencies, project managers gain valuable insights into the logical relationships between tasks and can effectively plan and manage project schedules."

This approach helps seamlessly integrate the content from the previous section into the current discussion, providing continuity for the reader while avoiding redundancy.

4.1.1. Task Dependency Constraints

Significance of Task Dependency Constraints:

Task dependency constraints serve several crucial purposes in project management:

- *Sequence Management:* Constraints define the logical order in which tasks should be performed, ensuring that project activities are sequenced correctly.

- *Schedule Optimization:* By specifying constraints, project managers can refine the project schedule, minimizing delays and maximizing efficiency.

- *Resource Allocation:* Constraints help in allocating resources effectively by synchronizing task dependencies with resource availability.

- *Risk Mitigation:* Certain constraints, such as those indicating mandatory dependencies, help in managing project risks by ensuring critical tasks are completed on time.

Managing Task Dependency Constraints in Microsoft Project:

Microsoft Project offers a range of features to manage task dependency constraints effectively:

1. Setting Constraint Types:

- Project managers can specify the type of constraint for each task in the project schedule. By default, tasks are set to the FS (Finish-to-Start) constraint, but this can be adjusted based on project requirements.

- In Microsoft Project, users can easily change the constraint type by selecting the task and modifying the "Constraint Type" field in the task information dialog box.

2. Adjusting Constraint Dates:

- Project managers can also set specific dates for task constraints, such as Start No Earlier Than (SNET) or Finish No Later Than (FNLT). These dates provide additional control over task scheduling.

- Microsoft Project allows users to enter constraint dates directly into the task information dialog box or the Gantt Chart view.

3. Resolving Scheduling Conflicts:

- In situations where task dependencies create scheduling conflicts, Microsoft Project provides tools to analyze and resolve these conflicts.

- Project managers can use the "Task Inspector" feature to identify scheduling conflicts and explore alternative scheduling options.

4. Utilizing Task Constraints in Resource Management:

- Task dependency constraints play a crucial role in resource management, ensuring that resources are allocated efficiently based on task dependencies.

- Microsoft Project's resource leveling feature takes task constraints into account when optimizing resource allocation, helping prevent overallocation and resource conflicts.

Best Practices for Managing Task Dependency Constraints:

To leverage task dependency constraints effectively in Microsoft Project, project managers should follow these best practices:

1. Understand Project Requirements:

  - Before applying task constraints, thoroughly understand the project requirements and dependencies to select the most appropriate constraint types.

  - Consult with stakeholders and team members to ensure alignment on task sequencing and dependencies.

2. Use Constraints Sparingly:

  - While constraints offer control over task scheduling, excessive use can lead to rigid schedules and reduced flexibility.

  - Use constraints judiciously and prioritize task relationships based on logical dependencies rather than arbitrary constraints.

3. Regularly Review and Adjust Constraints:

  - Project dynamics may change over time, necessitating adjustments to task constraints.

  - Regularly review the project schedule and constraints to accommodate changes in scope, resource availability, or project priorities.

4. Document Constraint Rationale:

  - Maintain documentation explaining the rationale behind each task constraint to facilitate communication and decision-making within the project team.

- Clearly communicate the impact of constraints on project scheduling and resource allocation.

By understanding the significance of task dependency constraints and effectively managing them within Microsoft Project, project managers can optimize project schedules, mitigate risks, and ensure successful project delivery.

4.2 Adjusting Task Durations and Deadlines

4.2.1. Modifying Task Durations

In project management, task durations play a pivotal role in defining the overall timeline and scheduling of a project. Mastering the art of adjusting task durations is essential for project managers to ensure timely completion of deliverables without compromising quality. This section delves into various strategies and considerations for modifying task durations effectively.

Understanding Task Durations

Before diving into the techniques for modifying task durations, it's crucial to have a clear understanding of what task duration represents in project management. Task duration refers to the amount of time required to complete a specific task or activity from start to finish. It is often estimated based on various factors such as resources allocated, complexity, dependencies, and historical data.

Factors Influencing Task Durations

Several factors can influence task durations, and understanding these factors is essential for accurate planning and scheduling:

1. Task Complexity: Tasks that are more complex in nature typically require a longer duration to complete. Complexity can stem from various factors such as technical intricacies, skill requirements, and interdependencies with other tasks.

2. Resource Availability: The availability of resources, including human resources, materials, and equipment, directly impacts task durations. Limited availability of critical resources may lead to extended durations.

3. Dependencies: Task dependencies, as discussed in the previous section, can affect task durations. Tasks that are dependent on the completion of preceding tasks may have their durations influenced by the duration of those preceding tasks.

4. Skill Level: The skill level and expertise of the individuals assigned to perform the task can significantly affect its duration. Highly skilled professionals may complete tasks more efficiently, thus reducing the duration.

5. Risks and Uncertainties: Unforeseen risks, uncertainties, and external factors can impact task durations. It's essential to account for contingencies and buffers to accommodate potential delays.

Techniques for Modifying Task Durations

Project managers have several techniques at their disposal for modifying task durations to align with project requirements and constraints:

1. Resource Allocation: Adjusting the number and type of resources allocated to a task can directly impact its duration. Increasing resources may shorten durations, while resource constraints may lead to longer durations.

2. Task Splitting: Breaking down tasks into smaller, more manageable subtasks can sometimes reduce overall duration. By parallelizing or overlapping subtasks, project managers can expedite progress.

3. Optimization of Processes: Streamlining processes and workflows associated with tasks can lead to efficiency gains and, consequently, reduced durations. Continuous process improvement efforts can yield significant time savings over the project lifecycle.

4. Negotiation and Prioritization: Prioritizing tasks and negotiating deadlines with stakeholders can help in reallocating resources and focusing efforts on critical activities, thereby optimizing durations.

5. Technology Utilization: Leveraging project management tools and software can automate repetitive tasks, facilitate communication and collaboration, and provide insights for optimizing task durations.

6. Risk Management: Proactively identifying and mitigating risks that could potentially impact task durations is essential. Developing risk response strategies can minimize the likelihood and impact of disruptions.

Best Practices for Modifying Task Durations

Incorporating best practices can enhance the effectiveness of modifying task durations:

1. Data-Driven Decision Making: Utilize historical data, benchmarks, and performance metrics to inform decisions regarding task durations. Data-driven approaches provide valuable insights for realistic planning and scheduling.

2. Stakeholder Communication: Maintain open and transparent communication with stakeholders regarding any proposed changes to task durations. Collaboration and alignment with stakeholders' expectations are key to successful modification.

3. Flexibility and Adaptability: Recognize that project dynamics may change, necessitating adjustments to task durations. Embrace a flexible mindset and be prepared to adapt plans as needed to accommodate evolving circumstances.

4. Continuous Monitoring and Evaluation: Regularly monitor progress against planned durations and evaluate the effectiveness of modifications. Adjustments may be required based on real-time feedback and performance metrics.

5. Documentation: Document all changes to task durations along with the rationale behind them. Clear documentation ensures accountability, facilitates knowledge transfer, and serves as a reference for future projects.

Case Study: Modifying Task Durations in Action

Let's illustrate the concepts discussed above with a hypothetical case study:

Scenario: A software development project is facing delays due to resource constraints and unexpected technical challenges. The project manager needs to modify task durations to mitigate these issues and ensure timely delivery.

Approach:

1. Resource Reallocation: The project manager reallocates additional developers to critical tasks to accelerate progress.

2. Task Splitting: Complex development tasks are broken down into smaller modules to facilitate parallel development and reduce overall duration.

3. Optimization of Processes: The development workflow is restructured to minimize dependencies and streamline code review and testing processes.

4. Negotiation with Stakeholders: The project manager engages with stakeholders to revise project milestones and deadlines, taking into account the updated task durations.

5. Utilization of Technology: Project management software is utilized to automate repetitive tasks, track progress, and identify bottlenecks in real-time.

Outcome: By implementing these strategies, the project team successfully mitigates delays, and the project is delivered on schedule, meeting stakeholders' expectations.

Conclusion

Modifying task durations is a fundamental aspect of project management, requiring careful consideration of various factors and the application of appropriate techniques. By understanding the influences on task durations, employing effective modification strategies, and adhering to best practices, project managers can optimize schedules, mitigate risks, and ensure project success.

Here's a step-by-step guide on how to perform task duration modifications using Microsoft Project:

Modifying Task Durations in Microsoft Project

Step 1: Open Your Project File

Launch Microsoft Project and open the project file you want to work on. Ensure that you're in the Gantt Chart view, which is the default view for most projects.

Step 2: Navigate to the Task Information Window

- Select the task whose duration you want to modify by clicking on it in the Gantt Chart.

- Right-click on the selected task, and a context menu will appear.

- From the context menu, choose "Task Information." Alternatively, you can double-click on the task to open the Task Information window.

Step 3: Adjust Task Duration

- In the Task Information window, navigate to the "General" tab.

- Locate the "Duration" field. This field displays the current duration of the task.

- To modify the duration, click on the duration value in the "Duration" field. You can directly edit the duration by typing in the new value or using the up and down arrows to increase or decrease the duration.

Step 4: Specify Duration Units

- Optionally, you can specify the units for the duration. By default, Microsoft Project uses the duration unit defined in the project settings, which is typically in days. However, you can specify other units such as hours, weeks, or months by appending the appropriate abbreviation after the duration value (e.g., "2d" for 2 days, "4h" for 4 hours).

Step 5: Apply Changes

- Once you've entered the new duration, press "Enter" or click outside the Duration field to apply the changes. Microsoft Project will automatically update the task duration in the Gantt Chart and adjust the project schedule accordingly.

Step 6: Review Schedule Impact

- After modifying the task duration, review the project schedule to assess the impact of the changes. Check for any scheduling conflicts, dependencies, or resource overallocations that may arise due to the adjusted duration.

Step 7: Save Your Project

- Once you're satisfied with the modifications, save your project file to retain the changes. Go to the "File" menu and choose "Save" or use the keyboard shortcut "Ctrl + S" to save your project.

Step 8: Continue Monitoring and Adjusting

- Throughout the project lifecycle, continue monitoring task durations and make adjustments as necessary to ensure that the project remains on track. Use Microsoft

Project's scheduling tools and reports to track progress and identify any deviations from the planned timeline.

4.2.2. Setting Task Deadlines

Setting task deadlines is a crucial aspect of project management within Microsoft Project. Deadlines help project managers ensure that tasks are completed within a specified timeframe, thus contributing to the overall project timeline and objectives. In this section, we will delve into the importance of setting task deadlines, best practices for establishing realistic deadlines, and how to effectively manage deadlines within Microsoft Project.

Importance of Setting Task Deadlines

Task deadlines serve several purposes in project management:

1. Time Management: Deadlines provide a clear timeline for task completion, allowing project managers to allocate resources and manage dependencies effectively.

2. Goal Alignment: Deadlines help align individual tasks with broader project goals and objectives, ensuring that each task contributes to the overall project success.

3. Stakeholder Expectations: Deadlines communicate expectations to stakeholders regarding when specific tasks will be completed, fostering transparency and accountability.

4. Risk Mitigation: By setting deadlines, project managers can identify potential delays early and take proactive measures to mitigate risks and keep the project on track.

Best Practices for Setting Task Deadlines

When setting task deadlines, it's essential to follow best practices to ensure they are realistic and achievable:

1. Consider Task Dependencies: Take into account task dependencies and constraints when setting deadlines to avoid creating unrealistic expectations or bottlenecks in the project timeline.

2. Consult with Team Members: Collaborate with team members to understand their availability, workload, and any potential obstacles that may impact task deadlines.

3. Factor in Contingencies: Incorporate buffer time into deadlines to account for unforeseen circumstances or delays that may arise during task execution.

4. Use Historical Data: Utilize historical project data to inform deadline setting, analyzing past performance metrics to establish realistic timelines for similar tasks.

5. Communicate Expectations: Clearly communicate task deadlines to team members, outlining the importance of meeting these deadlines and any consequences for missed deadlines.

Managing Deadlines in Microsoft Project

Microsoft Project offers several features to facilitate effective deadline management:

1. Deadline Field: Utilize the "Deadline" field in Microsoft Project to set specific deadlines for individual tasks. This field allows project managers to establish target dates for task completion.

2. Deadline Indicator: The deadline indicator in Microsoft Project visually highlights task deadlines, making it easy for project managers to identify critical deadlines and prioritize tasks accordingly.

3. Deadline Alerts: Configure deadline alerts in Microsoft Project to notify project managers when tasks are approaching or past their deadlines. These alerts serve as early warnings, allowing managers to take corrective actions promptly.

4. Critical Path Analysis: Leverage the critical path analysis feature in Microsoft Project to identify tasks that are crucial to project timelines and deadlines. By focusing on critical tasks, project managers can allocate resources effectively to ensure timely completion.

5. Resource Allocation: Use Microsoft Project's resource allocation tools to assign resources to tasks based on their deadlines, ensuring that adequate resources are available to meet project deadlines.

Conclusion

Setting task deadlines is an essential aspect of project management that contributes to project success. By following best practices for establishing realistic deadlines and leveraging Microsoft Project's features for deadline management, project managers can effectively monitor and control project timelines, ensuring that tasks are completed on schedule. Deadlines not only help keep projects on track but also promote accountability, stakeholder satisfaction, and overall project success.

Setting Task Deadlines in Microsoft Project:

1. Navigate to the Task Information Dialog Box: Double-click on the task you want to set a deadline for to open the Task Information dialog box.

2. Locate the Deadline Field: In the Task Information dialog box, navigate to the "Advanced" tab.

3. Enter the Deadline Date: In the "Deadline" field, enter the desired deadline date for the task.

4. Save Changes: Click "OK" to save the changes and close the Task Information dialog box.

Managing Deadlines in Microsoft Project:

1. View Deadline Indicators: In the Gantt Chart view, look for the small downward-facing arrow on the right side of a task bar. This arrow indicates that a task has a deadline set. You can hover over the arrow to view the deadline date.

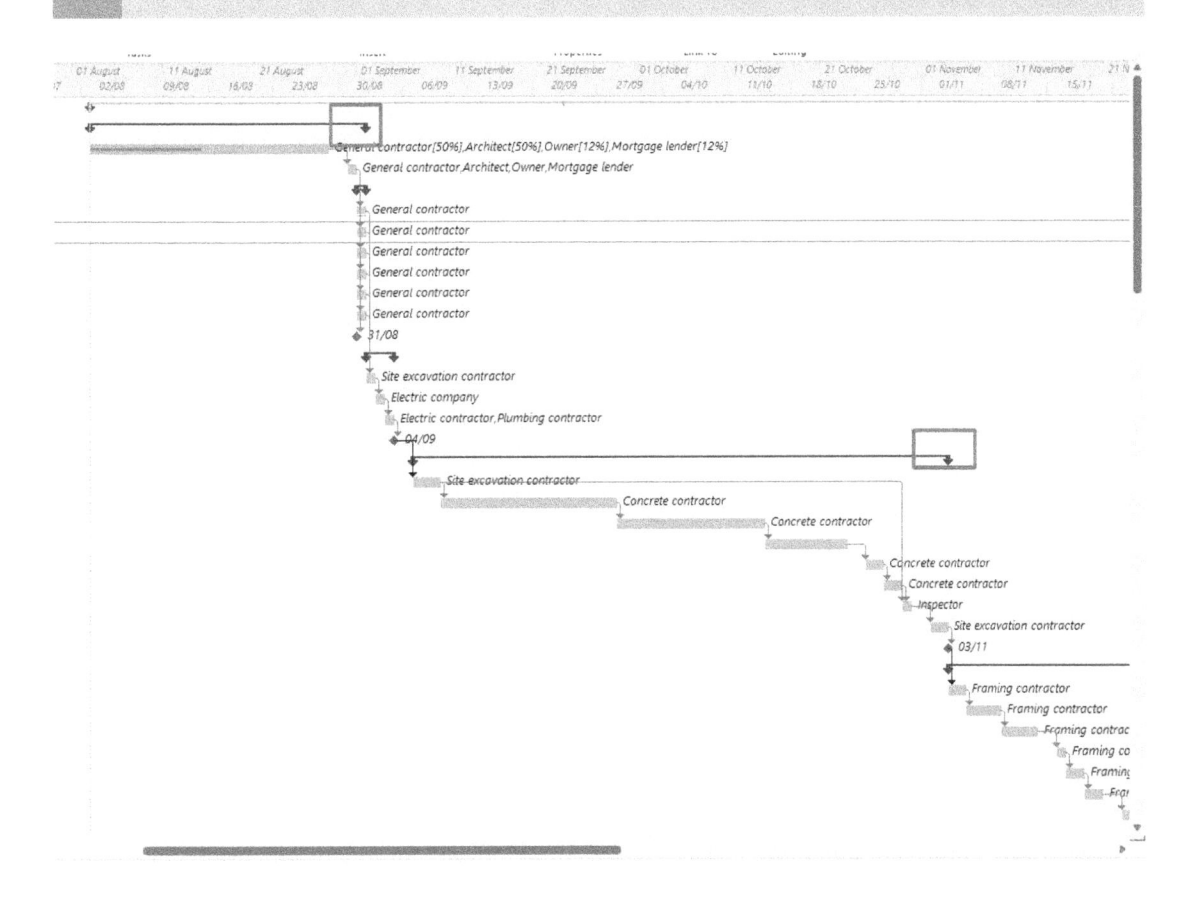

2. Configure Deadline Alerts: Go to the "File" tab, then select "Options." In the Project Options dialog box, click on "Advanced" and scroll down to the "Tasks" section. Here, you can specify when you want to be alerted about approaching or missed deadlines.

3. Critical Path Analysis: Go to the "View" tab and select "Critical." This will display the critical path in your project, which consists of tasks that directly impact the project's finish date. Focus on tasks along the critical path to ensure they meet their deadlines.

4. Resource Allocation: Navigate to the "Resource" tab and select "Resource Sheet." Here, you can assign resources to tasks by double-clicking on the cell where the resource and task intersect. Ensure that resources are allocated appropriately to meet task deadlines.

5. Monitoring Deadlines: Regularly review your project's Gantt Chart to monitor task deadlines. Identify any tasks that are at risk of missing their deadlines and take appropriate actions to address them.

By following these steps, you can effectively set and manage task deadlines within Microsoft Project, ensuring that your project stays on track and meets its objectives.

4.3 Managing Critical Paths

4.3.1. Identifying Critical Tasks

Once you've developed a schedule for your project, identifying critical tasks becomes paramount for effective project management. Critical tasks are those that, if delayed, will directly impact the project's overall timeline. Understanding and managing critical tasks are crucial to ensure the project stays on track and meets its deadlines.

Understanding Critical Paths

Before diving into identifying critical tasks, it's essential to grasp the concept of critical paths. A critical path is the longest sequence of dependent tasks and determines the shortest time in which a project can be completed. Any delay in a task on the critical path will result in a delay in the project's completion. Critical paths are crucial for project managers as they highlight areas where any slippage can have the most significant impact on project timelines.

Importance of Identifying Critical Tasks

Identifying critical tasks allows project managers to focus their attention and resources on activities that are vital to the project's success. By understanding which tasks are critical, project managers can allocate resources effectively, prioritize activities, and mitigate risks. Additionally, identifying critical tasks enables project managers to communicate potential bottlenecks and constraints to stakeholders, fostering transparency and alignment across the project team.

Methods for Identifying Critical Tasks

There are several methods for identifying critical tasks in a project schedule. These methods range from manual analysis to leveraging project management software tools such as Microsoft Project. Let's explore some common techniques:

1. Manual Analysis: Project managers can manually review the project schedule and identify tasks that have zero slack or float. Tasks with zero slack are those that cannot be delayed without impacting the project's timeline. While this method is straightforward, it may be time-consuming for large or complex projects.

2. Critical Path Method (CPM): CPM is a mathematical algorithm used to determine the longest sequence of dependent tasks and identify the critical path. CPM calculates the earliest start and finish times for each task, as well as the latest start and finish times, taking into account task dependencies and durations. Tasks with no slack are considered critical and are part of the critical path.

3. Project Management Software: Project management software such as Microsoft Project automates the process of identifying critical tasks. These tools use algorithms similar to CPM to analyze project schedules and highlight critical tasks. Project managers can easily view the critical path and make adjustments as needed to ensure project success.

Characteristics of Critical Tasks

Critical tasks exhibit several characteristics that distinguish them from non-critical tasks:

- *Zero Slack:* Critical tasks have zero slack or float, meaning any delay in these tasks will result in a delay in the project's completion.

- *Long Durations:* Critical tasks often have longer durations compared to non-critical tasks, as they represent the longest sequence of dependent activities in the project schedule.

- *High Impact:* Critical tasks have a high impact on the overall project timeline and success. Delays in critical tasks can cascade downstream and affect subsequent activities.

- *Dependency:* Critical tasks typically have multiple dependencies and are interconnected with other tasks in the project schedule.

Techniques for Managing Critical Tasks

Once critical tasks have been identified, project managers can employ various techniques to effectively manage them:

1. Resource Allocation: Allocate resources efficiently to critical tasks to ensure they are completed on time. Resource constraints can significantly impact critical tasks, so it's essential to monitor resource availability and adjust as needed.

2. Schedule Compression: Explore opportunities to compress the schedule for critical tasks by overlapping activities or fast-tracking certain activities. However, schedule compression should be done cautiously to avoid compromising quality or increasing risk.

3. Risk Management: Identify and mitigate risks associated with critical tasks to minimize the likelihood of delays. Proactively addressing potential risks can help maintain the integrity of the critical path and prevent schedule slippage.

4. Contingency Planning: Develop contingency plans for critical tasks in case of unexpected delays or issues. Having backup plans in place can help mitigate the impact of disruptions and keep the project on track.

5. Regular Monitoring and Reporting: Monitor critical tasks closely and provide regular updates to stakeholders on their progress. Early identification of issues allows for timely intervention and corrective action to prevent schedule delays.

Conclusion

Identifying and managing critical tasks are essential components of effective project management. By understanding the critical path and focusing attention on critical tasks, project managers can mitigate risks, allocate resources effectively, and ensure project success. Utilizing tools such as project management software and employing best practices in critical task management will enable project managers to deliver projects on time and within budget.

Absolutely! Let's illustrate the concepts discussed in the continuation with a hypothetical project scenario:

Example: Construction of a New Office Building

Background: ABC Construction Company has been contracted to build a new office building for a technology firm. The project involves multiple phases, including site preparation, foundation construction, building erection, interior finishing, and landscaping. The project has a strict deadline of 12 months, as the technology firm plans to move into the new office space by a specific date to coincide with their expansion plans.

Identifying Critical Tasks:

1. Site Survey and Preparation: Before construction can begin, the site must be surveyed, cleared, and prepared for building activities. Any delay in this phase will impact subsequent construction activities, making it a critical task.

2. Foundation Construction: The foundation is critical to the structural integrity of the building. Any delay in pouring the foundation or curing concrete can set back the entire project timeline.

3. Building Erection: Once the foundation is in place, the construction of the building itself begins. Tasks such as framing, roofing, and exterior cladding are critical, as they form the skeleton of the building.

4. Interior Finishing: Interior finishing tasks, including electrical wiring, plumbing installation, drywall installation, and painting, are critical to creating a functional office space. Delays in these tasks can delay occupancy.

5. Landscaping and Exterior Work: While landscaping may seem less critical, it contributes to the overall aesthetics and functionality of the office building. However, delays in landscaping can often be absorbed without impacting the project's completion date significantly.

Managing Critical Tasks:

1. Resource Allocation: ABC Construction allocates skilled labor and construction equipment to critical tasks such as foundation construction and building erection. They ensure that enough resources are available to complete these tasks on schedule.

2. Schedule Compression: To expedite the project, ABC Construction explores opportunities for schedule compression, such as overlapping certain tasks or working overtime during critical phases like foundation construction.

3. Risk Management: ABC Construction identifies potential risks such as adverse weather conditions, material shortages, or subcontractor delays that could impact critical tasks. They develop contingency plans, such as securing alternative suppliers or rescheduling work, to mitigate these risks.

4. Contingency Planning: ABC Construction maintains a buffer in the project schedule to account for unforeseen delays in critical tasks. They communicate this buffer to the client and stakeholders to manage expectations and ensure transparency.

5. Regular Monitoring and Reporting: Project managers at ABC Construction closely monitor the progress of critical tasks using project management software. They provide regular updates to the client, highlighting any deviations from the schedule and discussing mitigation strategies.

By effectively identifying and managing critical tasks, ABC Construction successfully completes the construction project within the specified timeframe, allowing the technology firm to move into their new office space as planned. This example demonstrates the importance of understanding critical paths and implementing strategies to ensure project success.

4.3.2. Optimizing Critical Path

Optimizing the critical path involves analyzing the sequence of critical tasks and identifying opportunities to streamline processes, allocate resources more effectively, and reduce overall project duration. By optimizing the critical path, project managers can enhance project performance, meet deadlines, and achieve project objectives efficiently. Below are some key strategies for optimizing the critical path:

1. Resource Leveling: Resource leveling is the process of smoothing out resource allocation to avoid overallocation or underallocation of resources. When resources are overallocated, it can lead to delays in critical tasks, thereby extending the project duration. By redistributing resources and balancing workloads, project managers can optimize the critical path and ensure smoother project execution.

2. Task Splitting: Task splitting involves breaking down large tasks into smaller, more manageable subtasks. By dividing complex tasks into smaller components, project managers can identify critical subtasks and allocate resources more efficiently. Task splitting can help in reducing task durations and minimizing dependencies, thereby optimizing the critical path and accelerating project progress.

3. Fast-Tracking: Fast-tracking involves overlapping sequential tasks that would typically be performed in series. By parallelizing tasks, project managers can reduce project duration and optimize the critical path. However, fast-tracking may increase project risks, as it can lead to resource conflicts and quality issues. Project managers should carefully evaluate the feasibility and impact of fast-tracking on project deliverables before implementation.

4. Crashing: Crashing involves allocating additional resources to critical tasks to expedite their completion. By adding extra resources such as manpower, equipment, or budget, project managers can accelerate critical tasks and compress the project schedule. However, crashing may incur additional costs and resource constraints, requiring careful cost-benefit analysis to ensure its effectiveness in optimizing the critical path.

5. Optimizing Task Sequencing: Analyzing task dependencies and optimizing task sequencing can help in identifying alternative paths through the project that may have shorter durations. By rearranging task sequences and minimizing dependencies, project managers can reduce project duration and optimize the critical path. Techniques such as the use of lead and lag time, as well as reevaluating task dependencies, can aid in optimizing task sequencing.

6. Risk Management: Proactively identifying and mitigating project risks can help in preventing potential delays and disruptions to critical tasks. By implementing risk management strategies such as contingency planning, risk mitigation, and issue resolution, project managers can minimize the impact of uncertainties on the critical path and ensure project success. Effective risk management contributes to optimizing the critical path by reducing the likelihood of delays and improving project resilience.

7. Continuous Monitoring and Control: Continuous monitoring and control of project activities are essential for optimizing the critical path. Project managers should regularly review project progress, identify deviations from the plan, and take corrective actions as needed to keep the project on track. By maintaining visibility into project performance and promptly addressing issues, project managers can optimize the critical path and mitigate potential risks to project success.

In conclusion, optimizing the critical path is vital for enhancing project efficiency, minimizing delays, and achieving project objectives within the stipulated timeline. By employing strategies such as resource leveling, task splitting, fast-tracking, crashing, optimizing task sequencing, risk management, and continuous monitoring, project managers can effectively optimize the critical path and drive project success. The optimization of the critical path requires proactive planning, diligent execution, and adaptive management to overcome challenges and deliver successful outcomes.

Optimizing Critical Path in Microsoft Project

1. Resource Leveling:

  - Open your project file in Microsoft Project.

  - Navigate to the "Resource" tab and select "Resource Leveling" from the drop-down menu.

  - In the Resource Leveling dialog box, choose the options for leveling, such as "Automatic" or "Manual."

  - Specify the leveling range and any constraints if needed.

  - Click "Level All" or "Level Selected" to start the resource leveling process.

  - Microsoft Project will analyze resource allocation and adjust task scheduling to resolve resource conflicts and optimize the critical path.

2. Task Splitting:

- Select the task you want to split in the Gantt Chart view.

- Right-click on the task and choose "Split Task" from the context menu.

- Click on the Gantt bar at the point where you want to split the task.

- Microsoft Project will split the task into two parts, allowing you to adjust each part independently.

- You can now allocate resources and adjust durations for each split task to optimize the critical path.

3. Fast-Tracking:

- Identify sequential tasks that can be overlapped to fast-track the project.

- Select the tasks you want to fast-track in the Gantt Chart view.

- Right-click on the selected tasks and choose "Task Information" from the context menu.

- In the Task Information dialog box, go to the "Advanced" tab.

- Check the "Mark task as critical" checkbox to indicate critical tasks.

- Click "OK" to apply the changes.

- Microsoft Project will automatically adjust task dependencies to fast-track the project and optimize the critical path.

4. Crashing:

- Identify critical tasks that require additional resources to expedite their completion.

- Select the critical tasks in the Gantt Chart view.

- Right-click on the selected tasks and choose "Assign Resources" from the context menu.

- Assign additional resources to the selected tasks to increase their productivity.

- Microsoft Project will recalculate task durations and optimize resource allocation to crash the critical path and accelerate project progress.

5. Optimizing Task Sequencing:

  - Review task dependencies and identify opportunities to optimize sequencing.

  - Select the tasks you want to resequence in the Gantt Chart view.

  - Use the "Predecessors" column to adjust task dependencies by adding or removing predecessors.

  - You can also adjust lead and lag time between tasks to optimize sequencing and minimize dependencies.

  - Microsoft Project will automatically update task sequencing based on your adjustments to optimize the critical path.

6. Risk Management:

  - Identify potential risks that may impact critical tasks and project timeline.

  - Create a risk management plan outlining strategies for mitigating identified risks.

  - Track risks using the "Risk" or "Issue" features in Microsoft Project.

  - Regularly review and update the risk register, and implement mitigation measures as needed.

  - Microsoft Project will help you monitor project risks and take proactive actions to minimize their impact on the critical path.

7. Continuous Monitoring and Control:

  - Use the "Tracking Gantt" view to monitor project progress and critical path.

- Regularly update task status, completion percentages, and actual durations.

- Compare actual progress with the baseline schedule to identify deviations.

- Take corrective actions to address deviations and keep the project on track.

- Microsoft Project provides real-time updates on project performance, allowing you to continuously monitor and control the critical path.

By following these step-by-step instructions, you can effectively optimize the critical path in Microsoft Project and improve project efficiency and delivery. Each optimization technique offers unique benefits and can be tailored to suit the specific requirements of your project.

PART V
Resource Allocation and Management

5.1 Adding Resources to Your Project

5.1.1. Resource Types and Categories

In project management, resources are the lifeblood of any endeavor. They encompass everything from human capital to physical assets and beyond. Understanding the various types and categories of resources is essential for effective resource allocation and management within Microsoft Project. In this section, we delve into the intricacies of resource types and categories, exploring their significance and how they impact project planning and execution.

Resource Types

Resources in Microsoft Project can be broadly categorized into two main types: work resources and material resources.

1. Work Resources:

Work resources represent the human element of a project. They include individuals or teams whose efforts contribute directly to task completion. Work resources are typically characterized by their availability in terms of time (hours per day, days per week) and their associated cost (hourly rate, salary). Examples of work resources include project managers, developers, designers, and consultants.

2. Material Resources:

Material resources, on the other hand, encompass tangible items or supplies required for project activities. These resources are consumed during the course of the project and may include raw materials, equipment, machinery, or any physical goods necessary for task execution. Unlike work resources, material resources are typically not associated with time-based constraints but are measured in units of quantity (e.g., liters, kilograms, units) and cost per unit.

Resource Categories

Within each resource type, further categorization can be beneficial for organizing and managing resources effectively. Microsoft Project offers several predefined categories, but users can also create custom categories tailored to their specific project needs. Let's explore some common resource categories:

1. Human Resources:

This category encompasses all work resources that involve human effort. It includes roles such as project managers, team members, contractors, and vendors. Human resources are typically characterized by factors such as availability (full-time, part-time), skill set, expertise level, and cost rates.

2. Equipment/Resources:

Under this category, you can include all material resources or equipment required for project tasks. This may include machinery, vehicles, computers, tools, or any other physical assets necessary for project execution. Each equipment/resource entry should specify details such as quantity, unit of measure, and associated costs.

3. Consumables:

Consumables represent resources that are depleted or consumed during project activities. This category can include items such as office supplies, fuel, stationery, or any materials that need replenishing over time. Tracking consumables ensures that project teams have access to essential supplies throughout the project lifecycle.

4. Facilities/Resources:

Facilities/resources category covers physical spaces or facilities required for project operations. This may include office space, meeting rooms, laboratories, or any infrastructure necessary for conducting project-related activities. Assigning facilities/resources ensures proper utilization of available space and facilitates scheduling of meetings and events.

5. External Services:

External services encompass resources provided by external vendors, subcontractors, or service providers. This category may include outsourced services such as consulting, training, legal advice, or any specialized expertise required to supplement internal capabilities. Managing external services involves contract negotiations, service level agreements, and tracking vendor performance.

Customizing Resource Categories

While Microsoft Project provides predefined resource categories, users can also create custom categories to align with their project's unique requirements. Custom categories offer flexibility in organizing resources based on specific criteria relevant to the project. To create custom categories:

1. Navigate to Resource Sheet: Access the Resource Sheet view in Microsoft Project.

2. Add New Field: Insert a new field to define resource categories. This could be a text field named "Resource Category."

3. Assign Categories: Populate the field with appropriate category labels for each resource entry. You can create categories such as "Technology," "Human Resources," "Facilities," etc.

4. Group Resources: Utilize the Group feature to organize resources by category, facilitating easier resource management and allocation.

By customizing resource categories, project managers can streamline resource management processes, improve resource visibility, and enhance overall project efficiency.

Conclusion

Resource types and categories play a pivotal role in Microsoft Project, serving as the foundation for effective resource allocation and management. Understanding the distinctions between work resources and material resources, as well as the various categories within each type, enables project managers to optimize resource utilization, minimize conflicts, and ensure project success. Whether it's assigning human resources to tasks, tracking material consumption, or managing external services, leveraging resource types and categories empowers project teams to navigate complexities and deliver results efficiently.

5.1.2. Adding Resources to Resource Pool

In Microsoft Project, the Resource Pool serves as a centralized repository for all resources that can be utilized across multiple projects within an organization. By maintaining a Resource Pool, project managers can efficiently manage and allocate resources, ensuring optimal utilization and avoiding overallocation or underutilization.

PART V: RESOURCE ALLOCATION AND MANAGEMENT

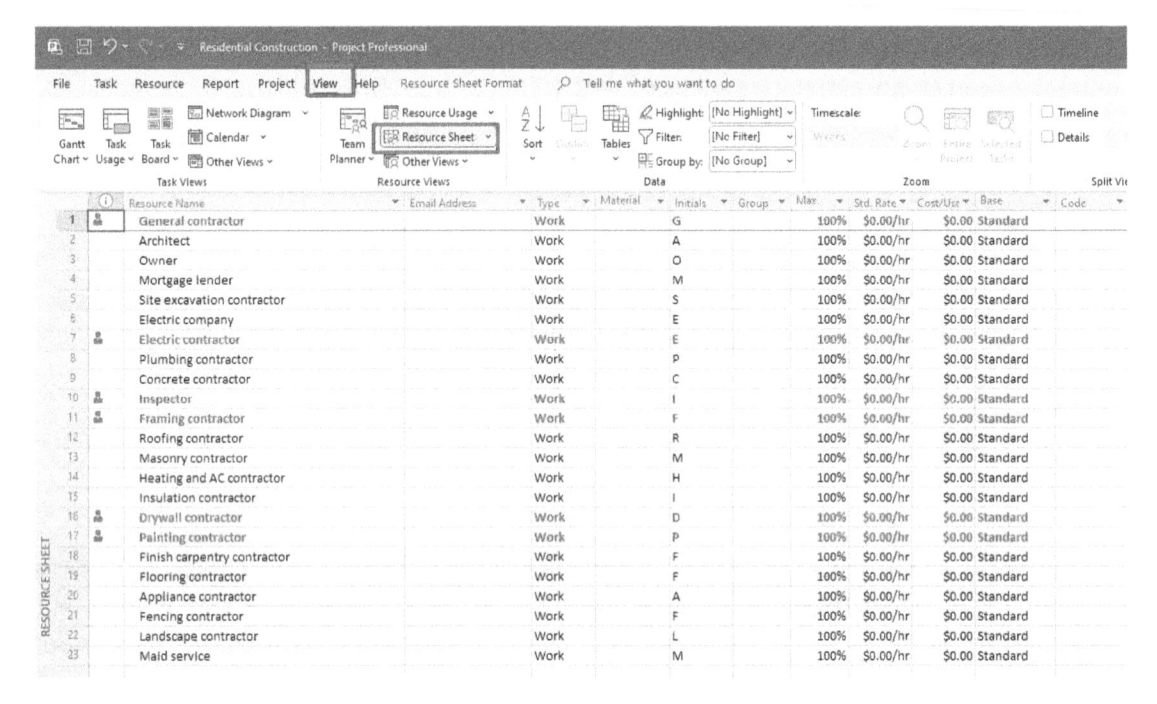

#	Resource Name	Type	Material	Initials	Group	Max	Std. Rate	Cost/Use	Base
1	General contractor	Work		G		100%	$0.00/hr	$0.00	Standard
2	Architect	Work		A		100%	$0.00/hr	$0.00	Standard
3	Owner	Work		O		100%	$0.00/hr	$0.00	Standard
4	Mortgage lender	Work		M		100%	$0.00/hr	$0.00	Standard
5	Site excavation contractor	Work		S		100%	$0.00/hr	$0.00	Standard
6	Electric company	Work		E		100%	$0.00/hr	$0.00	Standard
7	Electric contractor	Work		E		100%	$0.00/hr	$0.00	Standard
8	Plumbing contractor	Work		P		100%	$0.00/hr	$0.00	Standard
9	Concrete contractor	Work		C		100%	$0.00/hr	$0.00	Standard
10	Inspector	Work		I		100%	$0.00/hr	$0.00	Standard
11	Framing contractor	Work		F		100%	$0.00/hr	$0.00	Standard
12	Roofing contractor	Work		R		100%	$0.00/hr	$0.00	Standard
13	Masonry contractor	Work		M		100%	$0.00/hr	$0.00	Standard
14	Heating and AC contractor	Work		H		100%	$0.00/hr	$0.00	Standard
15	Insulation contractor	Work		I		100%	$0.00/hr	$0.00	Standard
16	Drywall contractor	Work		D		100%	$0.00/hr	$0.00	Standard
17	Painting contractor	Work		P		100%	$0.00/hr	$0.00	Standard
18	Finish carpentry contractor	Work		F		100%	$0.00/hr	$0.00	Standard
19	Flooring contractor	Work		F		100%	$0.00/hr	$0.00	Standard
20	Appliance contractor	Work		A		100%	$0.00/hr	$0.00	Standard
21	Fencing contractor	Work		F		100%	$0.00/hr	$0.00	Standard
22	Landscape contractor	Work		L		100%	$0.00/hr	$0.00	Standard
23	Maid service	Work		M		100%	$0.00/hr	$0.00	Standard

Adding resources to the Resource Pool is a straightforward process that involves creating resource entries with detailed information such as resource name, type, availability, cost rates, and any other relevant attributes. These resources can then be assigned to tasks across various projects, facilitating effective resource management and planning.

Creating Resource Entries

To add resources to the Resource Pool in Microsoft Project, follow these steps:

1. Open Microsoft Project: Launch Microsoft Project and open the project file where you want to create or update the Resource Pool.

2. Navigate to the Resource Sheet View: Click on the "View" tab in the ribbon at the top of the screen. Then, select the "Resource Sheet" view from the available options. This view displays a list of all resources in the project, including those in the Resource Pool.

3. Add New Resource: To add a new resource to the Resource Pool, click on the row below the last resource entry in the Resource Sheet. Alternatively, you can select any existing resource entry to update its information.

4. Enter Resource Details: Enter the details of the new resource in the appropriate columns of the Resource Sheet. The essential information includes:

  - *Resource Name:* Enter a descriptive name for the resource.

  - *Resource Type:* Specify whether the resource is a Work resource (e.g., a person or equipment) or a Material resource (e.g., raw materials or consumables).

  - *Max Units:* Define the maximum capacity or availability of the resource, usually expressed as a percentage (e.g., 100% for full-time availability).

  - *Standard Rate:* Enter the standard hourly rate for the resource, which is used for cost calculations.

  - *Overtime Rate:* If applicable, specify the hourly rate for overtime work.

  - *Cost Per Use:* Enter any additional cost associated with using the resource, such as setup fees or rental charges.

  - *Accrue At:* Define how costs associated with the resource are accrued over time, such as at the start or end of the task.

5. Save Resource Pool: Once you have added or updated resource entries, save the changes to the Resource Pool. Click on the "File" tab, select "Save As," and choose the option to save the file as a Resource Pool (.mpp) separate from your project files.

Illustrative Example: Adding Resources to the Resource Pool

Let's walk through the process of adding resources to the Resource Pool in Microsoft Project with an illustrative example. Suppose we're managing a construction project that requires various types of resources, including labor, equipment, and materials.

Step 1: Open Microsoft Project

Launch Microsoft Project on your computer to begin the process.

Step 2: Navigate to the Resource Sheet View

Click on the "View" tab in the ribbon at the top of the screen. From the drop-down menu, select "Resource Sheet" to switch to the Resource Sheet view.

Step 3: Add New Resource

Click on the first empty row in the Resource Sheet to add a new resource entry.

Step 4: Enter Resource Details

Now, let's enter the details of the new resource. For this example, we'll add a construction worker named John Smith.

- *Resource Name:* John S
- *Resource Type:* Work
- *Max Units:* 100% (Assuming John is available full-time)
- *Standard Rate:* $50 per hour

- *Overtime Rate:* $75 per hour (if applicable)

- *Cost Per Use:* $0

- *Accrue At:* Start (assuming costs accrue at the beginning of tasks)

Fill in these details in the respective columns of the Resource Sheet.

Step 5: Save Resource Pool

Once you've added John Smith as a resource, it's time to save the Resource Pool. Click on the "File" tab in the ribbon, then select "Save As." Choose the location where you want to save the Resource Pool file and give it a descriptive name, such as "Construction_Project_Resource_Pool."

Congratulations! You've successfully added a resource to the Resource Pool in Microsoft Project. Repeat these steps to add additional resources as needed for your project.

Best Practices Reminder: Remember to regularly update the Resource Pool with any changes in resource availability, rates, or other details to ensure accurate resource allocation and efficient project management.

By following these steps, you can effectively add resources to the Resource Pool in Microsoft Project, enabling centralized management and efficient allocation across multiple projects.

Best Practices for Managing the Resource Pool

Managing the Resource Pool effectively is essential for ensuring accurate resource allocation and optimal project performance. Here are some best practices to consider:

1. Regular Updates: Keep the Resource Pool up to date by regularly reviewing and updating resource information. This includes availability, rates, skills, and any changes in resource status or availability.

2. Standardization: Establish standard naming conventions and resource categorization to maintain consistency and facilitate easy identification of resources. This helps streamline resource management processes and enhances clarity and organization.

3. Resource Sharing: Encourage resource sharing and collaboration across projects by leveraging the centralized Resource Pool. This allows for better resource utilization and avoids duplication of effort or resources.

4. Capacity Planning: Use resource capacity planning tools and techniques to assess resource availability and identify potential bottlenecks or overallocations. Adjust resource assignments as needed to optimize resource utilization and prevent resource shortages or overloads.

5. Communication and Collaboration: Foster open communication and collaboration among project managers, resource managers, and team members to ensure alignment on resource priorities, availability, and allocations. This helps mitigate conflicts and ensures smooth resource management processes.

6. Regular Monitoring and Reporting: Monitor resource utilization and workloads regularly using built-in tracking tools and reports in Microsoft Project. Identify any discrepancies or issues early and take proactive measures to address them to prevent delays or resource shortages.

By adhering to these best practices, project managers can effectively manage the Resource Pool in Microsoft Project, optimize resource utilization, and enhance overall project success.

- *Overtime Rate:* $75 per hour (if applicable)

- *Cost Per Use:* $0

- *Accrue At:* Start (assuming costs accrue at the beginning of tasks)

Fill in these details in the respective columns of the Resource Sheet.

Step 5: Save Resource Pool

Once you've added John Smith as a resource, it's time to save the Resource Pool. Click on the "File" tab in the ribbon, then select "Save As." Choose the location where you want to save the Resource Pool file and give it a descriptive name, such as "Construction_Project_Resource_Pool."

Congratulations! You've successfully added a resource to the Resource Pool in Microsoft Project. Repeat these steps to add additional resources as needed for your project.

Best Practices Reminder: Remember to regularly update the Resource Pool with any changes in resource availability, rates, or other details to ensure accurate resource allocation and efficient project management.

By following these steps, you can effectively add resources to the Resource Pool in Microsoft Project, enabling centralized management and efficient allocation across multiple projects.

Best Practices for Managing the Resource Pool

Managing the Resource Pool effectively is essential for ensuring accurate resource allocation and optimal project performance. Here are some best practices to consider:

1. Regular Updates: Keep the Resource Pool up to date by regularly reviewing and updating resource information. This includes availability, rates, skills, and any changes in resource status or availability.

2. Standardization: Establish standard naming conventions and resource categorization to maintain consistency and facilitate easy identification of resources. This helps streamline resource management processes and enhances clarity and organization.

3. Resource Sharing: Encourage resource sharing and collaboration across projects by leveraging the centralized Resource Pool. This allows for better resource utilization and avoids duplication of effort or resources.

4. Capacity Planning: Use resource capacity planning tools and techniques to assess resource availability and identify potential bottlenecks or overallocations. Adjust resource assignments as needed to optimize resource utilization and prevent resource shortages or overloads.

5. Communication and Collaboration: Foster open communication and collaboration among project managers, resource managers, and team members to ensure alignment on resource priorities, availability, and allocations. This helps mitigate conflicts and ensures smooth resource management processes.

6. Regular Monitoring and Reporting: Monitor resource utilization and workloads regularly using built-in tracking tools and reports in Microsoft Project. Identify any discrepancies or issues early and take proactive measures to address them to prevent delays or resource shortages.

By adhering to these best practices, project managers can effectively manage the Resource Pool in Microsoft Project, optimize resource utilization, and enhance overall project success.

Conclusion

The Resource Pool in Microsoft Project serves as a central repository for managing and allocating resources across multiple projects. By adding resources to the Resource Pool and leveraging its capabilities, project managers can streamline resource management processes, optimize resource utilization, and ensure project success. By following best practices for managing the Resource Pool, project managers can effectively allocate resources, mitigate risks, and achieve project objectives efficiently.

5.2 Assigning Resources to Tasks

5.2.1. Resource Assignments Overview

Assigning resources to tasks is a critical aspect of project management within Microsoft Project. Effectively allocating resources ensures that tasks are completed efficiently and within the defined constraints of time, budget, and scope. In this section, we delve into the intricacies of assigning resources to tasks, covering various methodologies, best practices, and tools available in Microsoft Project.

Resource assignments involve the process of associating specific resources with individual tasks in your project. This linkage establishes who will be responsible for completing each task and the corresponding allocation of resources, whether it be human resources, equipment, or materials. A robust understanding of resource assignments is pivotal for project managers to optimize resource utilization and maintain project timelines.

Understanding Resource Assignments

Resource assignments serve as the foundation for resource management within Microsoft Project. Each task in your project requires specific resources to be completed successfully. By assigning resources to tasks, you delineate responsibilities, allocate workloads, and establish dependencies between tasks and resources.

Key Components of Resource Assignments

1. Resource Identification: Before assigning resources to tasks, it is imperative to identify the available resources and their respective skill sets, availability, and constraints. Resources can include personnel, equipment, and materials required to execute project tasks.

2. Task Requirements: Evaluate the requirements of each task to determine the resources needed for its completion. Consider factors such as skill level, availability, and duration when matching resources with tasks.

3. Resource Allocation: Assign resources to tasks based on their compatibility with the task requirements. Ensure that resources are allocated efficiently to optimize productivity and minimize resource conflicts.

4. Duration and Work Estimation: Assess the duration and work effort required for each task to accurately allocate resources. Consider factors such as resource availability and skill level to estimate task durations effectively.

5. Resource Leveling: Utilize resource leveling techniques to balance resource workloads and resolve overallocation issues. Resource leveling helps prevent resource burnout and ensures equitable distribution of work among team members.

Best Practices for Resource Assignments

1. Clear Communication: Communicate resource assignments clearly to team members to ensure everyone understands their roles and responsibilities. Transparency fosters accountability and encourages collaboration within the project team.

2. Regular Updates: Continuously monitor resource assignments and make adjustments as necessary to accommodate changes in project scope, schedule, or resource availability. Regular updates help maintain alignment between resources and tasks throughout the project lifecycle.

3. Utilize Resource Pools: Take advantage of resource pools to centralize resource management and streamline the allocation process across multiple projects. Resource pools enable efficient resource sharing and facilitate resource optimization at the organizational level.

4. Consider Constraints: Be mindful of resource constraints, such as availability, skill level, and geographical location, when making resource assignments. Consider alternative resources or adjust task schedules to accommodate resource constraints effectively.

5. Optimize Resource Utilization: Strive to maximize resource utilization while minimizing idle time and overallocation. Utilize Microsoft Project's resource management tools to analyze resource usage patterns and identify opportunities for optimization.

Tools and Techniques for Resource Assignments

Microsoft Project offers a plethora of tools and techniques to facilitate resource assignments and optimize resource management within your project. Some of the key features include:

1. Resource Sheet: The Resource Sheet provides a comprehensive overview of all resources available for your project, including their names, resource types, and availability. Use the Resource Sheet to identify suitable resources for task assignments.

2. Assign Resources Dialog Box: The Assign Resources dialog box allows you to assign resources to tasks quickly and efficiently. You can specify resource names, units, and work values directly within the dialog box, streamlining the assignment process.

3. Resource Usage View: The Resource Usage view displays resource assignments and workloads over time, providing insights into resource utilization and availability. Use the Resource Usage view to identify overallocated resources and adjust assignments accordingly.

4. Task Usage View: The Task Usage view offers a detailed breakdown of tasks and resource assignments, allowing you to visualize the relationship between tasks and resources. Use the Task Usage view to fine-tune resource assignments and optimize task schedules.

5. Resource Leveling: Microsoft Project's resource leveling feature automatically adjusts task schedules to resolve resource overallocation issues. Utilize resource leveling to optimize resource utilization and maintain project timelines effectively.

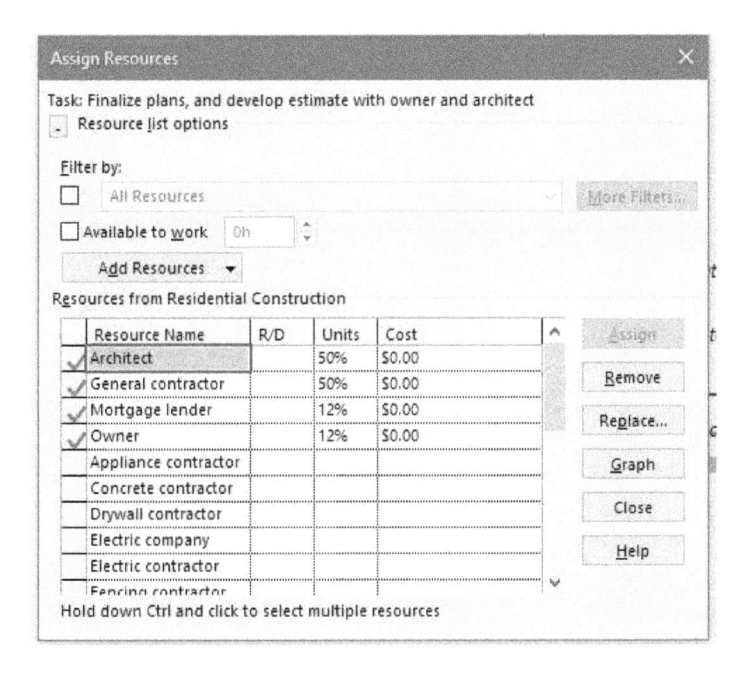

Conclusion

Resource assignments play a pivotal role in project management, enabling project managers to allocate resources effectively and optimize project performance. By understanding the fundamentals of resource assignments and leveraging the tools and techniques available in Microsoft Project, project managers can streamline resource management processes, mitigate risks, and ensure the successful execution of project tasks. Mastering resource assignments is essential for achieving project objectives and delivering value to stakeholders.

5.2.2. Assigning Resources to Tasks

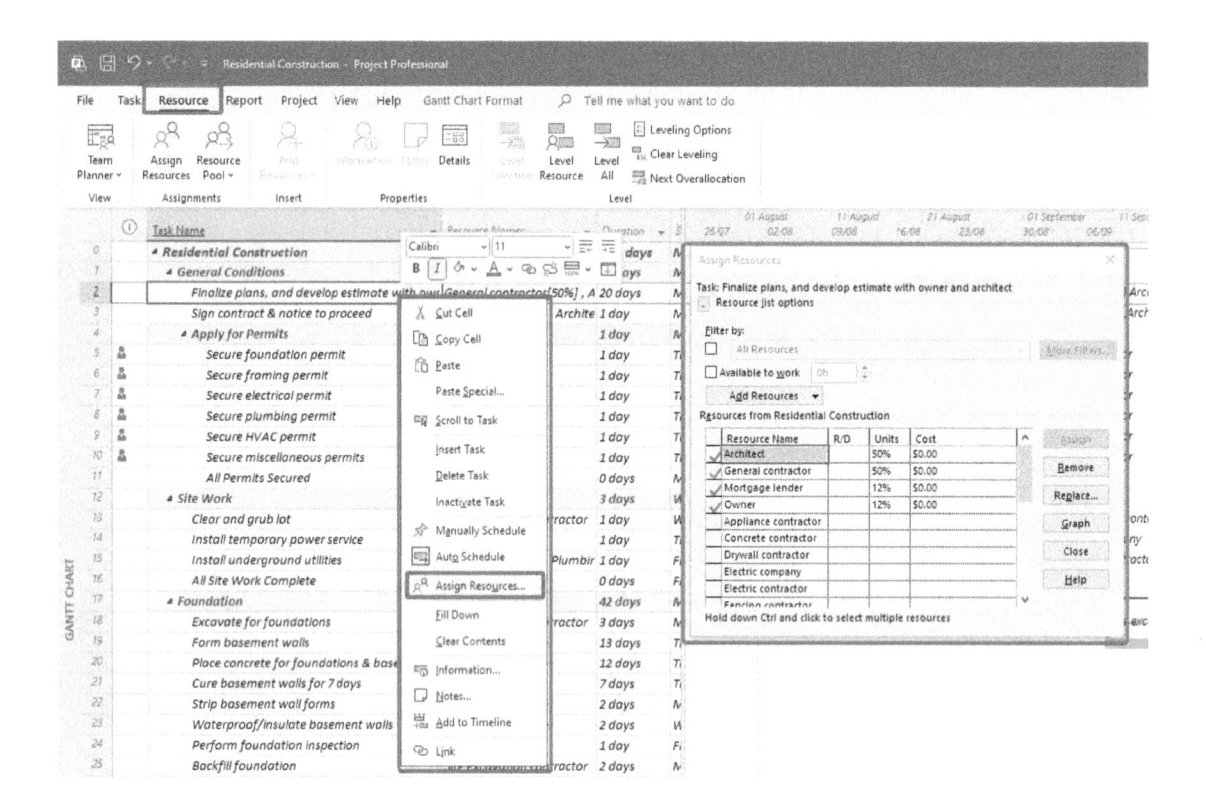

Assigning resources to tasks is a crucial aspect of project management in Microsoft Project. It involves associating the right people or materials with specific project activities to ensure that they are completed effectively and efficiently. This section will delve into the process of assigning resources to tasks, exploring best practices, common challenges, and strategies for optimization.

Understanding Resource Assignments

Before diving into the practical aspects of assigning resources to tasks, it's essential to grasp the concept of resource assignments within the context of Microsoft Project.

Resource Assignment Overview:

In Microsoft Project, a resource assignment refers to the allocation of a specific resource to a particular task for a defined duration. This allocation establishes a relationship between the resource, the task, and the project timeline, enabling the software to calculate resource utilization, workload, and project costs accurately.

Key Components of a Resource Assignment:

- *Resource Name:* The individual, equipment, or material assigned to the task.

- *Task Name:* The activity or work item to which the resource is allocated.

- *Start Date:* The date when the resource is scheduled to begin working on the task.

- *Finish Date*: The date when the resource is expected to complete work on the task.

- *Work Hours/Units:* The amount of time or effort the resource is expected to dedicate to the task, usually measured in hours or percentage of availability.

Best Practices for Resource Assignment

Effective resource assignment is vital for project success. Here are some best practices to optimize this process:

1. Understand Resource Skills and Availability: Before assigning resources, assess their skills, availability, and workload. This ensures that you allocate the right people with the necessary expertise to each task without overburdening them.

2. Utilize Resource Pools: Microsoft Project allows you to create and manage a centralized pool of resources that can be shared across multiple projects. Utilizing resource pools promotes consistency, reduces duplication of effort, and facilitates efficient resource allocation.

3. Consider Dependencies: When assigning resources, consider task dependencies and constraints. Some tasks may rely on others to be completed first, impacting resource availability and sequencing.

4. Optimize Work Distribution: Distribute work evenly among resources to prevent overloading certain team members while others remain underutilized. Resource leveling tools in Microsoft Project can assist in smoothing out resource workloads.

5. Monitor and Adjust Assignments: Continuously monitor resource assignments throughout the project lifecycle. Be prepared to adjust allocations as project requirements evolve, priorities shift, or unexpected issues arise.

6. Communicate Changes: Transparent communication is essential when making changes to resource assignments. Notify team members promptly about any modifications to their workload, ensuring clarity and alignment.

Common Challenges and Solutions

Despite careful planning, resource assignment in Microsoft Project can encounter various challenges. Here are some common issues and strategies to address them:

1. Resource Overallocation: When a resource is assigned to multiple tasks simultaneously, leading to overallocation or excessive workload. To resolve this, utilize resource leveling tools to adjust task scheduling and redistribute work more evenly.

2. Limited Resource Availability: Sometimes, essential resources may have limited availability due to other commitments or constraints. In such cases, explore alternative resources, adjust task timelines, or renegotiate priorities to accommodate constraints.

3. Skill Mismatches: Assigning resources without considering their skillsets can lead to inefficiencies and delays. Verify that assigned resources possess the necessary expertise and qualifications to perform the required tasks effectively.

4. Unclear Responsibilities: Lack of clarity regarding task responsibilities can result in confusion and inefficiency. Ensure that resource assignments are clearly defined, including roles, expectations, and deliverables, to avoid misunderstandings.

5. Resistance to Change: Team members may resist changes to their resource assignments, especially if they perceive them as disruptive or unfair. Address concerns proactively, emphasize the rationale behind changes, and involve team members in the decision-making process where possible.

Strategies for Optimization

To streamline resource assignment processes and enhance project outcomes, consider implementing the following optimization strategies:

1. Automate Assignment Where Possible: Leverage Microsoft Project's automation features to streamline resource assignment based on predefined criteria such as skill requirements, availability, and workload.

2. Implement Resource Levelling: Use resource leveling techniques to resolve resource overallocation issues and optimize work distribution across the project timeline. This ensures a balanced workload and prevents burnout among team members.

3. Utilize Resource Pools Effectively: Establish a centralized resource pool containing information about available resources, skills, and availability. Regularly update and maintain the resource pool to ensure accuracy and reliability.

4. Invest in Training and Development: Enhance the skills and capabilities of your project team through training and professional development initiatives. Well-equipped resources are better prepared to tackle project challenges and contribute to overall success.

5. Regularly Review and Refine Processes: Conduct periodic reviews of resource assignment processes to identify areas for improvement and optimization. Solicit feedback from project team members and stakeholders to refine strategies and enhance efficiency.

6. Embrace Collaboration Tools: Utilize collaboration tools and platforms to facilitate communication, coordination, and transparency among project team members. Effective collaboration enhances synergy and fosters a cohesive project environment.

Here's a step-by-step guide on how to assign resources to tasks using Microsoft Project:

Step 1: Open Your Project File

1. Launch Microsoft Project on your computer.

2. Open the project file you want to work on by clicking on "File" in the top menu bar, then selecting "Open" and navigating to the location of your project file. Double-click on the file to open it.

Step 2: Navigate to the Gantt Chart View

3. Once your project file is open, navigate to the Gantt Chart view. You can do this by clicking on the "View" tab in the top menu bar and selecting "Gantt Chart" from the available view options.

Step 3: Select the Task You Want to Assign Resources To

4. In the Gantt Chart view, locate the task to which you want to assign resources. Click on the row corresponding to the task to select it.

Step 4: Access the Resource Sheet

5. Next, navigate to the "Resource" tab in the top menu bar. Click on "Resource Sheet" in the toolbar to access the Resource Sheet view.

Step 5: Identify Available Resources

6. In the Resource Sheet view, review the list of available resources. This includes individuals, equipment, or materials that have been entered into the project.

Step 6: Assign Resources to the Selected Task

7. Return to the Gantt Chart view by clicking on the "View" tab and selecting "Gantt Chart" if you're not already there.

8. With the task still selected, locate the "Assign Resources" button in the toolbar or ribbon. Click on it to open the Assign Resources dialog box.

Step 7: Choose Resources to Assign

9. In the Assign Resources dialog box, you'll see a list of available resources from the Resource Sheet.

10. Select the checkbox next to each resource you want to assign to the task. You can assign multiple resources if needed.

Step 8: Adjust Resource Allocation

11. For each selected resource, specify the units or percentage of their availability to allocate to the task. You can do this by entering values in the "Units" column next to each resource.

Step 9: Finalize Resource Assignments

12. Once you've selected the desired resources and adjusted their allocation, click "OK" to finalize the resource assignments for the selected task.

Step 10: Review Resource Assignments

13. Back in the Gantt Chart view, review the task to ensure that the assigned resources are displayed correctly. You should see the assigned resources listed under the task name.

Step 11: Save Your Changes

14. After making resource assignments, remember to save your project file to retain the changes. Click on "File" in the top menu bar and select "Save" or "Save As" to save the file to your desired location.

Step 12: Repeat for Other Tasks (Optional)

15. If you have additional tasks that require resource assignments, repeat the above steps for each task as needed.

By following these step-by-step instructions, you can efficiently assign resources to tasks in Microsoft Project, ensuring proper resource utilization and effective project management.

Conclusion

Resource assignment is a fundamental aspect of project management in Microsoft Project, influencing project outcomes and team performance significantly. By understanding the principles of resource allocation, implementing best practices, addressing common challenges, and optimizing processes, project managers can maximize resource utilization, minimize risks, and achieve project objectives efficiently. Effective resource assignment fosters a productive work environment, empowers team members, and contributes to project success.

In the next section, we will explore techniques for tracking resource workloads and optimizing resource management throughout the project lifecycle.

5.3 Tracking Resource Workloads

5.3.1. Resource Workload Analysis

Resource workload analysis is a crucial aspect of project management that involves assessing the utilization and capacity of resources over time. By conducting workload analysis, project managers can ensure that resources are allocated efficiently, prevent overloading of individuals or teams, and identify potential bottlenecks in project execution. This section delves into the techniques and tools used for resource workload analysis in Microsoft Project.

Understanding Resource Workloads

Before delving into the analysis techniques, it's essential to understand what constitutes a resource workload. A resource workload refers to the amount of work assigned to a resource within a specific timeframe, usually depicted in hours or days. Workloads can vary based on factors such as task duration, resource availability, and task dependencies.

Resource workloads are dynamic and can change throughout the project lifecycle. Initially, during project planning, workloads might be evenly distributed among resources. However, as the project progresses, adjustments may be necessary due to changes in task priorities, resource availability, or unexpected delays.

Analyzing Resource Workloads in Microsoft Project

Microsoft Project offers several features and tools to facilitate resource workload analysis. These tools enable project managers to visualize resource allocations, identify potential conflicts, and make informed decisions to optimize resource utilization. Below are some key techniques for analyzing resource workloads in Microsoft Project:

Resource Usage View:

The Resource Usage view in Microsoft Project provides a detailed overview of resource assignments, workloads, and allocations. It displays information such as the tasks assigned to each resource, the duration and work hours for each task, and the total workload for each resource over time. By examining this view, project managers can identify resource overloads, underutilized resources, and potential scheduling conflicts.

Resource Graphs:

Microsoft Project offers various graphing tools that allow project managers to visualize resource workloads graphically. Resource graphs display information such as resource availability, workloads, and allocations in a graphical format, making it easier to identify trends and patterns. Common types of resource graphs include workload histograms, resource availability charts, and resource usage graphs.

Resource Reports:

Microsoft Project includes a wide range of pre-built reports specifically designed for analyzing resource workloads. These reports provide comprehensive insights into resource utilization, assignments, and allocations across different timeframes. Project managers can customize these reports to focus on specific resources, tasks, or time periods, enabling them to generate actionable insights quickly.

Resource Leveling:

Resource leveling is a technique used to optimize resource utilization and balance workloads across the project schedule. Microsoft Project offers built-in resource leveling tools that automatically adjust task assignments and schedules to resolve resource overloads and conflicts. By applying resource leveling, project managers can ensure that resources are allocated efficiently without overburdening individuals or teams.

Best Practices for Resource Workload Analysis

In addition to utilizing the tools and techniques provided by Microsoft Project, project managers should follow best practices to effectively analyze resource workloads:

- Regular Monitoring: Continuously monitor resource workloads throughout the project lifecycle to identify changes and trends promptly. Regular monitoring enables proactive management of resource allocations and helps prevent potential issues before they escalate.

- Collaboration: Foster collaboration between project managers, resource managers, and team members to ensure accurate and up-to-date information on resource availability and workloads. Collaboration facilitates effective resource planning and allocation decisions based on real-time data and insights.

- Flexibility: Maintain flexibility in resource allocations and schedules to accommodate changes in project requirements, priorities, and constraints. Be prepared to adjust resource assignments and workloads as needed to adapt to evolving circumstances and optimize project performance.

- Communication: Communicate transparently with stakeholders, particularly regarding resource constraints, overloads, and conflicts. Keep stakeholders informed about resource allocation decisions, potential impacts on project timelines, and mitigation strategies to address resource-related issues.

Conclusion

Resource workload analysis is a critical aspect of project management that enables efficient allocation and management of resources. By leveraging the tools and techniques available in Microsoft Project and following best practices, project managers can effectively analyze resource workloads, optimize resource utilization, and ensure successful project outcomes. Prioritizing resource workload analysis empowers project managers to proactively identify and address potential challenges, ultimately enhancing project performance and stakeholder satisfaction.

5.3.2. Resource Leveling Techniques

Resource workload tracking is a critical aspect of project management, ensuring that resources are allocated efficiently and effectively throughout the project lifecycle. In this section, we delve into resource leveling techniques, which are essential for balancing resource workloads and optimizing project schedules.

Resource leveling is the process of redistributing tasks and adjusting schedules to resolve resource overallocations and ensure a smoother workflow. This technique is particularly valuable in complex projects where resources are limited or shared among multiple tasks. By optimizing resource utilization, project managers can prevent burnout, minimize delays, and enhance overall productivity. Here are some key resource leveling techniques:

1. Task Dependencies:

Understanding task dependencies is fundamental to effective resource leveling. Tasks with dependencies must be sequenced appropriately to avoid conflicts and ensure that resources are available when needed. By identifying dependencies and establishing logical relationships between tasks, project managers can allocate resources more efficiently and minimize idle time.

2. Critical Path Analysis:

The critical path method (CPM) is a powerful tool for identifying critical tasks that directly impact project duration. By analyzing the critical path, project managers can prioritize tasks and allocate resources accordingly. Resource leveling often involves adjusting non-critical tasks to accommodate the needs of critical tasks without delaying the project's overall timeline.

3. Resource Smoothing:

Resource smoothing focuses on optimizing resource utilization without altering the project's critical path. This technique involves redistributing resource assignments within permissible limits to eliminate peaks and valleys in resource workloads. By smoothing out resource demands, project managers can minimize resource overallocations and ensure a more balanced workload distribution.

4. Resource Constraints:

Resource constraints refer to limitations on resource availability, such as maximum working hours or skill requirements. When allocating resources, project managers must consider these constraints to prevent overutilization and maintain project feasibility. By prioritizing tasks and adjusting schedules based on resource constraints, project managers can optimize resource allocation and mitigate potential risks.

5. Resource Leveling Heuristics:

Resource leveling heuristics are practical rules or guidelines used to resolve resource conflicts and prioritize task assignments. These heuristics often consider factors such as task duration, resource availability, and project objectives. Common heuristics include delaying non-critical tasks, splitting tasks into smaller subtasks, and reallocating resources based on task priorities.

6. Resource Levelling Software:

Project management software, such as Microsoft Project, often includes built-in features for resource leveling. These tools automate the process of identifying resource overallocations, suggesting schedule adjustments, and optimizing resource utilization. By leveraging resource leveling software, project managers can streamline the resource leveling process and focus on strategic decision-making.

7. Collaboration and Communication:

Effective collaboration and communication are essential for successful resource leveling. Project managers must work closely with team members, stakeholders, and resource managers to identify potential conflicts, negotiate resource allocations, and resolve scheduling issues. By fostering open communication and collaboration, project teams can adapt to changing resource demands and maintain project momentum.

8. Continuous Monitoring and Adjustment:

Resource leveling is an iterative process that requires continuous monitoring and adjustment throughout the project lifecycle. Project managers should regularly review resource allocations, monitor resource workloads, and identify emerging conflicts or bottlenecks. By proactively addressing resource issues and making timely adjustments, project managers can optimize resource utilization and ensure project success.

In conclusion, resource leveling techniques are essential for optimizing resource utilization, balancing workloads, and minimizing project delays. By applying these techniques strategically and leveraging appropriate tools and methodologies, project managers can effectively manage resource constraints, mitigate risks, and deliver successful projects on time and within budget.

Example: Software Development Project

Let's consider a software development project to illustrate the concept of tracking resource workloads and applying resource leveling techniques.

Project Overview:

Imagine a project to develop a new mobile application for a client. The project involves designing, coding, testing, and deploying the application within a six-month timeframe.

Resource Allocation:

The project team consists of developers, testers, designers, and a project manager. Each team member has specific skills and expertise required for different phases of the project.

Initial Resource Allocation:

- Two developers (Developer A and Developer B)

- One tester (Tester X)

- One designer (Designer D)

- One project manager (Manager M)

Task Assignments:

Tasks are assigned to team members based on their skills and availability:

- Developer A and Developer B: coding and programming tasks

- Tester X: testing and quality assurance

- Designer D: UI/UX design

- Manager M: project planning, coordination, and communication

Resource Workloads:

As the project progresses, resource workloads are tracked to ensure optimal utilization and prevent overallocations:

- Developer A: Assigned coding tasks for the first two months, then shifts focus to debugging and optimization.

- Developer B: Initially assists with coding tasks but also handles technical support and troubleshooting as needed.

- Tester X: Conducts ongoing testing throughout the project lifecycle to identify bugs and ensure quality.

- Designer D: Works on UI/UX design in the early stages, then provides support for graphic assets and visual elements.

- Manager M: Oversees project progress, facilitates team meetings, and addresses any issues or concerns.

Resource Overallocations:

Midway through the project, resource overallocations become apparent:

- Developer A is overloaded with coding tasks, leading to delays in debugging and optimization.

- Tester X is overwhelmed with testing requirements, resulting in a backlog of unresolved issues.

- Designer D faces competing priorities and struggles to meet deadlines for graphic design tasks.

- Manager M experiences challenges in balancing project oversight with other responsibilities.

Resource Leveling Techniques:

To address resource overallocations and optimize resource utilization, the project manager implements resource leveling techniques:

1. Task Dependencies: Identifies critical tasks and adjusts dependencies to prioritize debugging and testing activities.

2. Resource Smoothing: Redistributes coding tasks between Developer A and Developer B to balance workloads and reduce bottlenecks.

3. Resource Constraints: Establishes realistic deadlines and milestones based on resource availability and skill sets.

4. Collaboration and Communication: Facilitates regular team meetings to discuss resource allocations, identify challenges, and adjust schedules as needed.

5. Continuous Monitoring and Adjustment: Monitors resource workloads regularly and makes real-time adjustments to prevent resource overallocations and ensure project progress.

Outcome:

By applying resource leveling techniques, the project manager successfully resolves resource overallocations, balances workloads, and maintains project momentum. The team collaborates effectively, communicates openly, and adapts to changing resource demands, ultimately delivering the mobile application on time and within budget.

Analysis:

This example demonstrates the importance of tracking resource workloads and applying resource leveling techniques to optimize resource utilization and mitigate risks in project management. By proactively addressing resource constraints and leveraging appropriate strategies, project managers can overcome challenges, minimize delays, and achieve project success.

PART VI
Budgeting and Cost Management

6.1 Estimating Project Costs

6.1.1. Cost Estimation Techniques

Cost estimation is a critical aspect of project management, as it lays the foundation for budgeting and resource allocation throughout the project lifecycle. Accurate cost estimation ensures that projects are adequately funded and completed within budget constraints. However, estimating project costs can be challenging due to various uncertainties and variables. In this section, we will explore various cost estimation techniques commonly used by project managers.

1. Analogous Estimation

Analogous estimation, also known as top-down estimation, relies on historical data from similar projects to estimate costs for the current project. This technique is useful when detailed information is not available or when there is limited time for estimation. By comparing the current project with past projects in terms of scope, size, and complexity, project managers can derive cost estimates quickly. However, the accuracy of analogous estimation depends on the similarity between the current and past projects.

2. Parametric Estimation

Parametric estimation involves using statistical relationships between historical data and project parameters to estimate costs. Instead of relying on overall project characteristics like in analogous estimation, parametric estimation uses specific metrics or variables to calculate costs. For example, in software development projects, cost per line of code or cost per function point can be used as parameters for estimation. Parametric models are developed based on historical data analysis and are continuously refined as more data becomes available. While parametric estimation provides more accuracy than analogous estimation, it requires detailed data and may not be applicable to all project types.

3. Bottom-Up Estimation

Bottom-up estimation, also known as detailed estimation, involves breaking down the project into smaller, more manageable components and estimating the costs for each component individually. Project managers collaborate with team members to identify all tasks, activities, and resources required for the project and estimate their costs. These individual estimates are then aggregated to determine the total project cost. Bottom-up estimation is highly accurate as it considers the specific requirements of the project. However, it is also time-consuming and may not be feasible for large or complex projects.

4. Three-Point Estimation

Three-point estimation, also known as PERT (Program Evaluation and Review Technique) estimation, accounts for uncertainty by considering three estimates for each task: optimistic, pessimistic, and most likely. These estimates are then used to calculate the expected cost using the formula:

Expected Cost = (Optimistic Cost + 4 Most Likely Cost + Pessimistic Cost) / 6

The three-point estimation technique is particularly useful for tasks with high levels of uncertainty, as it provides a range of possible costs rather than a single point estimate. This approach encourages project managers to account for risk and variability in their cost estimates.

5. Expert Judgment

Expert judgment involves consulting with subject matter experts, stakeholders, or industry professionals to obtain cost estimates based on their experience and expertise. These experts may have valuable insights into the specific requirements and challenges of the project, which can inform more accurate cost estimates. Expert judgment can be used in conjunction with other estimation techniques to validate estimates and identify potential risks or opportunities.

6. Vendor Bids and Quotations

For projects involving procurement of goods or services from external vendors, cost estimation can be based on bids and quotations provided by vendors. Project managers solicit bids from multiple vendors and evaluate them based on factors such as cost, quality, and timeline. Vendor bids provide real-world cost estimates based on market rates and vendor capabilities. However, project managers should carefully analyze and compare bids to ensure they accurately reflect the project requirements and deliverables.

7. Reserve Analysis

Reserve analysis involves setting aside contingency reserves to account for unforeseen risks or changes in project scope that may impact costs. These reserves act as a buffer to cover additional expenses that were not included in the initial cost estimates. Reserve analysis can be based on historical data, expert judgment, or risk assessments. By allocating contingency reserves based on the level of uncertainty and risk exposure, project managers can mitigate the impact of cost overruns and ensure project success.

Conclusion

Effective cost estimation is essential for the success of any project, as it provides the foundation for budgeting, resource allocation, and decision-making. By employing a combination of cost estimation techniques such as analogous estimation, parametric estimation, bottom-up estimation, three-point estimation, expert judgment, vendor bids, and reserve analysis, project managers can develop accurate and reliable cost estimates that support project objectives and stakeholders' expectations. Additionally, regular monitoring and control of project costs throughout the project lifecycle are essential to ensure that the project remains within budget constraints and delivers value to the organization.

6.1.2. Cost Baseline and Contingency Planning

Cost estimation is an essential aspect of project management, but it's not enough to simply estimate costs; you also need a plan to manage those costs throughout the project lifecycle. This is where the cost baseline and contingency planning come into play. In this section, we'll delve into the importance of establishing a cost baseline and developing contingency plans to deal with unforeseen circumstances that may impact the project budget.

Establishing the Cost Baseline

The cost baseline serves as a benchmark against which actual project costs are measured and compared. It represents the approved, time-phased budget for the project, including all estimated costs for labor, materials, equipment, and other resources. Establishing a cost baseline is a critical step in project planning as it provides a clear financial roadmap for the project and helps project managers track and control expenditures.

Components of the Cost Baseline

1. Direct Costs: These are expenses directly attributable to the project, such as labor costs, material costs, equipment costs, and subcontractor fees. Direct costs are usually estimated based on resource requirements identified in the project plan.

2. Indirect Costs: Also known as overhead costs, these are expenses that are not directly tied to a specific project activity but are necessary for the project's completion. Indirect costs may include utilities, administrative expenses, and overhead for shared resources.

3. Contingency Reserves: Contingency reserves are funds set aside to cover unforeseen events or risks that may impact the project. These reserves are included in the cost baseline to ensure that the project has a buffer to address unexpected expenses without exceeding the approved budget.

4. Management Reserves: Management reserves are additional funds allocated for unknown unknowns—risks that are unforeseeable at the time of project planning. Unlike contingency reserves, which are managed by the project manager, management reserves are typically controlled by senior management and are not included in the cost baseline.

Importance of Contingency Planning

Despite thorough cost estimation and baseline establishment, projects are inherently prone to uncertainties and unforeseen events that can disrupt the planned budget. Contingency planning involves identifying potential risks and developing strategies to mitigate their impact on project costs. By anticipating and preparing for potential risks, project managers can minimize cost overruns and ensure that the project stays within budget constraints.

Steps in Contingency Planning

1. Risk Identification: The first step in contingency planning is to identify potential risks that could affect the project budget. Risks can arise from various sources, including external factors such as market changes, environmental conditions, or regulatory requirements, as well as internal factors such as resource constraints, scope changes, or technical challenges.

2. Risk Assessment: Once risks are identified, they must be assessed in terms of their likelihood of occurrence and potential impact on project costs. Risks with high probability and high impact should be prioritized for mitigation, while risks with low probability and low impact may be accepted or monitored with less intensive mitigation efforts.

3. Risk Mitigation Strategies: After assessing risks, project managers must develop appropriate mitigation strategies to address identified threats to the project budget. Mitigation strategies may include risk avoidance (eliminating the risk altogether), risk mitigation (reducing the likelihood or impact of the risk), risk transfer (shifting the risk to another party through insurance or contracts), or risk acceptance (acknowledging the risk and its potential impact).

4. Contingency Reserve Allocation: Based on the identified risks and mitigation strategies, project managers allocate contingency reserves to cover potential cost overruns associated with specific risks. Contingency reserves should be allocated strategically to address the most significant threats to the project budget while maintaining overall budgetary discipline.

Monitoring and Control

Once the cost baseline and contingency plans are established, it's crucial to monitor and control project costs throughout the project lifecycle. This involves regularly tracking actual expenditures against the cost baseline, identifying variances, and taking corrective action when necessary to keep the project on track financially.

Earned Value Management (EVM)

Earned Value Management is a technique used to monitor and control project performance by integrating cost, schedule, and scope measurements. EVM provides a comprehensive view of project progress and performance by comparing planned value (PV), earned value (EV), and actual cost (AC) of work performed. Key metrics derived from EVM include the Cost Performance Index (CPI) and the Schedule Performance Index (SPI), which indicate whether the project is meeting, exceeding, or falling short of cost and schedule targets.

Variance Analysis

Variance analysis involves comparing actual project costs to the cost baseline and identifying discrepancies or variances. Positive variances (where actual costs are lower than planned) may indicate cost savings or efficiency gains, while negative variances (where actual costs exceed planned) may signal cost overruns or inefficiencies. By analyzing variances and their root causes, project managers can take corrective action to address budgetary deviations and ensure that the project remains financially viable.

Conclusion

In conclusion, establishing a cost baseline and developing contingency plans are essential aspects of effective cost management in project management. By setting clear financial benchmarks and preparing for potential risks, project managers can better control project costs and minimize the impact of unforeseen events on project budgets. Through diligent monitoring, analysis, and control, project managers can ensure that projects are completed within budgetary constraints while delivering the intended value to stakeholders.

6.2 Tracking Expenses and Budgets

6.2.1. Expense Tracking Methods

Tracking expenses is a critical aspect of project management, as it allows project managers to monitor where the project stands in terms of budget utilization. By diligently tracking expenses, project managers can identify potential cost overruns early and take corrective actions to ensure that the project stays within budget constraints. In this section, we will explore various expense tracking methods commonly used by project managers.

1. Manual Expense Tracking:

Manual expense tracking involves recording project expenses manually using spreadsheets, paper forms, or dedicated expense tracking software. While this method may seem archaic compared to automated systems, it offers simplicity and flexibility, especially for small-scale projects with limited resources.

Advantages:

- *Cost-Effective:* Manual expense tracking doesn't require investment in specialized software or tools.

- *Customizable:* Project managers can tailor expense tracking formats to suit their specific project needs.

- *Accessibility:* Data can be easily accessed and modified using commonly available tools like Microsoft Excel.

Disadvantages:

- *Prone to Errors:* Manual data entry increases the risk of errors, such as typos or miscalculations.

- *Time-Consuming:* Recording and updating expenses manually can be time-consuming, especially for large projects.

- *Limited Scalability:* Manual methods may not be suitable for complex projects with high transaction volumes.

2. Spreadsheet-Based Tracking:

Spreadsheet-based expense tracking involves using spreadsheet software like Microsoft Excel or Google Sheets to record and manage project expenses. Project managers can create customized templates with predefined fields for expense categories, amounts, dates, and descriptions.

Advantages:

- *Flexibility:* Spreadsheets can be customized to accommodate various expense tracking requirements.

- *Calculation Capabilities:* Spreadsheet formulas enable automatic calculation of totals, subtotals, and other financial metrics.

- *Visualization:* Data can be presented visually through charts and graphs for easier analysis and reporting.

Disadvantages:

- *Version Control:* Managing multiple versions of a spreadsheet can lead to confusion and data discrepancies.

- *Security Risks:* Spreadsheets may lack robust security features, making them vulnerable to unauthorized access or data breaches.

- *Limited Collaboration:* Simultaneous collaboration on a single spreadsheet can be challenging, especially with large project teams.

3. Dedicated Expense Tracking Software:

Dedicated expense tracking software, also known as expense management software, is specifically designed to streamline the process of recording, categorizing, and analyzing expenses. These tools often integrate with project management software or accounting systems to provide a comprehensive view of project finances.

Advantages:

- *Automation*: Expense tracking software automates many aspects of expense management, reducing manual effort and minimizing errors.

- *Integration:* Seamless integration with other project management tools enables real-time synchronization of financial data.

- *Customization:* Users can configure expense categories, approval workflows, and reporting formats to align with project requirements.

Disadvantages:

- *Cost:* Dedicated expense tracking software may involve subscription fees or licensing costs, which can be prohibitive for small organizations or projects.

- *Learning Curve:* Users may require training to fully utilize the features and functionalities of the software.

- *Dependency:* Relying on third-party software vendors introduces dependency and potential risks associated with service outages or discontinuation of support.

4. Mobile Expense Tracking Apps:

Mobile expense tracking apps provide on-the-go convenience for capturing and managing project expenses using smartphones or tablets. These apps typically offer features such as receipt scanning, mileage tracking, and expense report generation.

Advantages:

- *Accessibility:* Users can record expenses anytime, anywhere, using their mobile devices, eliminating the need for manual data entry.

- *Real-Time Updates:* Expense data is instantly synchronized with the central database, providing up-to-date visibility for project stakeholders.

- *Receipt Management:* Built-in camera functionality allows users to capture receipts and attach them directly to expense records for verification and audit purposes.

Disadvantages:

- *Device Compatibility:* Compatibility issues may arise with different mobile devices and operating systems, affecting user experience.

- *Data Security:* Storing sensitive financial data on mobile devices poses security risks in case of loss, theft, or unauthorized access.

- *Dependency on Connectivity:* Mobile expense tracking apps require internet connectivity for data synchronization, which may not be available in remote or offline environments.

Conclusion:

Effective expense tracking is essential for maintaining project financial health and ensuring successful project delivery. Project managers must select the most appropriate expense tracking method based on the project's size, complexity, and resource constraints. Whether opting for manual methods, spreadsheet-based solutions, dedicated software, or mobile apps, the key is to establish robust processes and controls to accurately capture, monitor, and analyze project expenses throughout the project lifecycle. By doing so, project managers can make informed decisions, mitigate financial risks, and ultimately achieve project success within budgetary constraints.

This concludes our exploration of expense tracking methods in project management. In the next section, we will delve into the concept of budget vs. actual analysis and its significance in project cost management.

6.2.2. Budget vs. Actual Analysis

Budget vs. actual analysis is a critical component of financial management within project management. It involves comparing the planned budget for a project with the actual expenses incurred during its execution. This analysis provides valuable insights into how well a project is performing financially and helps project managers make informed decisions to keep the project on track.

Understanding Budget vs. Actual Analysis

At its core, budget vs. actual analysis compares what was planned (the budget) with what actually happened (the actual expenses). This comparison allows project managers to identify discrepancies, understand variances, and take corrective actions if necessary. By monitoring these differences throughout the project lifecycle, project managers can proactively manage resources, control costs, and optimize project performance.

Importance of Budget vs. Actual Analysis

1. Performance Evaluation: Budget vs. actual analysis provides a clear picture of a project's financial performance. It allows project managers to assess whether the project is meeting its financial objectives and staying within the allocated budget.

2. Early Detection of Issues: Discrepancies between the budget and actual expenses may indicate underlying issues such as cost overruns, resource mismanagement, or scope creep. Early detection of these issues enables timely intervention to address them before they escalate.

3. Decision Making: The insights gained from budget vs. actual analysis empower project managers to make data-driven decisions. Whether it involves reallocating resources, renegotiating contracts, or revising project scope, informed decisions can mitigate risks and optimize project outcomes.

4. Stakeholder Communication: Transparent reporting of budget vs. actual performance fosters trust and transparency among stakeholders. Project managers can effectively communicate project financials, justify resource allocations, and manage stakeholder expectations.

Components of Budget vs. Actual Analysis

1. Budgeted Costs: This includes the planned expenses outlined in the project budget. It encompasses various cost elements such as labor, materials, equipment, overhead, and contingency reserves.

2. Actual Costs: Actual costs refer to the real expenses incurred during the execution of the project. These may differ from the budgeted costs due to factors such as changes in resource rates, unexpected delays, or scope modifications.

3. Variances: Variances represent the differences between budgeted costs and actual costs. They can be either favorable (cost savings) or unfavorable (cost overruns) and are typically expressed in both monetary terms and percentages.

4. Root Cause Analysis: Identifying the root causes of variances is crucial for effective corrective action. It involves investigating the factors contributing to the discrepancies and understanding their impact on project performance.

Techniques for Budget vs. Actual Analysis

1. Variance Analysis: This technique involves comparing individual cost items in the budget with their corresponding actual expenses. Variances are calculated for each cost category, allowing project managers to pinpoint areas where deviations occur.

2. Trend Analysis: Trend analysis involves tracking the pattern of budget vs. actual variances over time. It helps project managers identify recurring issues, assess the effectiveness of corrective actions, and anticipate future financial trends.

3. Benchmarking: Benchmarking involves comparing the project's performance against industry standards or similar projects. This comparative analysis provides context for interpreting budget vs. actual variances and identifying areas for improvement.

Steps for Conducting Budget vs. Actual Analysis

1. Gather Data: Collect comprehensive data on both budgeted costs and actual expenses. Ensure accuracy and consistency in recording financial information to facilitate meaningful analysis.

2. Calculate Variances: Determine the differences between budgeted costs and actual expenses for each cost category. Analyze both the magnitude and direction of variances to understand their implications.

3. Identify Causes: Investigate the root causes of variances by examining factors such as changes in scope, resource utilization, market conditions, or project constraints.

4. Evaluate Impact: Assess the impact of variances on project performance, schedule, and quality. Consider both short-term implications and long-term consequences to make informed decisions.

5. Develop Action Plans: Based on the analysis, develop action plans to address identified variances and mitigate their impact on the project. Collaborate with relevant stakeholders to implement corrective measures effectively.

6. Monitor Progress: Continuously monitor the implementation of action plans and track the progress of budget vs. actual performance. Adjust strategies as needed to ensure alignment with project objectives and financial targets.

Best Practices for Effective Budget vs. Actual Analysis

1. Establish Clear Baselines: Define clear baselines for budgeted costs and performance metrics to serve as reference points for analysis.

2. Regular Monitoring: Conduct regular reviews of budget vs. actual performance throughout the project lifecycle to detect issues early and facilitate timely interventions.

3. Communication: Foster open communication channels with project team members, stakeholders, and financial stakeholders to facilitate collaboration and transparency in budget management.

4. Flexibility: Remain flexible in adapting to changing project dynamics and evolving financial conditions. Adjust budgetary allocations and resource plans as needed to align with project priorities and objectives.

5. Continuous Improvement: Learn from past experiences and incorporate lessons learned into future budgeting and cost management practices. Continuously strive for improvement in financial performance and project outcomes.

Conclusion

Budget vs. actual analysis is a fundamental tool for effective financial management in project management. By comparing planned budgets with actual expenses, project managers can evaluate performance, identify variances, and take proactive measures to optimize project outcomes. By following best practices and leveraging appropriate techniques, project managers can enhance their ability to control costs, mitigate risks, and deliver successful projects within budgetary constraints.

6.3 Analyzing Cost Variances

6.3.1. Cost Variance Calculation

Welcome6.3. Analyzing Cost Variances

Cost variance analysis is a crucial aspect of project management, providing insights into how well a project is performing in terms of budget adherence. By comparing actual costs with planned costs, project managers can identify discrepancies early on and take corrective actions to keep the project on track financially. In this section, we will delve into the process of calculating cost variances and interpreting the results to make informed decisions.

6.3.1. Cost Variance Calculation

Cost variance (CV) is a measure used to assess the variance between the actual costs incurred and the budgeted costs for the work performed during a specific time period. It indicates whether the project is under budget (positive CV) or over budget (negative CV). The formula for calculating cost variance is:

CV = EV - AC

Where:

- CV = Cost Variance

- EV = Earned Value

- AC = Actual Cost

Let's break down each component of the formula:

1. Earned Value (EV): Earned Value represents the value of the work completed at a specific point in time, expressed in monetary terms. It is determined by multiplying the percent complete of each task or activity by its planned budgeted cost. The formula for calculating Earned Value is:

EV = % Complete x BAC

Where:

- % Complete = Percentage of completion of the task or activity

- BAC = Budget at Completion (total budget for the project)

For example, if a task was budgeted to cost $1,000 and it is 50% complete, the Earned Value would be $500.

2. Actual Cost (AC): Actual Cost refers to the total expenditure incurred for completing the work at a specific point in time. It includes all costs associated with the project, such as labor, materials, equipment, overhead, and any other direct or indirect expenses. Actual Cost can be calculated by summing up all the costs incurred up to the reporting date.

Once the Earned Value (EV) and Actual Cost (AC) are determined, the Cost Variance (CV) can be calculated using the formula provided earlier.

Interpreting Cost Variance Results:

The interpretation of cost variance results depends on whether the value is positive, negative, or zero:

1. Positive Cost Variance (CV > 0): A positive cost variance indicates that the project is under budget, meaning that the actual costs are less than the budgeted costs for the work performed. This is generally considered favorable, as it means cost savings are being realized. However, it's essential to investigate the reasons behind the variance to ensure that quality and scope haven't been compromised to achieve cost savings.

2. Negative Cost Variance (CV < 0): A negative cost variance suggests that the project is over budget, meaning that the actual costs exceed the budgeted costs for the work performed. This is considered unfavorable and requires immediate attention from the project manager to identify the root causes of the variance and implement corrective actions to bring the project back on track financially.

3. Zero Cost Variance (CV = 0): A zero cost variance indicates that the actual costs are equal to the budgeted costs. While this may seem ideal, it's essential to remember that it doesn't necessarily mean the project is on track. It's possible for the project to be meeting budget targets while facing other issues such as schedule delays or quality issues.

Using Cost Variance for Decision Making:

Cost variance analysis provides valuable insights that can guide decision-making throughout the project lifecycle. By regularly monitoring and analyzing cost variances, project managers can:

- Identify cost-saving opportunities and areas of cost overruns.

- Assess the effectiveness of cost control measures.

- Allocate resources more efficiently to minimize cost overruns.

- Forecast future project costs more accurately.

- Communicate project financial status to stakeholders effectively.

Key Considerations and Best Practices:

To ensure accurate and meaningful cost variance analysis, project managers should consider the following best practices:

1. Establish Baselines: Define clear cost baselines at the beginning of the project to serve as reference points for comparison. This includes creating a budget baseline and a schedule baseline against which actual performance can be measured.

2. Regular Monitoring: Implement a robust project monitoring system to track actual costs, earned value, and planned costs regularly. This allows for early detection of cost variances and timely intervention.

3. Root Cause Analysis: Conduct thorough investigations to identify the root causes of cost variances. This may involve reviewing project records, consulting with team members, and analyzing external factors that may have contributed to the variances.

4. Document Variance Reasons: Document the reasons behind cost variances along with the actions taken to address them. This helps in learning from past experiences and improving cost estimation and control processes for future projects.

5. Communicate Effectively: Communicate cost variance analysis findings transparently to project stakeholders, including senior management, clients, and team members. Provide clear explanations of the implications of cost variances and proposed corrective actions.

6. Adjust Budgets as Needed: Based on the insights gained from cost variance analysis, be prepared to adjust project budgets and resource allocations as needed to ensure financial viability and project success.

In conclusion, cost variance analysis is a powerful tool for project managers to monitor, control, and optimize project costs. By calculating cost variances and interpreting the results effectively, project managers can make informed decisions, mitigate financial risks, and steer projects towards successful outcomes within budget constraints.

6.3.2. Cost Performance Index (CPI) Analysis

Cost Performance Index (CPI) is a crucial metric in project management, especially in the realm of cost control and forecasting. It provides project managers with insights into how efficiently the project is utilizing its budget. In simple terms, CPI indicates whether the project is under or over budget at a specific point in time. Understanding CPI and effectively analyzing its implications can significantly contribute to proactive decision-making and successful project outcomes.

Understanding Cost Performance Index (CPI)

CPI is a ratio that compares the actual work completed to the actual costs incurred. Mathematically, it is calculated by dividing the Earned Value (EV) by the Actual Cost (AC):

CPI = EV / AC

Where:

- **EV (Earned Value)** represents the value of the work performed up to a certain point in time, usually measured in terms of the budgeted cost of work scheduled (BCWS) or planned value.

- **AC (Actual Cost)** is the total cost incurred in completing the work up to the same point in time.

A CPI value of 1 indicates that the project is exactly on budget. A CPI greater than 1 signifies that the project is under budget, meaning that it is delivering more value than what was spent. Conversely, a CPI less than 1 suggests that the project is over budget, indicating inefficiencies in cost management.

Interpreting CPI Values

Interpreting CPI values requires context and an understanding of the project's objectives and constraints. While a CPI greater than 1 is generally desirable, it could also imply that resources are not being fully utilized, which might not align with project goals. On the other hand, a CPI less than 1 raises concerns about cost overruns and the need for corrective actions to bring the project back on track.

Here are some common interpretations of CPI values:

1. CPI = 1: The project is on budget. The actual costs incurred are proportional to the value of work completed.

2. CPI > 1: The project is under budget. More value has been earned than what was spent. While this might seem positive, it could also indicate resource inefficiencies or underestimated budgets.

3. CPI < 1: The project is over budget. The actual costs exceed the value of work completed. This situation requires immediate attention to identify cost-saving measures or reallocate resources effectively.

Benefits of CPI Analysis

Analyzing CPI offers several benefits to project managers and stakeholders:

1. Early Warning System: CPI serves as an early warning system for potential cost overruns. By monitoring CPI regularly, project managers can identify budgetary issues before they escalate, allowing for timely interventions.

2. Performance Evaluation: CPI provides a quantitative measure of project performance in terms of cost efficiency. It helps assess whether the project is meeting its financial objectives and allows for comparisons across different phases or projects.

3. Decision Support: Armed with CPI data, project managers can make informed decisions regarding resource allocation, scope management, and procurement. For instance, if CPI indicates significant cost overruns, project managers can explore options such as renegotiating contracts or revising the project scope to control costs.

4. Continuous Improvement: By analyzing CPI trends over time, project teams can identify patterns and areas for improvement in cost estimation, budgeting, and resource management. This facilitates continuous learning and refinement of project management processes.

Strategies for CPI Improvement

Improving CPI involves a combination of proactive measures aimed at enhancing cost efficiency and effectiveness. Here are some strategies to consider:

1. Enhanced Cost Estimation: Invest time and resources in improving the accuracy of cost estimates during project planning. Utilize historical data, expert judgment, and risk analysis techniques to develop realistic budgets and contingency reserves.

2. Resource Optimization: Ensure optimal utilization of resources throughout the project lifecycle. Avoid resource bottlenecks or underutilization by closely monitoring resource allocation and adjusting staffing levels as needed.

3. Scope Management: Implement robust scope management processes to prevent scope creep and unnecessary changes that can inflate project costs. Clearly define project deliverables and establish change control procedures to manage scope changes effectively.

4. Vendor Management: Negotiate favorable terms with vendors and suppliers to optimize procurement costs. Regularly review vendor performance and seek opportunities for cost savings through competitive bidding or alternative sourcing strategies.

5. Risk Management: Identify and mitigate potential risks that could impact project costs. Develop contingency plans and reserves to address unforeseen events or uncertainties that may lead to cost overruns.

6. Performance Monitoring: Establish a system for regular monitoring and reporting of project performance metrics, including CPI. Analyze CPI trends to identify deviations from the baseline and take corrective actions as necessary.

Case Study: Applying CPI Analysis in Practice

To illustrate the practical application of CPI analysis, consider the following case study:

Project: Development of a mobile application for a client in the retail sector.

Objective: Deliver the application within the specified budget and timeline to meet client requirements.

Key Metrics: CPI, EV, AC, Budget at Completion (BAC), Planned Value (PV).

In this scenario, the project team regularly tracks EV and AC to calculate CPI at various stages of the project. Early in the project lifecycle, CPI indicates that the project is slightly under budget, which is attributed to efficient resource allocation and streamlined development processes.

However, as the project progresses, CPI begins to decline due to unforeseen technical challenges and scope changes requested by the client. By closely monitoring CPI trends, the project manager identifies the deteriorating cost performance and initiates corrective actions, such as revising the project scope, reallocating resources, and renegotiating vendor contracts.

Through proactive intervention and diligent cost management, the project team successfully improves CPI and brings the project back on track, ultimately delivering the mobile application within the budgetary constraints.

Conclusion

Cost Performance Index (CPI) analysis is a powerful tool for project managers to monitor and control project costs effectively. By comparing the value of work completed to the actual costs incurred, CPI provides valuable insights into cost efficiency and helps identify potential budgetary issues early in the project lifecycle.

Understanding CPI and its implications allows project managers to make informed decisions, implement corrective actions, and ultimately improve project outcomes. By incorporating CPI analysis into project management practices, organizations can enhance cost control, optimize resource utilization, and increase the likelihood of project success.

PART VII
Reporting and Analysis

7.1 Generating Project Reports

7.1.1. Built-in Report Templates

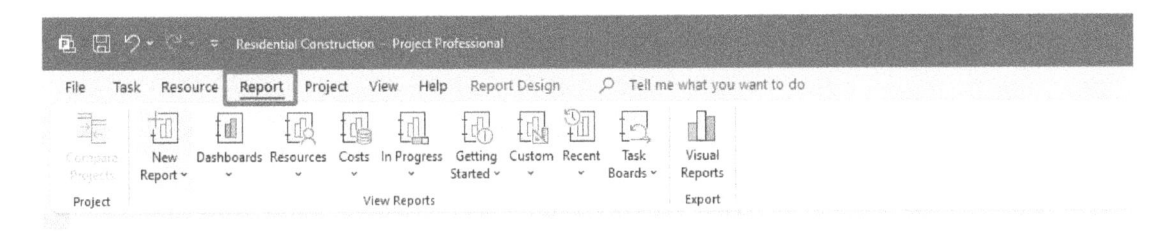

Built-in report templates in Microsoft Project serve as powerful tools for project managers to quickly generate insightful reports without the need for extensive customization. These templates cover various aspects of project management, from task progress to resource allocation, providing a comprehensive overview of project performance. In this section, we will explore the built-in report templates available in Microsoft Project and discuss their functionalities.

Overview of Built-in Report Templates

PART VII: REPORTING AND ANALYSIS

Mon 03/08/20 - Wed 03/03/21

BURNDOWN

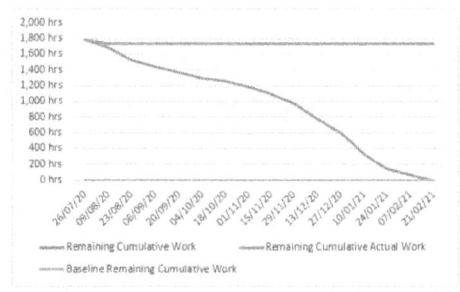

WORK BURNDOWN
Shows how much work you have completed and how much you have left. If the remaining cumulative work line is steeper, then the project may be late. Is your baseline zero?

Try setting a baseline

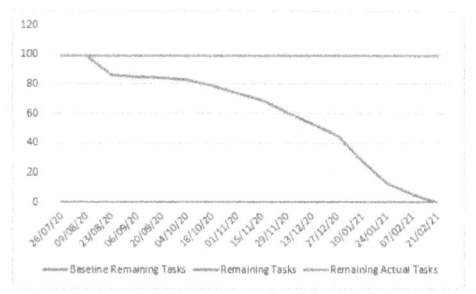

TASK BURNDOWN
Shows how many tasks you have completed and how many you have left. If the remaining tasks line is steeper, then your project may be late.

Learn more

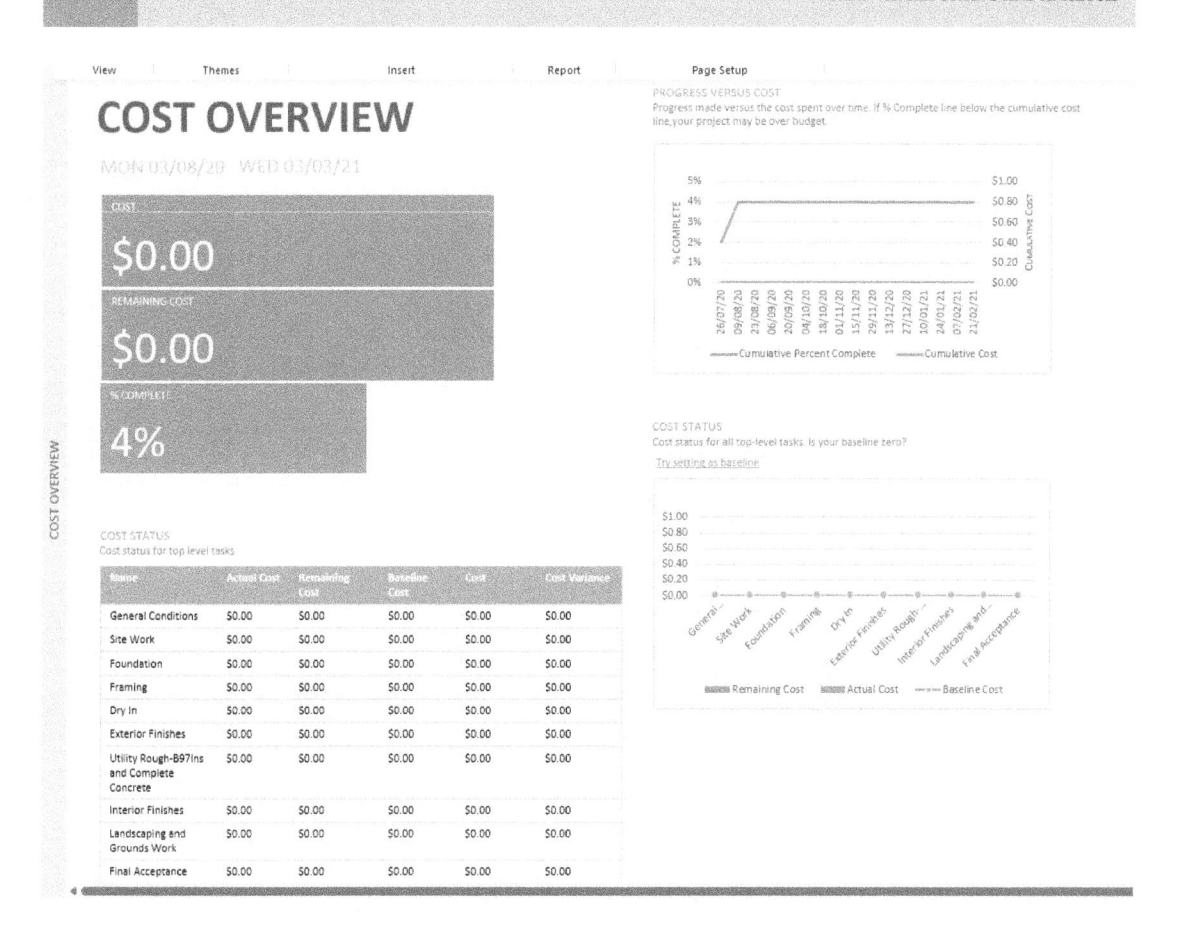

PART VII: REPORTING AND ANALYSIS

| View | Themes | Insert | Report | Page Setup |

COST OVERVIEW

MON 03/08/20 — WED 03/03/21

COST
$0.00

REMAINING COST
$0.00

% COMPLETE
4%

PROGRESS VERSUS COST
Progress made versus the cost spent over time. If % Complete line below the cumulative cost line, your project may be over budget.

— Cumulative Percent Complete   — Cumulative Cost

COST STATUS
Cost status for all top-level tasks. Is your baseline zero?
Try setting as baseline

COST STATUS
Cost status for top level tasks

Name	Actual Cost	Remaining Cost	Baseline Cost	Cost	Cost Variance
General Conditions	$0.00	$0.00	$0.00	$0.00	$0.00
Site Work	$0.00	$0.00	$0.00	$0.00	$0.00
Foundation	$0.00	$0.00	$0.00	$0.00	$0.00
Framing	$0.00	$0.00	$0.00	$0.00	$0.00
Dry In	$0.00	$0.00	$0.00	$0.00	$0.00
Exterior Finishes	$0.00	$0.00	$0.00	$0.00	$0.00
Utility Rough-B97Ins and Complete Concrete	$0.00	$0.00	$0.00	$0.00	$0.00
Interior Finishes	$0.00	$0.00	$0.00	$0.00	$0.00
Landscaping and Grounds Work	$0.00	$0.00	$0.00	$0.00	$0.00
Final Acceptance	$0.00	$0.00	$0.00	$0.00	$0.00

— Remaining Cost   — Actual Cost   — Baseline Cost

PART VII: REPORTING AND ANALYSIS

PROJECT OVERVIEW

MON 03/08/20   WED 03/03/21

% COMPLETE

4%

MILESTONES DUE
Milestones that are coming soon.

Name	Finish
All Permits Secured	Mon 31/08/20
All Site Work Complete	Fri 04/09/20
Foundation Complete	Tue 03/11/20
Framing Complete	Thu 03/12/20
Dry In Complete	Fri 01/01/21
<Exterior Finishes Complete	Thu 28/01/21
Utility Rough-ins Complete	Wed 09/12/20
Interior Finishes Complete	Fri 12/02/21
Landscaping & Grounds Work Complete	Fri 19/02/21
Residential Construction Project Complete	Wed 03/03/21

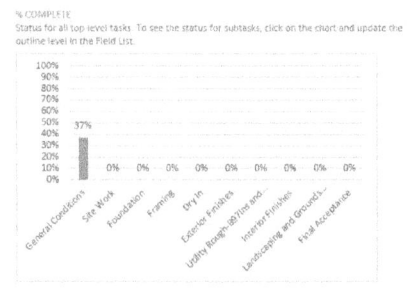

% COMPLETE
Status for all top-level tasks. To see the status for subtasks, click on the chart and update the outline level in the Field List.

LATE TASKS
Tasks that are past due.

Name	Start	Finish	Duration	% Complete	Resource Names
Finalize plans, and develop estimate with owner and architect	Mon 03/08/20	Fri 28/08/20	20 days	50%	General contractor[50%],Architect[50%],Owner[12%],Mortgage lender[12%]

PART VII: REPORTING AND ANALYSIS

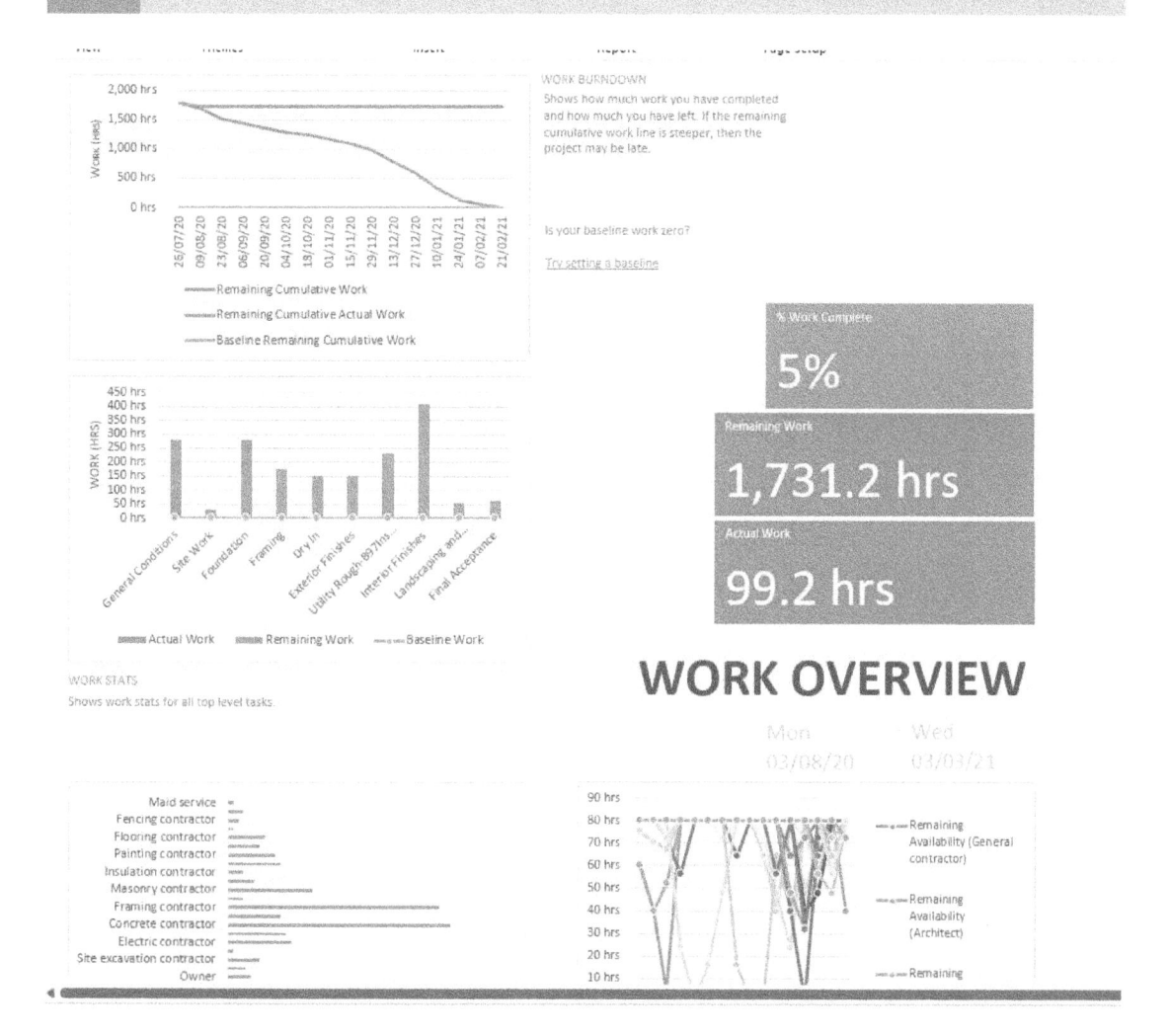

WORK BURNDOWN
Shows how much work you have completed and how much you have left. If the remaining cumulative work line is steeper, then the project may be late.

Is your baseline work zero?

Try setting a baseline

% Work Complete
5%

Remaining Work
1,731.2 hrs

Actual Work
99.2 hrs

WORK STATS
Shows work stats for all top level tasks.

WORK OVERVIEW

Mon 03/08/20   Wed 03/03/21

- Remaining Availability (General contractor)
- Remaining Availability (Architect)
- Remaining

PART VII: REPORTING AND ANALYSIS

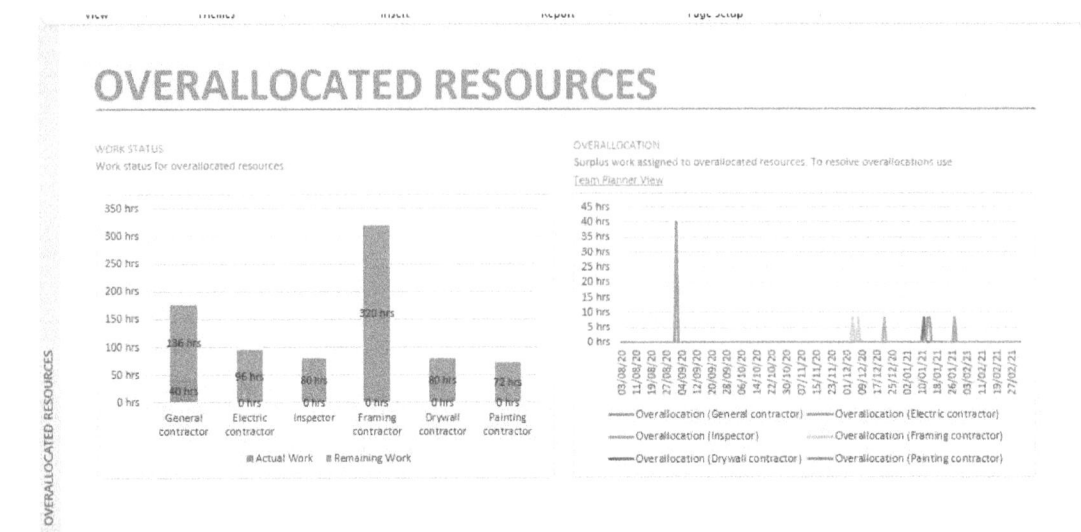

OVERALLOCATED RESOURCES

WORK STATUS
Work status for overallocated resources

OVERALLOCATION
Surplus work assigned to overallocated resources. To resolve overallocations use Team Planner View.

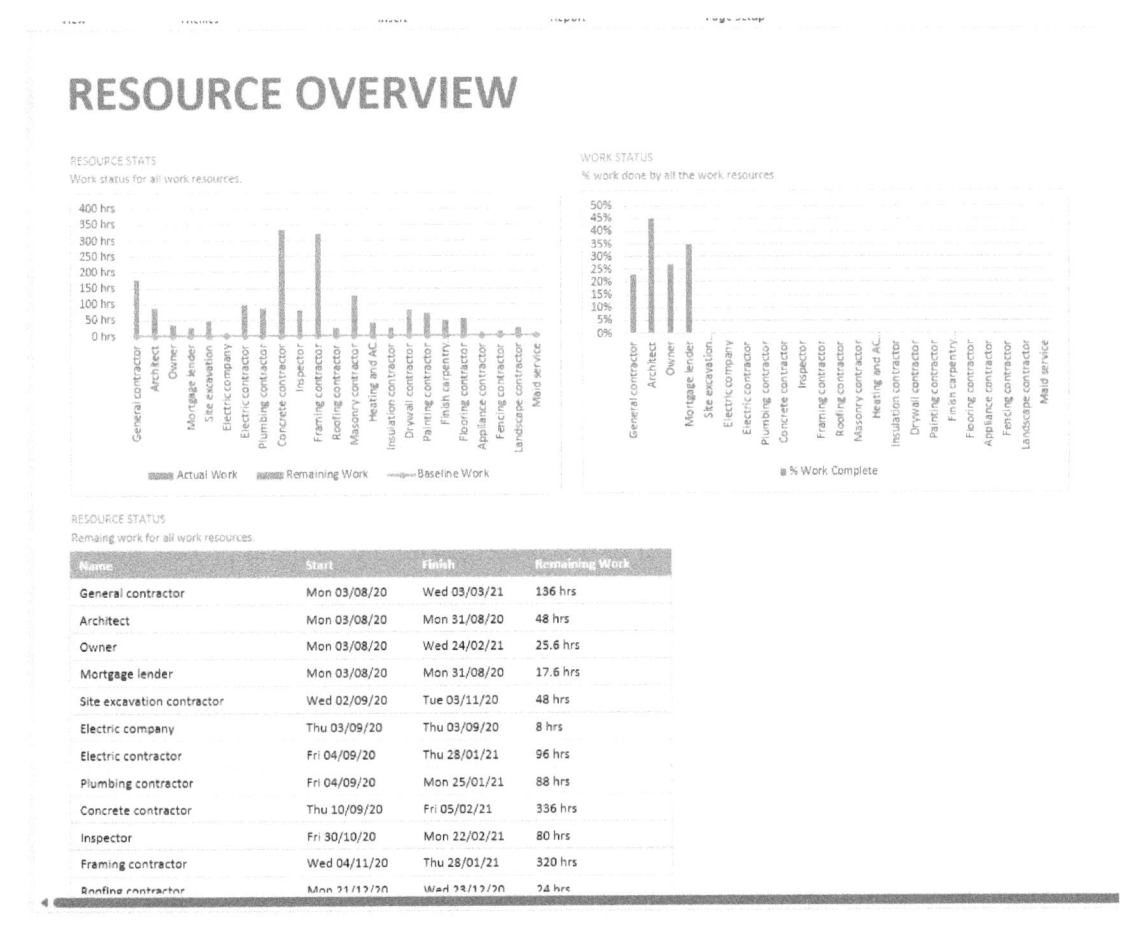

PART VII: REPORTING AND ANALYSIS

[Screenshot of Microsoft Project "Resource Overview" report showing Resource Stats bar chart, Work Status pie/bar chart, and Resource Status table with columns: Name, Start, Finish, Remaining Work]

Name	Start	Finish	Remaining Work
General contractor	Mon 03/08/20	Wed 03/03/21	136 hrs
Architect	Mon 03/08/20	Mon 31/08/20	48 hrs
Owner	Mon 03/08/20	Wed 24/02/21	25.6 hrs
Mortgage lender	Mon 03/08/20	Mon 31/08/20	17.6 hrs
Site excavation contractor	Wed 02/09/20	Tue 03/11/20	48 hrs
Electric company	Thu 03/09/20	Thu 03/09/20	8 hrs
Electric contractor	Fri 04/09/20	Thu 28/01/21	96 hrs
Plumbing contractor	Fri 04/09/20	Mon 25/01/21	88 hrs
Concrete contractor	Thu 10/09/20	Fri 05/02/21	336 hrs
Inspector	Fri 30/10/20	Mon 22/02/21	80 hrs
Framing contractor	Wed 04/11/20	Thu 28/01/21	320 hrs
Roofing contractor	Mon 21/12/20	Wed 23/12/20	24 hrs

Microsoft Project offers a diverse range of built-in report templates designed to meet the needs of different stakeholders involved in a project. These templates are conveniently categorized based on the type of information they present, such as task-centric reports, resource-centric reports, and financial reports. Let's delve into each category to understand the scope of available templates.

Task-Centric Reports

Task-centric reports focus on tracking and analyzing task-related data within a project. They provide insights into task progress, dependencies, and critical path analysis. Some commonly used task-centric report templates include:

1. Task Progress Report: This report provides a summary of task completion status, including percentage complete, actual duration, and remaining duration. It helps project managers monitor the overall progress of tasks and identify potential delays.

2. Task Usage Report: The task usage report offers a detailed breakdown of task assignments, showing the allocation of resources to individual tasks over time. It aids in resource management and workload balancing by highlighting resource utilization patterns.

3. Critical Tasks Report: Identifying critical tasks is crucial for ensuring project success. This report highlights tasks that are critical to the project timeline, helping project managers prioritize their efforts and allocate resources effectively.

Resource-Centric Reports

Resource-centric reports focus on analyzing resource allocation, availability, and utilization within a project. They assist project managers in optimizing resource allocation and resolving resource-related bottlenecks. Some common resource-centric report templates include:

1. Resource Overview Report: This report provides an overview of resource availability and allocation across different tasks. It helps project managers identify resource overloads or underutilization and make necessary adjustments to resource assignments.

2. Resource Workload Report: The resource workload report offers insights into the workload distribution among resources, highlighting potential resource conflicts or overallocations. It enables project managers to balance workload across resources and ensure optimal resource utilization.

3. Resource Cost Overview: Managing project costs associated with resources is essential for budget control. This report summarizes resource costs, including labor costs, material costs, and other expenses, helping project managers track project expenditures and manage budget constraints effectively.

Financial Reports

Financial reports focus on analyzing project costs, budget allocations, and financial performance. They help project managers monitor project finances and make informed decisions to ensure cost efficiency. Some common financial report templates include:

1. Cost Overview Report: This report provides a comprehensive overview of project costs, including budgeted costs, actual costs, and variance analysis. It helps project managers track cost performance and identify cost-saving opportunities or budget overruns.

2. Budget vs. Actual Report: Comparing budgeted costs with actual expenditures is essential for evaluating project financial performance. This report compares budgeted costs to actual costs incurred during project execution, highlighting any discrepancies and enabling project managers to take corrective actions as needed.

3. Earned Value Analysis Report: Earned value management (EVM) is a powerful technique for assessing project performance against planned objectives. This report applies EVM principles to analyze project progress, cost performance, and schedule performance, providing valuable insights into project health and forecasting future outcomes.

Customizing Built-in Report Templates

While the built-in report templates in Microsoft Project offer valuable insights, project managers may need to customize these templates to suit their specific requirements or stakeholder preferences. Microsoft Project provides robust customization options, allowing users to tailor report layouts, data fields, and visualizations according to their needs.

Report Customization Options

Microsoft Project offers various customization options for modifying built-in report templates:

1. Layout Customization: Users can customize the layout of reports by adding, removing, or rearranging data fields and columns. This allows project managers to focus on the most relevant information and present it in a clear and concise manner.

2. Visual Customization: Visual elements such as charts, graphs, and tables can be customized to enhance the readability and effectiveness of reports. Users can choose from different chart types, color schemes, and formatting styles to create visually appealing and informative reports.

3. Filtering and Sorting: Microsoft Project allows users to apply filters and sorting criteria to report data, enabling them to focus on specific tasks, resources, or time periods. This helps project managers extract relevant insights from large datasets and identify trends or patterns more effectively.

Creating Dashboard Views

In addition to traditional reports, Microsoft Project enables users to create interactive dashboard views for real-time monitoring and decision-making. Dashboards provide a consolidated view of project metrics, KPIs, and critical indicators, allowing project managers to track project performance at a glance and take proactive measures to address issues.

To create a dashboard view in Microsoft Project, follow these steps:

1. Select Dashboard Components: Identify the key metrics and KPIs that you want to display on the dashboard. These may include task progress, resource allocation, budget status, and schedule performance.

2. Customize Dashboard Layout: Arrange the selected components on the dashboard layout, taking into account their relative importance and relevance to project stakeholders. You can organize components into panels, tabs, or sections for easy navigation and accessibility.

3. Configure Data Visualization: Choose appropriate data visualization techniques, such as charts, graphs, or gauges, to represent each metric or KPI effectively. Ensure that the visualizations are clear, intuitive, and actionable for users to interpret and act upon.

4. Enable Interactivity: Add interactive features to the dashboard, such as drill-down capabilities, filters, and dynamic updates, to enhance user engagement and usability. This allows stakeholders to explore data in more detail and gain deeper insights into project performance.

5. Review and Test Dashboard: Before deploying the dashboard to project stakeholders, thoroughly review and test its functionality, layout, and content to ensure accuracy and usability. Solicit feedback from team members and stakeholders to identify any areas for improvement or refinement.

By creating customized dashboard views in Microsoft Project, project managers can provide stakeholders with real-time visibility into project performance and facilitate data-driven decision-making.

Step-by-Step Guide to Generating Project Reports in Microsoft Project

1. Open Microsoft Project:

   - Launch Microsoft Project software on your computer.

2. Select the Project:

   - Open the project for which you want to generate reports.

   - If the project is not already open, navigate to "File" > "Open" and select the desired project file (.mpp).

3. Navigate to the "Report" Tab:

   - Click on the "Report" tab located in the ribbon menu at the top of the Microsoft Project window.

4. Choose a Built-in Report Template:

   - In the "Report" tab, you will see a list of built-in report templates categorized based on their focus areas (e.g., Task-centric, Resource-centric, Financial).

   - Click on the category that aligns with the type of report you need (e.g., Task Progress Report, Resource Overview Report).

5. Select a Specific Report Template:

   - Within the chosen category, browse through the available report templates.

   - Click on the specific report template that best suits your reporting needs (e.g., Task Progress Report, Resource Workload Report).

6. Review the Report Preview:

- Once you select a report template, Microsoft Project will generate a preview of the report in the main window.

- Review the report preview to ensure it includes the desired information and meets your requirements.

7. Customize Report (Optional):

- If necessary, customize the report according to your preferences or specific requirements.

- Click on the "Design" tab within the report preview window to access customization options.

- Customize the layout, data fields, visualizations, and other elements as needed.

8. Generate the Report:

- After customizing the report (if required), click on the "Run" or "Generate" button to generate the final report.

- Microsoft Project will compile the report based on the selected template and any customization applied.

9. Review and Save the Report:

- Once the report is generated, review it to ensure accuracy and completeness.

- If satisfied with the report, you can save it by clicking on the "Save As" option and specifying the file format and location.

10. Share or Print the Report:

- After saving the report, you can share it with project stakeholders by sending the file via email or sharing it through a collaborative platform.

- Alternatively, you can print the report by selecting the "Print" option from the menu and choosing the printer settings.

11. Close the Report:

   - After generating, saving, and sharing/printing the report, you can close the report window to return to the main Microsoft Project interface.

12. Repeat for Additional Reports (Optional):

   - If you need to generate multiple reports for different aspects of the project, repeat the above steps for each report template as needed.

13. Save Project Changes (if applicable):

   - If you made any changes to the project data while generating reports, remember to save the project file to preserve the updates.

14. Exit Microsoft Project:

   - Once you have completed generating reports and saved any necessary changes, you can exit Microsoft Project software.

By following these step-by-step instructions, you can effectively generate project reports using Microsoft Project software, providing valuable insights into project progress, resource utilization, and financial performance.

Conclusion

Built-in report templates in Microsoft Project offer a convenient and efficient way to generate insightful reports for project management. By leveraging these templates, project managers can track project progress, analyze resource utilization, and monitor financial performance effectively. Additionally, customization options allow users to tailor reports to their specific requirements and stakeholder preferences, ensuring that the information presented is relevant and actionable. Furthermore, the ability to create interactive dashboard views enhances real-time monitoring and decision-making, enabling project managers to proactively manage project risks and optimize project outcomes. Overall, mastering the use of built-in report templates in Microsoft Project is essential for project managers seeking to enhance their project management capabilities and achieve project success.

7.1.2. Custom Report Creation

Custom report creation in Microsoft Project offers project managers the flexibility to tailor reports to meet specific project requirements and stakeholder preferences. While the built-in report templates provide a solid foundation for reporting, custom reports enable users to extract and present project data in unique formats, enhancing clarity and relevance. In this section, we delve into the process of creating custom reports in Microsoft Project, exploring various customization options and best practices for effective reporting.

Understanding Custom Report Creation

Custom reports in Microsoft Project allow project managers to design reports tailored to the unique needs of their projects and stakeholders. Whether it's showcasing project progress, resource utilization, or financial metrics, custom reports offer the flexibility to highlight key insights effectively. By leveraging the extensive data stored within the project plan, custom reports can provide comprehensive visibility into project performance and facilitate informed decision-making.

Steps to Create Custom Reports

Creating custom reports in Microsoft Project involves several steps, ranging from selecting the desired data fields to designing the report layout. Below is a step-by-step guide to help project managers navigate the process:

1. Define Reporting Requirements:

Before diving into report creation, it's essential to clarify the specific information stakeholders require. Identify the key metrics, data points, and visualizations necessary to convey project progress and performance effectively. Consider the preferences of different stakeholders to ensure the report meets diverse needs.

2. Access Report Creation Tools:

Microsoft Project offers a range of tools and features for report creation, accessible from the "Report" tab in the ribbon menu. Navigate to the "Custom Reports" section to access options for designing and customizing reports according to project requirements.

3. Select Data Fields:

Choose the relevant data fields to include in the custom report. Microsoft Project provides a comprehensive list of data fields covering various aspects of the project, including tasks, resources, durations, and costs. Select fields that align with the reporting objectives and desired insights.

4. Customize Report Layout:

Design the layout of the custom report to optimize readability and clarity. Arrange the selected data fields in a logical sequence, grouping related information together. Utilize formatting options such as font styles, colors, and borders to enhance visual appeal and highlight critical data points.

5. Apply Filters and Sorts:

Apply filters and sorts to refine the data displayed in the custom report. Filters enable users to focus on specific subsets of data based on criteria such as task status, resource assignments, or date ranges. Sorting options allow for organizing data in ascending or descending order to facilitate analysis.

6. Incorporate Visualizations:

Enhance the effectiveness of the custom report by incorporating visualizations such as charts and graphs. Microsoft Project offers various chart types, including Gantt charts, pie charts, and bar graphs, to represent project data visually. Choose the most suitable visualization formats based on the nature of the data and the insights you intend to convey.

7. Preview and Review:

Before finalizing the custom report, preview the layout and content to ensure accuracy and relevance. Review the report from the perspective of different stakeholders to gauge its effectiveness in communicating key information. Make adjustments as needed to address any discrepancies or enhance clarity.

8. Save and Share:

Once satisfied with the custom report, save it for future use and sharing. Microsoft Project allows users to save custom reports as templates or export them in various formats such as PDF or Excel. Share the report with relevant stakeholders to provide insights into project performance and facilitate decision-making.

Best Practices for Custom Report Creation

To maximize the effectiveness of custom reports in Microsoft Project, project managers can adopt the following best practices:

- Align with Stakeholder Needs: Tailor custom reports to meet the specific requirements and preferences of different stakeholders, ensuring the relevance and utility of the information presented.

- Maintain Consistency: Establish a standardized format and layout for custom reports to promote consistency across projects and reporting periods. Consistent reporting practices facilitate easier comparison and analysis of project data.

- Focus on Key Metrics: Prioritize key metrics and performance indicators in custom reports to highlight critical insights and facilitate decision-making. Avoid cluttering the report with unnecessary data that may obscure important information.

- Visualize Data Effectively: Leverage visualizations such as charts, graphs, and diagrams to present project data in a clear and intuitive manner. Choose visualization formats that enhance comprehension and enable stakeholders to grasp insights quickly.

- Review and Iterate: Regularly review custom reports to assess their effectiveness and relevance. Solicit feedback from stakeholders and incorporate suggestions for improvement to enhance the quality of future reports.

Conclusion

Custom report creation in Microsoft Project empowers project managers to tailor reporting to the specific needs and preferences of stakeholders, facilitating effective communication of project progress and performance. By following best practices and leveraging the customization options available, project managers can create insightful and visually compelling reports that support informed decision-making and drive project success.

7.2 Customizing Reports and Dashboards

Microsoft Project provides a range of customization options to refine the appearance, content, and functionality of project reports. Understanding and utilizing these options enable project managers to produce tailored reports that align with organizational objectives and stakeholder expectations. From adjusting layout settings to incorporating specific data fields, the following subsections delve into the diverse customization features available for enhancing project reports.

7.2.1. Report Customization Options

Layout Customization

The layout of a report significantly influences its readability and usability. Microsoft Project offers several layout customization options to structure reports according to individual preferences. Project managers can modify the arrangement of data fields, headers, and footers to optimize the visual presentation of information. Furthermore, the software allows for the inclusion of graphical elements such as charts, graphs, and images to enhance the overall appeal and comprehensibility of reports.

Data Field Selection

The selection of data fields determines the content and depth of information included in project reports. Microsoft Project offers extensive flexibility in choosing relevant data fields to be displayed within reports. Project managers can select from a vast array of predefined data fields covering various aspects of project management, including task duration, resource allocation, and cost estimation. Additionally, custom fields can be created to accommodate unique project requirements or specific metrics relevant to stakeholders.

Filtering and Sorting

Filtering and sorting functionalities empower project managers to focus on pertinent data and streamline the reporting process. Microsoft Project enables users to apply filters to project data based on criteria such as task status, resource assignments, or date ranges. By refining data through filtering, reports can present targeted insights tailored to specific stakeholders or project phases. Similarly, sorting options allow for the arrangement of data in a logical sequence, enhancing the clarity and coherence of reports.

Conditional Formatting

Conditional formatting enhances the visual representation of data within project reports by highlighting important information or trends. Microsoft Project offers robust conditional formatting capabilities, enabling users to apply formatting rules based on predefined conditions. For example, task deadlines nearing expiration can be visually emphasized using distinct colors or font styles, drawing immediate attention to critical milestones or potential delays. By leveraging conditional formatting, project managers can effectively communicate key insights and facilitate informed decision-making.

Grouping and Subtotaling

Grouping and subtotaling features facilitate the organization and summarization of project data within reports. Microsoft Project allows users to group related tasks or resources based on common attributes such as category, phase, or priority. This hierarchical structuring enhances the readability of reports by presenting data in a logical and structured manner. Additionally, subtotaling functionality enables the calculation of summary values for grouped data, providing aggregated metrics such as total duration, cost, or resource utilization. By leveraging grouping and subtotaling, project managers can generate comprehensive reports that convey both high-level overviews and detailed insights.

Template Customization

Template customization offers project managers the ability to create standardized report formats tailored to specific project requirements or organizational standards. Microsoft Project provides a range of built-in report templates that can be customized and saved for future use. Project managers can modify template layouts, data fields, and formatting options to create personalized reporting formats aligned with stakeholder preferences. Customized templates streamline the reporting process, ensuring consistency and efficiency in generating project reports across different projects or teams.

Integration with Other Applications

Integration with other applications extends the functionality of Microsoft Project by enabling seamless data exchange and collaboration. Project managers can leverage integration capabilities to incorporate data from external sources or export project reports to other software applications for further analysis or presentation. Common integration options include Microsoft Excel for advanced data manipulation, Microsoft PowerPoint for interactive presentations, and SharePoint for centralized document management. By integrating with complementary tools and platforms, project managers can enhance the accessibility, usability, and value of project reports.

Conclusion

Customizing reports and dashboards in Microsoft Project empowers project managers to deliver tailored insights that drive informed decision-making and enhance project performance. By leveraging the diverse customization options available, project managers can refine the appearance, content, and functionality of project reports to meet the unique needs of stakeholders and project requirements. Whether adjusting layout settings, selecting data fields, applying conditional formatting, or integrating with other applications, Microsoft Project provides a comprehensive toolkit for optimizing the reporting process and maximizing the effectiveness of project communication. By mastering report customization techniques, project managers can elevate their project management capabilities and achieve greater success in delivering projects on time, within budget, and to stakeholders' satisfaction.

7.2.2. Creating Dashboard Views

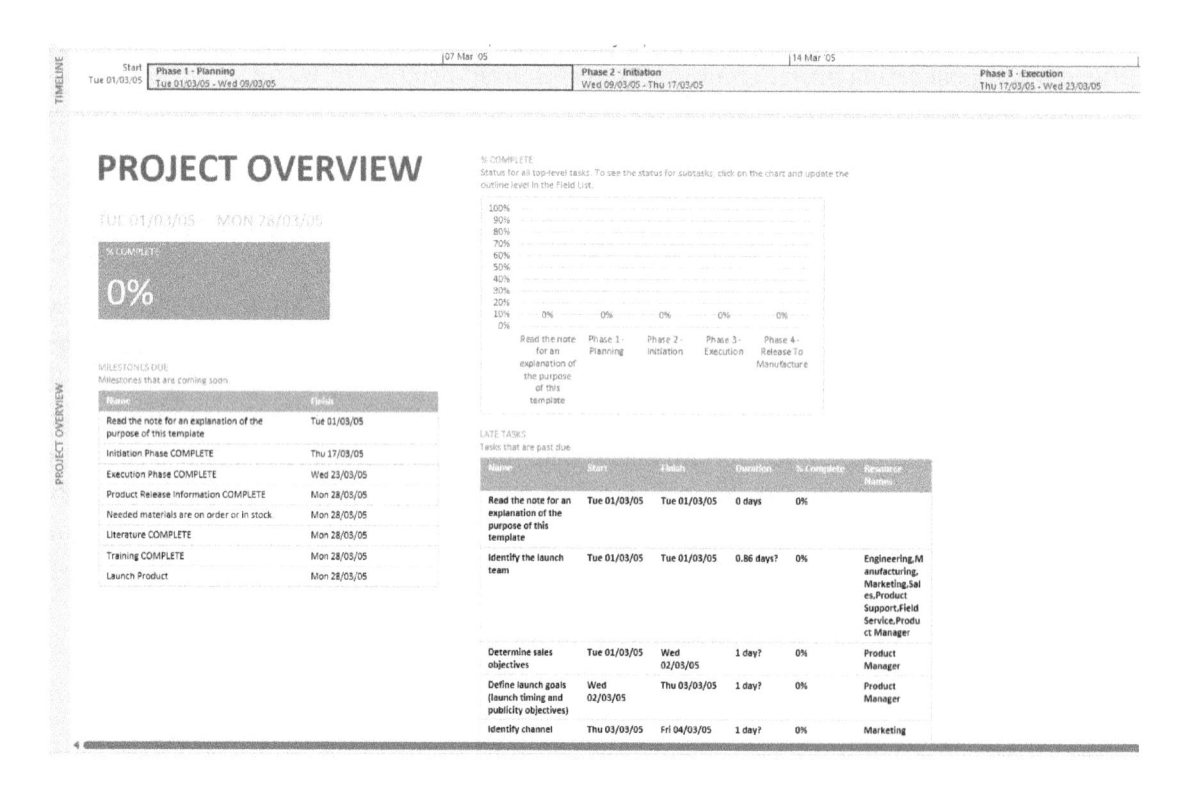

Dashboard views serve as comprehensive visual representations of project data, offering stakeholders a quick and concise overview of project status, performance metrics, and key indicators. By harnessing the power of Microsoft Project, project managers can design custom dashboard views tailored to the unique requirements of their projects and stakeholders.

Understanding Dashboard Views

Dashboard views in Microsoft Project enable project managers to consolidate essential project information into a single, easily digestible interface. These views typically comprise charts, graphs, tables, and other visual elements that provide insights into various aspects of project performance.

Before delving into the specifics of creating dashboard views, it's essential to understand the key components that contribute to their effectiveness:

1. Data Visualization: Dashboard views leverage data visualization techniques to transform complex project data into intuitive charts and graphs. Visual representations such as bar charts, pie charts, and line graphs facilitate quick comprehension of trends, patterns, and performance metrics.

2. Customization Options: Microsoft Project offers a plethora of customization options for dashboard views, allowing project managers to tailor the layout, content, and visual elements to align with stakeholders' preferences and information needs.

3. Interactive Elements: Interactive elements enhance the usability of dashboard views by enabling stakeholders to explore data dynamically. Features such as drill-down capabilities, filters, and tooltips empower users to delve deeper into specific areas of interest within the project.

4. Real-time Updates: Dashboard views can be configured to display real-time project data, ensuring that stakeholders have access to the most current information at all times. This dynamic updating capability enhances transparency and enables proactive decision-making based on the latest insights.

Creating Custom Dashboard Views

Microsoft Project offers a streamlined process for creating custom dashboard views, allowing project managers to design visually compelling displays of project information. The following steps outline the process of creating custom dashboard views in Microsoft Project:

1. Define Dashboard Objectives: Before embarking on the dashboard creation process, clearly define the objectives and intended audience for the dashboard. Determine the key metrics, performance indicators, and information requirements that the dashboard should address.

2. Select Data Sources: Identify the data sources within your Microsoft Project file that contain the information necessary for the dashboard. This may include task lists, resource allocations, timelines, and other project-related data.

3. Choose Visual Elements: Select the appropriate visual elements, such as charts, graphs, tables, and indicators, to convey the desired information effectively. Consider the best-suited visualization types for each type of data to ensure clarity and readability.

4. Design Layout and Composition: Design the layout and composition of the dashboard view to optimize usability and visual appeal. Arrange visual elements logically, grouping related information together and maintaining consistency in formatting and styling.

5. Configure Interactivity: Implement interactive features, such as filters, slicers, and dynamic controls, to enhance user engagement and enable exploration of the data. Ensure that interactive elements are intuitive and user-friendly, facilitating seamless navigation and data analysis.

6. Preview and Test: Preview the dashboard view to assess its appearance and functionality. Conduct thorough testing to identify any issues or discrepancies and make necessary adjustments to refine the dashboard's performance and usability.

7. Finalize and Publish: Once satisfied with the custom dashboard view, finalize the design and publish it for stakeholder access. Ensure that the dashboard is easily accessible to relevant parties and provide guidance on interpreting the displayed information.

Best Practices for Dashboard Design

While creating custom dashboard views in Microsoft Project, adhering to best practices can enhance the effectiveness and usability of the dashboards. Consider the following guidelines when designing dashboard views:

1. Keep it Simple: Strive for simplicity in dashboard design by focusing on presenting the most relevant and actionable information. Avoid clutter and unnecessary complexity that may hinder comprehension.

2. Maintain Consistency: Maintain consistency in visual elements, formatting, and terminology across the dashboard to promote coherence and facilitate navigation. Consistent design principles enhance usability and reduce cognitive load for users.

3. Prioritize Key Metrics: Prioritize key metrics and performance indicators that align with project objectives and stakeholder priorities. Highlight critical information prominently to draw attention and facilitate informed decision-making.

4. Provide Context: Provide context and interpretation for the data presented in the dashboard to ensure that stakeholders understand its significance. Incorporate annotations, descriptions, and commentary where necessary to elucidate complex concepts or trends.

5. Enable Drill-down Capability: Implement drill-down capability to allow stakeholders to explore detailed information underlying summary metrics. Hierarchical navigation enables users to delve deeper into specific areas of interest without overwhelming the dashboard with excessive detail.

6. Facilitate Customization: Offer customization options that allow users to tailor the dashboard views to their individual preferences and information needs. Flexible layouts, adjustable parameters, and personalized settings enhance user satisfaction and engagement.

7. Iterate and Improve: Continuously iterate on dashboard design based on user feedback, evolving project requirements, and changing stakeholder needs. Regularly assess the effectiveness of dashboard views and incorporate improvements to enhance their utility and relevance.

Case Study: Custom Dashboard for Construction Project Management

To illustrate the practical application of custom dashboard views in Microsoft Project, let's consider a case study involving the construction industry. Imagine a construction project management team tasked with overseeing the development of a commercial office building. The project involves multiple phases, including planning, design, procurement, construction, and commissioning.

Dashboard Objectives

The primary objectives of the custom dashboard for the construction project management team are as follows:

1. Monitor Project Progress: Provide real-time visibility into the progress of key project activities, milestones, and deliverables across different phases of the construction project.

2. Track Resource Utilization: Track the allocation and utilization of resources, including manpower, equipment, and materials, to ensure optimal resource management and identify potential bottlenecks or constraints.

3. Manage Budget and Costs: Monitor project expenditures, budget allocations, and cost variances to control costs effectively and prevent budget overruns.

4. Assess Schedule Adherence: Evaluate adherence to project schedules and timelines, identifying any delays or deviations from the planned timeline and implementing corrective actions as necessary.

5. Visualize Risk Exposure: Visualize project risks, hazards, and uncertainties, highlighting areas of high risk and implementing risk mitigation strategies to minimize potential impacts on project outcomes.

Dashboard Components

Based on the defined objectives, the custom dashboard for construction project management comprises the following components:

1. Project Overview: A summary section providing an overview of key project metrics, including overall progress, milestones achieved, and upcoming deadlines.

2. Timeline Visualization: A Gantt chart displaying the project timeline, with tasks, dependencies, and critical path highlighted to visualize project scheduling and identify potential delays.

3. Resource Allocation Heatmap: A heatmap illustrating resource allocation across different project phases, with color-coded indicators representing resource availability and utilization levels.

4. Cost Performance Dashboard: A series of charts and graphs depicting project costs, budget allocations, expenditure trends, and cost variances to monitor financial performance and adherence to budget constraints.

5. Risk Matrix: A risk matrix matrix displaying project risks categorized based on likelihood and impact, with corresponding risk mitigation strategies and contingency plans outlined to manage risk exposure effectively.

Creating the Custom Dashboard

The construction project management team leverages Microsoft Project to create the custom dashboard, following a systematic approach:

1. Dashboard Planning: The team conducts a thorough analysis of project requirements and stakeholder expectations to define the objectives and scope of the custom dashboard.

2. Data Integration: Project data, including task lists, resource allocations, cost estimates, and risk registers, are imported into Microsoft Project to serve as the foundation for dashboard development.

3. Dashboard Design: Using the built-in customization tools in Microsoft Project, the team designs the layout and composition of the dashboard, selecting appropriate visual elements and arranging them to optimize usability and readability.

4. Visualization Configuration: Charts, graphs, and tables are configured to visualize project data effectively, with interactive features such as filters and drill-down capabilities implemented to enhance user engagement and exploration.

5. Testing and Validation: The custom dashboard undergoes rigorous testing to ensure functionality, accuracy, and usability. Feedback from stakeholders is solicited and incorporated into the dashboard design to address any identified issues or enhancements.

6. Deployment and Training: Once finalized, the custom dashboard is deployed for stakeholder access, accompanied by training sessions and user guides to facilitate adoption and utilization.

Conclusion

Custom dashboard views in Microsoft Project empower project managers to transform project data into actionable insights, facilitating informed decision-making and effective communication with stakeholders. By following best practices and leveraging the robust customization capabilities of Microsoft Project, project managers can create visually compelling dashboard views tailored to the unique requirements of their projects and stakeholders. Whether tracking project progress, monitoring resource utilization, managing costs, or assessing risks, custom dashboard views serve as invaluable tools for enhancing project management efficiency and driving project success.

7.3 Analyzing Project Performance

Analyzing project performance is essential for project managers to ensure that their projects stay on track and meet their objectives. Key Performance Indicators (KPIs) are invaluable tools in this regard, providing quantifiable measures of a project's success or failure. By monitoring KPIs throughout the project lifecycle, project managers can identify areas of concern early and take corrective actions to keep the project on course. In this section, we will explore the concept of KPIs in project management, their significance, and how to effectively use them to analyze project performance.

7.3.1. Key Performance Indicators (KPIs)

Key Performance Indicators, commonly referred to as KPIs, are specific metrics used to evaluate the performance of a project, team, or organization. KPIs are selected based on the goals and objectives of the project and are typically tied to critical success factors. They provide valuable insights into various aspects of project performance, including schedule adherence, budget management, quality, and stakeholder satisfaction.

Importance of KPIs in Project Management

The importance of KPIs in project management cannot be overstated. They serve as a means of quantifying progress towards project objectives and help in identifying potential issues before they escalate into major problems. By tracking KPIs regularly, project managers can make data-driven decisions, allocate resources effectively, and ensure that the project stays aligned with organizational goals.

Types of KPIs

KPIs can be broadly categorized into several types, each serving a different purpose in evaluating project performance:

1. Schedule Performance KPIs: These KPIs assess the project's adherence to the planned schedule. Common metrics include schedule variance (SV), schedule performance index (SPI), and milestone adherence.

2. Cost Performance KPIs: Cost performance KPIs focus on evaluating the project's budget management. Key metrics include cost variance (CV), cost performance index (CPI), and budget utilization.

3. Quality KPIs: Quality KPIs measure the level of conformance to specified quality standards and requirements. Metrics may include defect density, customer satisfaction scores, and rework rates.

4. Stakeholder Satisfaction KPIs: These KPIs gauge the satisfaction levels of project stakeholders, including customers, sponsors, and team members. Surveys, feedback mechanisms, and Net Promoter Score (NPS) are commonly used to assess stakeholder satisfaction.

5. Risk Management KPIs: Risk management KPIs track the effectiveness of risk identification, assessment, and mitigation strategies. Metrics may include risk exposure, risk response timeliness, and risk impact.

6. Resource Utilization KPIs: Resource utilization KPIs evaluate the efficiency of resource allocation and utilization throughout the project lifecycle. Metrics include resource utilization rates, resource availability, and overtime percentages.

Selecting Relevant KPIs

Choosing the right KPIs is crucial for effective project performance analysis. KPIs should be aligned with the project's objectives, measurable, and relevant to key stakeholders. When selecting KPIs, project managers should consider the following factors:

1. Relevance: KPIs should directly reflect the project's goals and objectives. They should provide meaningful insights into critical aspects of project performance.

2. Measurability: KPIs must be quantifiable and measurable using objective data. Clear criteria for measurement should be established to ensure consistency and accuracy.

3. Actionability: KPIs should be actionable, meaning that they should provide information that can lead to specific actions or interventions. Project managers should be able to use KPI data to make informed decisions and drive improvements.

4. Timeliness: KPIs should provide timely information to facilitate proactive management and decision-making. Delays in KPI reporting can impede the ability to address issues promptly.

5. Balance: A balanced set of KPIs should encompass various aspects of project performance, including schedule, cost, quality, and stakeholder satisfaction. Overemphasis on one aspect at the expense of others can lead to skewed perceptions of overall project health.

Implementing KPI Monitoring

Once relevant KPIs have been identified, project managers must establish processes for monitoring and reporting on these metrics throughout the project lifecycle. The following steps outline a typical approach to implementing KPI monitoring:

1. Define Measurement Criteria: Clearly define how each KPI will be measured, including the data sources, calculation methods, and frequency of measurement.

2. Establish Baselines: Establish baseline values for each KPI based on initial project plans and expectations. Baselines serve as reference points for evaluating performance over time.

3. Set Targets: Establish target values or thresholds for each KPI to indicate desired levels of performance. Targets should be realistic and achievable within the project constraints.

4. Implement Tracking Mechanisms: Put in place systems and tools for collecting, recording, and analyzing KPI data. Automated project management software such as Microsoft Project can streamline this process by generating reports and dashboards.

5. Regular Monitoring: Monitor KPIs regularly throughout the project lifecycle to track progress and identify deviations from the plan. Regular monitoring enables early detection of issues and timely intervention.

6. Analyze Trends: Analyze trends and patterns in KPI data to identify underlying causes of performance changes. Understanding the root causes allows project managers to implement targeted corrective actions.

7. Communicate Results: Communicate KPI results and insights to project stakeholders through regular reporting mechanisms. Transparent communication fosters accountability and enables stakeholders to stay informed about project performance.

8. Continuous Improvement: Continuously review and refine KPIs based on feedback and changing project dynamics. Adjust targets and measurement criteria as needed to ensure relevance and effectiveness.

Case Study: Using KPIs to Analyze Project Performance

To illustrate the practical application of KPIs in project management, let's consider a hypothetical case study of a software development project:

Project: Development of a New Mobile Application

Objective: To develop and launch a new mobile application within a six-month timeframe, meeting quality standards and stakeholder expectations.

Selected KPIs:

1. Schedule Performance: Schedule Variance (SV), Schedule Performance Index (SPI)

2. Cost Performance: Cost Variance (CV), Cost Performance Index (CPI)

3. Quality: Defect Density, Customer Satisfaction Score

4. Stakeholder Satisfaction: Net Promoter Score (NPS)

5. Risk Management: Risk Exposure, Risk Response Timeliness

6. Resource Utilization: Resource Utilization Rate, Overtime Percentage

Implementation:

- Measurement Criteria: SV and CV are measured in monetary terms, while SPI and CPI are calculated ratios. Defect Density is measured as defects per thousand lines of code, and Customer Satisfaction Score is based on survey responses. NPS is calculated from stakeholder feedback, and risk metrics are derived from risk registers. Resource utilization metrics track the allocation and utilization of human resources.

- Baseline and Targets: Baseline values and targets are established for each KPI based on project plans and stakeholder expectations. For example, a target SPI of 1.0 indicates on-time schedule performance, while a target NPS of 70 reflects a high level of stakeholder satisfaction.

- Monitoring and Reporting: KPI data is monitored regularly using project management software, with automated reports generated to track performance against targets. Deviations from targets are investigated promptly, and corrective actions are implemented as necessary.

- Analysis and Improvement: Trends in KPI data are analyzed to identify areas of improvement and optimize project performance. For example, recurring quality issues may prompt process improvements or additional testing measures.

Conclusion

Key Performance Indicators (KPIs) are indispensable tools for project managers seeking to analyze and improve project performance. By selecting relevant KPIs, establishing measurement criteria, and implementing robust monitoring processes, project managers can gain valuable insights into various aspects of project execution. Effective use of KPIs enables proactive management, informed decision-making, and continuous improvement, ultimately increasing the likelihood of project success.

In the next section, we will delve into another critical aspect of project performance analysis: Earned Value Management (EVM) Analysis.

7.3.2. Earned Value Management (EVM) Analysis

Earned Value Management (EVM) is a powerful technique used by project managers to measure and track project performance against the project baseline. It integrates project scope, schedule, and cost measures to provide a comprehensive view of project progress. In this section, we will delve deeper into EVM analysis, understanding its key concepts, formulas, and how to interpret the results effectively.

Understanding Earned Value Management (EVM)

At its core, Earned Value Management (EVM) compares the value of work accomplished (earned value) against the actual costs incurred (actual cost) and the planned costs (planned value) to assess the project's performance. It helps project managers answer crucial questions such as: Are we on schedule? Are we within budget? How effectively are we utilizing resources?

Key EVM Formulas

1. Planned Value (PV): Planned Value represents the authorized budget assigned to scheduled work. It is also referred to as the Budgeted Cost of Work Scheduled (BCWS).

   - Formula: PV = Planned % Complete × Total Budget

2. **Earned Value (EV)**: Earned Value represents the value of the work actually accomplished. It is also referred to as the Budgeted Cost of Work Performed (BCWP).

   - Formula: EV = % Complete × Total Budget

3. **Actual Cost (AC)**: Actual Cost represents the total costs incurred for the work performed.

   - Formula: AC = Total Actual Costs

4. **Schedule Variance (SV)**: Schedule Variance measures the variance between the earned value and the planned value, indicating whether the project is ahead or behind schedule.

   - Formula: SV = EV - PV

5. **Cost Variance (CV)**: Cost Variance measures the variance between the earned value and the actual cost, indicating whether the project is under or over budget.

   - Formula: CV = EV - AC

6. **Schedule Performance Index (SPI)**: Schedule Performance Index measures the efficiency of schedule performance, indicating how well the project is progressing against the schedule.

   - Formula: SPI = EV / PV

7. **Cost Performance Index (CPI)**: Cost Performance Index measures the efficiency of cost performance, indicating how well the project is utilizing its budget.

   - Formula: CPI = EV / AC

Interpreting EVM Results

1. Schedule Variance (SV)

   - SV > 0: The project is ahead of schedule.

   - SV = 0: The project is on schedule.

   - SV < 0: The project is behind schedule.

2. Cost Variance (CV)

   - CV > 0: The project is under budget.

   - CV = 0: The project is on budget.

   - CV < 0: The project is over budget.

3. Schedule Performance Index (SPI)

   - SPI > 1: The project is ahead of schedule.

   - SPI = 1: The project is on schedule.

   - SPI < 1: The project is behind schedule.

4. Cost Performance Index (CPI)

   - CPI > 1: The project is under budget.

   - CPI = 1: The project is on budget.

   - CPI < 1: The project is over budget.

Benefits of EVM Analysis

1. Early Identification of Issues: EVM provides early warning indicators, allowing project managers to identify and address issues promptly.

2. Objective Performance Measurement: EVM offers objective metrics to measure project performance, reducing subjectivity.

3. Better Decision Making: With EVM insights, project managers can make informed decisions to reallocate resources or adjust schedules to keep the project on track.

4. Enhanced Stakeholder Communication: EVM analysis facilitates clear and transparent communication with stakeholders regarding project progress and performance.

Implementing EVM in Microsoft Project

Microsoft Project offers robust features to facilitate EVM analysis. Users can input project data, including budgeted costs, actual costs, and percent complete, to generate EVM metrics automatically. Additionally, customizable reports and dashboards enable project managers to visualize and communicate EVM results effectively to stakeholders.

Conclusion

Earned Value Management (EVM) is a valuable technique for project managers to assess project performance objectively. By integrating schedule, cost, and scope measures, EVM provides a comprehensive view of project progress and enables timely decision-making. Understanding key EVM concepts, formulas, and interpreting results effectively are essential for leveraging EVM to its full potential in project management. With the right tools and methodologies, such as those offered by Microsoft Project, project managers can effectively implement EVM to drive project success.

PART VIII
Collaboration and Integration

8.1 Sharing Projects with Team Members

8.1.1. Collaborative Project Setup

Collaborative project management has become increasingly vital in today's dynamic work environment. Teams are often dispersed across different locations, making it essential to establish seamless communication channels and efficient workflows. Microsoft Project offers robust features for collaborative project setup, enabling project managers to streamline coordination, enhance transparency, and maximize team productivity. In this section, we delve into the key steps and best practices for setting up collaborative projects in Microsoft Project.

Understanding Collaborative Project Setup

Before diving into the technical aspects of setting up collaborative projects in Microsoft Project, it's crucial to grasp the underlying principles and benefits of collaboration in project management.

Benefits of Collaborative Project Management:

1. Enhanced Communication: Collaborative project setup fosters open communication channels among team members, stakeholders, and project managers. It facilitates real-time

updates, feedback exchange, and issue resolution, thereby reducing misunderstandings and enhancing project clarity.

2. Improved Coordination: By centralizing project information and resources, collaborative setups enable seamless coordination among team members. Everyone stays on the same page regarding project progress, timelines, and deliverables, fostering a cohesive team environment.

3. Increased Transparency: Collaborative project management promotes transparency by providing stakeholders with visibility into project activities, milestones, and performance metrics. This transparency builds trust and confidence among stakeholders and encourages active engagement throughout the project lifecycle.

4. Efficient Resource Allocation: By leveraging collaborative tools and platforms, project managers can optimize resource allocation and utilization. They can assign tasks, allocate resources, and track progress in real-time, ensuring that project resources are effectively deployed to meet project objectives.

Key Components of Collaborative Project Setup:

1. Team Structure: Define the project team structure, roles, and responsibilities to ensure clarity and accountability among team members. Establish clear communication channels and escalation paths to facilitate smooth collaboration and issue resolution.

2. Communication Plan: Develop a comprehensive communication plan outlining the communication protocols, frequency, and mediums for project updates, meetings, and discussions. Ensure that all stakeholders are aware of the communication plan and adhere to it throughout the project lifecycle.

3. Collaboration Tools: Identify and implement the appropriate collaboration tools and platforms to support project communication, document sharing, task management, and collaboration. Microsoft Project offers integration with various collaboration tools such as Microsoft Teams, SharePoint, and OneDrive, enabling seamless data sharing and collaboration.

Setting Up Collaborative Projects in Microsoft Project

Microsoft Project provides several features and functionalities to facilitate collaborative project management. Here's a step-by-step guide to setting up collaborative projects in Microsoft Project:

Step 1: Define Project Scope and Objectives

Before initiating project setup in Microsoft Project, ensure that you have a clear understanding of the project scope, objectives, deliverables, and timelines. Collaborate with stakeholders to gather requirements and define project success criteria.

Step 2: Create a Project Plan

Using Microsoft Project, create a comprehensive project plan outlining the project tasks, dependencies, milestones, and resource requirements. Leverage the Gantt chart view to visualize the project timeline and task dependencies, making adjustments as needed to optimize project scheduling.

Step 3: Assign Resources and Roles

Assign resources to project tasks based on their availability, skills, and role requirements. Define roles and responsibilities for each team member to ensure clarity and accountability. Utilize resource leveling and allocation features in Microsoft Project to optimize resource utilization and avoid overallocation.

Step 4: Set Up Collaboration Tools

Integrate Microsoft Project with collaboration tools such as Microsoft Teams, SharePoint, and OneDrive to facilitate seamless communication and document sharing. Configure permissions and access controls to ensure that team members have the appropriate level of access to project information and resources.

Step 5: Establish Communication Channels

Establish communication channels within Microsoft Project to facilitate real-time communication and collaboration among team members. Utilize features such as task comments, status updates, and notifications to keep everyone informed of project progress and updates.

Step 6: Monitor and Track Progress

Continuously monitor and track project progress using Microsoft Project's tracking features. Update task statuses, track milestones, and adjust schedules as needed to ensure that the project stays on track. Utilize reporting and analytics tools to gain insights into project performance and identify areas for improvement.

Step 7: Collaborate and Iterate

Encourage collaboration and feedback exchange among team members throughout the project lifecycle. Conduct regular project meetings, reviews, and retrospectives to gather feedback, address issues, and make necessary adjustments to the project plan. Iterate and refine project processes based on lessons learned and stakeholder input.

Best Practices for Collaborative Project Setup

To maximize the effectiveness of collaborative project setup in Microsoft Project, consider the following best practices:

1. Define Clear Communication Protocols: Establish clear communication protocols and guidelines to ensure consistent and effective communication among team members.

2. Promote Transparency and Accountability: Foster a culture of transparency and accountability by providing stakeholders with visibility into project activities, progress, and performance metrics.

3. Encourage Collaboration and Feedback: Encourage collaboration, feedback exchange, and knowledge sharing among team members to leverage collective expertise and insights.

4. Utilize Collaborative Tools Effectively: Leverage the full capabilities of collaborative tools and platforms to streamline communication, document sharing, and task management.

5. Adapt and Iterate: Be flexible and adaptive in your approach to collaborative project management. Continuously assess and iterate project processes based on feedback and lessons learned.

By following these best practices and leveraging the collaborative features of Microsoft Project, project managers can effectively streamline communication, enhance coordination, and maximize team productivity in collaborative project environments.

8.1.2. Sharing Options and Permissions

Sharing your project with team members is a fundamental aspect of project management collaboration. However, it's crucial to control access and permissions to ensure data integrity and security. Microsoft Project offers various sharing options and permission settings to tailor access levels according to team roles and responsibilities. In this section, we delve into the sharing options and permissions available in Microsoft Project, empowering project managers to manage collaboration effectively.

Sharing Options

Microsoft Project provides multiple avenues for sharing projects with team members, each offering distinct benefits and functionalities. Understanding these options enables project managers to choose the most suitable method based on project requirements and team dynamics.

1. Sharing via Microsoft Project Online: Microsoft Project Online is a cloud-based project management solution that facilitates real-time collaboration among team members. Project managers can upload their project files to Project Online, granting team members access to view and edit project data from anywhere with an internet connection. This option ensures seamless communication and updates, enhancing project visibility and coordination.

2. Sharing via SharePoint Integration: SharePoint integration enables seamless project sharing within the organization's SharePoint environment. Project managers can publish project files to SharePoint libraries, granting team members access based on SharePoint permissions. This integration fosters centralized document management and collaboration, leveraging SharePoint's robust features for file sharing, version control, and document collaboration.

3. Sharing via Email: For quick communication and collaboration, project managers can share project files via email. Microsoft Project allows users to send project snapshots or entire project files as attachments directly from the application. While email sharing is convenient for distributing project information, it lacks real-time synchronization and version control features compared to cloud-based solutions.

4. Sharing via File Storage Services: Project managers can leverage file storage services like OneDrive, Google Drive, or Dropbox to share project files with team members. These platforms offer collaboration features such as file sharing links, access control, and version history, facilitating secure and efficient project sharing. Integrating Microsoft Project with file storage services streamlines document management and accessibility for distributed teams.

Permission Settings

Controlling access permissions is essential for maintaining data integrity and confidentiality within a project. Microsoft Project provides flexible permission settings that empower project managers to define access levels and restrictions for team members.

1. Read-Only Access: Users with read-only access can view project data but cannot make any changes. This permission level is suitable for stakeholders, clients, or team members who require project visibility without editing capabilities. Read-only access ensures that project information remains accurate and consistent, minimizing the risk of unauthorized modifications.

2. Edit Access: Team members with edit access can view and modify project data, enabling active participation in project planning and execution. This permission level is typically assigned to project team members responsible for task updates, schedule adjustments, and resource allocations. However, project managers should exercise caution when granting edit access to prevent unintended changes or conflicts in the project plan.

3. Full Control Access: Project managers and administrators typically have full control access, allowing them to modify project settings, add or remove tasks, and adjust resource assignments. This permission level grants complete authority over the project, empowering users to manage all aspects of project planning and execution. Full control access is reserved for individuals entrusted with overall project management responsibilities.

4. Custom Permissions: Microsoft Project offers the flexibility to define custom permission levels tailored to specific user roles or project requirements. Project managers can create custom permission groups with unique access rights and restrictions, ensuring granular control over project data and functionality. Custom permissions enable project managers to align access levels with team hierarchies and project workflows effectively.

Best Practices for Sharing and Permission Management

Effective sharing and permission management are integral to successful project collaboration. To optimize the use of Microsoft Project's sharing options and permission settings, project managers can follow these best practices:

1. Define Clear Access Policies: Establish clear guidelines and policies regarding access permissions to ensure consistency and accountability across the project team. Clearly communicate the roles and responsibilities associated with each permission level to avoid confusion and misuse.

2. Regularly Review and Update Permissions: Periodically review and update permission settings based on project progress, team dynamics, and organizational changes. Adjust access levels as needed to accommodate new team members, changes in responsibilities, or evolving project requirements.

3. Limit Access to Sensitive Information: Exercise caution when granting edit or full control access to sensitive project data, such as budget information, confidential documents, or strategic plans. Limit access to authorized individuals or teams responsible for handling sensitive information to prevent unauthorized disclosure or misuse.

4. Utilize Role-Based Permissions: Implement role-based permissions tailored to different project stakeholders and team members. Assign access levels based on user roles, such as project manager, team lead, developer, or client, to ensure that each individual has the appropriate level of access to project resources and information.

5. Educate Users on Security Practices: Provide training and guidance on security best practices to promote responsible data handling and mitigate the risk of security breaches or data leaks. Educate team members on the importance of safeguarding project information, avoiding phishing attempts, and adhering to company policies regarding data protection.

Here's a step-by-step guide on how to perform each action in Microsoft Project:

1. Sharing via Microsoft Project Online:

   a. Open your project in Microsoft Project.

   b. Navigate to the "File" tab in the top-left corner of the screen.

   c. Select "Share" from the menu options.

   d. Choose "Save to Project Web App" or "Save to SharePoint" depending on your organization's setup.

   e. Follow the prompts to sign in to your Microsoft Project Online or SharePoint account.

f. Select the destination location for your project file and click "Save" to upload it to the cloud.

g. Specify the sharing settings, such as who can view or edit the project, and adjust permissions accordingly.

h. Click "Share" or "Save" to finalize the sharing process.

2. Sharing via SharePoint Integration:

a. Open your project in Microsoft Project.

b. Navigate to the "File" tab.

c. Select "Save As" from the menu options.

d. Choose "Browse" and navigate to your organization's SharePoint site.

e. Select the SharePoint document library where you want to save the project file.

f. Click "Save" to publish the project to SharePoint.

g. Access the SharePoint document library and configure permissions for the project file, granting access to team members as needed.

3. Sharing via Email:

a. Open your project in Microsoft Project.

b. Navigate to the "File" tab.

c. Select "Share" from the menu options.

d. Choose "Send using Email" or "Send a Snapshot" depending on your preference.

e. Enter the recipient's email address(es) in the designated field.

f. Optionally, add a message to accompany the email.

g. Click "Send" to email the project snapshot or file as an attachment.

4. Sharing via File Storage Services:

a. Save your project file locally on your computer.

b. Open the file storage service of your choice (e.g., OneDrive, Google Drive, Dropbox).

c. Upload the project file to the appropriate folder within the file storage service.

d. Configure sharing settings for the uploaded file, such as generating a shareable link or inviting specific collaborators via email.

e. Copy the shareable link or send invitations to team members to access the project file.

f. Optionally, set permissions for collaborators, specifying whether they can view or edit the file.

5. Permission Settings:

a. Open your project in Microsoft Project.

b. Navigate to the "File" tab.

c. Select "Info" from the menu options.

d. Click on "Manage Permissions" or "Share Project" depending on the version of Microsoft Project you're using.

e. Choose the user or group for which you want to modify permissions.

f. Select the desired permission level from the available options (e.g., Read, Write, Full Control).

g. Click "OK" or "Apply" to save the changes.

h. Repeat the process for other users or groups as needed.

By leveraging Microsoft Project's sharing options and permission settings effectively, project managers can facilitate seamless collaboration, enhance communication, and drive project success. Empowering team members with the right level of access and ensuring data security fosters a culture of trust, transparency, and accountability within the project team.

8.2 Integrating with Microsoft Office Suite

Integration with the Microsoft Office Suite is a cornerstone of maximizing efficiency and productivity in project management. Microsoft Project, with its robust capabilities, seamlessly collaborates with other Office applications such as Excel, Outlook, and SharePoint. This section delves into the intricacies of importing and exporting data between Microsoft Project and other Office tools, highlighting the benefits and best practices for seamless integration.

8.2.1. Importing and Exporting Data

Importing and exporting data between Microsoft Project and other Office applications is a vital function for project managers. It streamlines workflows, enhances communication, and ensures data accuracy across platforms. Understanding the methods, formats, and considerations involved in this process is essential for leveraging the full potential of integration within the Microsoft Office Suite.

Importing Data into Microsoft Project:

Importing data into Microsoft Project allows project managers to incorporate information from various sources, such as Excel spreadsheets or Outlook tasks, into their project plans. This streamlines the initial setup process and ensures that all relevant data is centralized within the project management environment.

1. Importing from Excel:

   - Microsoft Excel is a commonly used tool for organizing and analyzing project-related data. Importing data from Excel into Microsoft Project facilitates the transition from planning to execution.

- To import data from Excel, navigate to the "Task" tab in Microsoft Project and select "Import Data" from the "External Data" group. Choose the Excel file containing the desired data and follow the prompts to map fields and customize import settings.

  - It's crucial to ensure that the data in the Excel file aligns with the structure and requirements of the Microsoft Project plan. Field mapping allows for seamless integration and prevents data discrepancies.

2. Importing from Outlook:

  - Outlook tasks often serve as a repository for individual and team assignments. Importing tasks from Outlook into Microsoft Project provides visibility and alignment within the project plan.

  - In Microsoft Project, go to the "Task" tab and click on "Import Outlook Tasks" in the "External Data" group. Select the Outlook task folder containing the relevant tasks and configure import settings as needed.

  - Considerations such as task dependencies, deadlines, and resource assignments should be reviewed and adjusted during the import process to maintain consistency and accuracy in the project plan.

Exporting Data from Microsoft Project:

Exporting data from Microsoft Project enables project managers to share project information with stakeholders, collaborate with team members, and integrate project data into reports or presentations. Understanding the export options and their implications is crucial for effective communication and decision-making.

1. Exporting to Excel:

  - Exporting project data to Excel allows for further analysis, reporting, and customization beyond the capabilities of Microsoft Project.

- To export data to Excel, navigate to the "File" tab, select "Save As," and choose the desired Excel format (e.g., .xlsx). Customize export settings such as data range and formatting options to meet specific requirements.

  - Excel provides flexibility in organizing and presenting project data, making it accessible to stakeholders with varying levels of technical expertise.

2. Exporting to Outlook:

  - Exporting project tasks to Outlook enables team members to view and manage their assignments within their familiar email environment.

  - From the "Task" tab in Microsoft Project, select "Sync" and choose "Sync to Outlook." Follow the prompts to specify the task list and synchronization options.

  - Team members can then access project tasks alongside their other commitments in Outlook, promoting visibility and accountability.

3. Exporting to SharePoint:

  - SharePoint serves as a centralized platform for document management, collaboration, and communication within organizations. Exporting project data to SharePoint facilitates seamless integration with other business processes and workflows.

  - In Microsoft Project, go to the "File" tab, select "Save As," and choose "Save Project as Web Page." Follow the prompts to specify the SharePoint site and document library for the export.

  - Project data exported to SharePoint can be accessed, shared, and updated by authorized users, fostering collaboration and alignment across teams.

Best Practices for Data Integration:

- Standardize Data Formats: Establish consistent data formats and conventions across Office applications to ensure compatibility and accuracy during import and export processes.

- Validate Data Integrity: Conduct regular checks and validations to verify the integrity and consistency of imported and exported data, minimizing errors and discrepancies.

- Document Procedures: Document import and export procedures, including field mappings, settings, and validation steps, to facilitate knowledge transfer and ensure continuity in data management practices.

- Train Users: Provide training and resources to users on data integration techniques and best practices to empower them to leverage Office integration effectively in their project management activities.

Conclusion:

Integrating Microsoft Project with the Office Suite enhances collaboration, streamlines workflows, and improves decision-making in project management. Importing and exporting data between Microsoft Project and other Office applications enables project managers to centralize information, facilitate communication, and leverage the strengths of each tool to achieve project success. By understanding the methods, considerations, and best practices for data integration, project managers can harness the full potential of the Microsoft Office Suite to drive efficiency and productivity in their projects.

8.2.2. Integration with Excel, Outlook, and SharePoint

Integration with Microsoft Office Suite is a hallmark feature of Microsoft Project, enhancing its versatility and usability for project managers. By seamlessly connecting with widely-used Office applications such as Excel, Outlook, and SharePoint, Microsoft Project empowers project teams to streamline communication, data management, and collaboration. This section explores the intricacies of integrating Microsoft Project with

Excel, Outlook, and SharePoint, unlocking a myriad of possibilities for project management efficiency.

Excel Integration

Excel is a ubiquitous tool for data analysis and reporting, making it an invaluable asset for project managers seeking to visualize and manipulate project data. Microsoft Project offers robust integration capabilities with Excel, facilitating seamless data exchange between the two applications. Here's how you can harness the power of Excel integration within Microsoft Project:

1. Exporting Data to Excel: Microsoft Project enables users to export project data to Excel effortlessly. This feature allows project managers to generate customized reports, perform in-depth analysis, and present information in a format tailored to their stakeholders' needs. Whether it's task lists, resource allocations, or Gantt charts, exporting data to Excel provides flexibility and agility in data management.

2. Creating Dynamic Dashboards: Excel's flexibility in creating dynamic charts and graphs complements Microsoft Project's project tracking capabilities. By exporting project data to Excel, project managers can create interactive dashboards that visualize key performance indicators, project milestones, and resource utilization. These dashboards not only enhance project monitoring but also facilitate informed decision-making by presenting data in a visually appealing format.

3. Performing Advanced Analysis: Excel's robust calculation features empower project managers to perform advanced analysis on project data exported from Microsoft Project. Whether it's forecasting project timelines, analyzing resource constraints, or conducting scenario planning, Excel's analytical capabilities augment Microsoft Project's functionality, enabling comprehensive project management.

4. Synchronization: Microsoft Project offers seamless synchronization with Excel, ensuring that project data exported to Excel remains up-to-date. This synchronization mechanism eliminates the need for manual data updates, minimizing errors and enhancing data integrity across both platforms. Project managers can leverage this feature to maintain consistency between their project plans in Microsoft Project and their analytical models in Excel.

Outlook Integration

Email communication plays a pivotal role in project management, facilitating collaboration, task assignment, and progress tracking among project stakeholders. Microsoft Project's integration with Outlook streamlines email communication within the project management framework, fostering efficient collaboration and information exchange. Here's how you can leverage Outlook integration within Microsoft Project:

1. Task Assignment and Reminders: Microsoft Project allows project managers to seamlessly assign tasks to team members directly from within the application. By integrating with Outlook, assigned tasks are automatically synchronized with team members' Outlook calendars and task lists. This integration ensures that team members receive timely notifications and reminders about upcoming tasks, promoting accountability and adherence to project timelines.

2. Meeting Scheduling: Microsoft Project enables project managers to schedule project-related meetings and appointments directly within the application. By integrating with Outlook's calendar functionality, project meetings are automatically synchronized with participants' Outlook calendars, eliminating the need for manual scheduling and reducing scheduling conflicts. This integration enhances communication and coordination among project team members, ensuring that meetings are convened efficiently and attended by relevant stakeholders.

3. Email Notifications: Microsoft Project offers the ability to configure email notifications for project-related events such as task assignments, deadline changes, or budget updates. By integrating with Outlook, these email notifications are seamlessly delivered to project stakeholders' Outlook inboxes, keeping them informed about project developments in real-time. This integration enhances communication transparency and ensures that stakeholders stay engaged and informed throughout the project lifecycle.

4. Status Updates: Microsoft Project allows team members to provide status updates on their assigned tasks directly within the application. By integrating with Outlook, these status updates can be automatically communicated to project managers and relevant stakeholders via email. This integration streamlines the status reporting process, ensuring that project managers have real-time visibility into task progress and can proactively address any issues or delays.

5. Document Sharing: Outlook integration facilitates seamless document sharing among project team members. Microsoft Project enables users to attach project-related documents, such as schedules, reports, or meeting agendas, to project-related emails sent via Outlook. This integration centralizes document management within the project management framework, ensuring that all project-related communication and documentation are easily accessible to team members.

SharePoint Integration

SharePoint serves as a centralized hub for document management, collaboration, and information sharing within organizations. Microsoft Project's integration with SharePoint enhances project team collaboration and document management by providing seamless access to project-related resources. Here's how you can leverage SharePoint integration within Microsoft Project:

1. Document Repository: Microsoft Project allows project managers to create a SharePoint site dedicated to the project, serving as a centralized repository for project-related documents, files, and resources. This integration enables project team members to access, share, and collaborate on project documents in real-time, regardless of their location or device.

2. Version Control: SharePoint's version control capabilities ensure that project documents stored within the SharePoint site remain organized and up-to-date. Microsoft Project automatically syncs project-related documents with the SharePoint site, enabling team members to access the latest versions of documents and track changes effectively. This integration minimizes versioning issues and enhances document traceability throughout the project lifecycle.

3. Collaborative Workspaces: SharePoint integration facilitates the creation of collaborative workspaces within the project SharePoint site, allowing team members to collaborate on documents, participate in discussions, and share updates in a centralized environment. Microsoft Project provides seamless access to these collaborative workspaces, promoting teamwork, knowledge sharing, and cross-functional collaboration among project stakeholders.

4. Task Management: SharePoint integration enables project managers to create and manage project tasks directly within the SharePoint site. Microsoft Project syncs project tasks with the SharePoint task list, allowing team members to view, update, and track task progress within the familiar SharePoint interface. This integration enhances task visibility and accountability, empowering project managers to effectively manage project workflows and dependencies.

5. Integration with Project Portfolios: SharePoint serves as a platform for managing project portfolios, providing project managers with comprehensive visibility and governance over multiple projects within an organization. Microsoft Project's integration with SharePoint extends to project portfolio management, enabling seamless integration and

synchronization of project data between the two platforms. Here's how you can leverage SharePoint integration for project portfolio management within Microsoft Project:

1. Portfolio Dashboards: SharePoint integration allows project managers to create interactive portfolio dashboards within the SharePoint site, providing stakeholders with a centralized view of project portfolios, key performance indicators, and strategic objectives. Microsoft Project seamlessly syncs project data with the SharePoint dashboard, enabling stakeholders to monitor portfolio health, track progress, and make informed decisions regarding resource allocation and prioritization.

2. Resource Management: SharePoint integration enhances resource management capabilities within Microsoft Project by providing access to centralized resource pools and allocation calendars. Project managers can leverage SharePoint's resource management features to identify resource availability, allocate resources to projects, and track resource utilization across the portfolio. This integration facilitates efficient resource allocation and optimization, ensuring that projects are adequately staffed and resourced to meet organizational objectives.

3. Risk and Issue Management: SharePoint serves as a platform for managing project risks and issues, providing project managers with tools to identify, assess, and mitigate project-related risks. Microsoft Project seamlessly integrates with SharePoint's risk and issue management capabilities, allowing project managers to link project tasks, milestones, and deliverables to corresponding risks and issues within the SharePoint site. This integration enhances risk visibility and facilitates proactive risk management across the project portfolio.

4. Document Collaboration: SharePoint integration enables seamless document collaboration and version control within the project portfolio. Microsoft Project syncs project-related documents with SharePoint document libraries, providing project team members with centralized access to project documentation, templates, and best practices. This integration promotes collaboration, knowledge sharing, and document traceability across the project portfolio, enhancing productivity and reducing duplication of effort.

5. Project Governance: SharePoint serves as a platform for establishing project governance frameworks and workflows, ensuring that projects adhere to organizational standards and policies. Microsoft Project integrates with SharePoint's governance features, allowing project managers to define project workflows, approval processes, and governance gates within the SharePoint site. This integration facilitates consistent project governance, compliance, and accountability across the project portfolio, fostering alignment with organizational objectives and regulatory requirements.

6. Issue Tracking and Resolution: SharePoint integration enhances issue tracking and resolution within Microsoft Project by providing a centralized platform for logging, tracking, and resolving project issues. Project managers can leverage SharePoint's issue tracking capabilities to create issue logs, assign ownership, and track resolution status across the project portfolio. This integration promotes transparency, accountability, and timely resolution of project issues, mitigating potential risks and disruptions to project delivery.

7. Collaborative Decision-making: SharePoint integration facilitates collaborative decision-making within the project portfolio by providing tools for capturing, documenting, and reviewing key decisions. Microsoft Project seamlessly syncs decision records with SharePoint decision repositories, enabling stakeholders to access decision documentation, rationale, and outcomes within the SharePoint site. This integration promotes transparency, consensus-building, and accountability in decision-making processes across the project portfolio.

8. Performance Reporting: SharePoint serves as a platform for generating and distributing project performance reports to stakeholders within the organization. Microsoft Project integrates with SharePoint's reporting capabilities, allowing project managers to create customized performance reports, dashboards, and scorecards within the SharePoint site. This integration enables stakeholders to access real-time project performance metrics, track progress against objectives, and make data-driven decisions to optimize project outcomes.

9. Integration with Project Management Methodologies: SharePoint integration extends to supporting various project management methodologies, such as Agile, Waterfall, and Hybrid approaches. Microsoft Project seamlessly integrates with SharePoint's project management templates, workflows, and methodologies, enabling project managers to align project execution with organizational standards and best practices. This integration enhances consistency, efficiency, and scalability in project delivery, regardless of the chosen methodology.

10. Collaborative Project Planning: SharePoint integration enhances collaborative project planning within Microsoft Project by providing tools for collecting input, feedback, and approvals from project stakeholders. Project managers can leverage SharePoint's collaborative features to engage stakeholders in the planning process, gather requirements, and solicit feedback on project scope, schedules, and resource allocations. This integration promotes stakeholder engagement, buy-in, and alignment with project objectives, fostering a culture of collaboration and transparency.

In conclusion, Microsoft Project's integration with Excel, Outlook, and SharePoint empowers project managers with robust capabilities for data analysis, communication, collaboration, and information management. By seamlessly connecting with widely-used Office applications and collaboration platforms, Microsoft Project enhances project management efficiency, transparency, and effectiveness, enabling project teams to achieve their goals with greater agility and confidence.

8.3 Syncing with Project Management Tools

In today's diverse project management landscape, utilizing a single tool to manage all aspects of a project is often impractical. Teams may find themselves using a combination of specialized tools tailored to their unique needs, from Agile project management platforms to issue tracking systems. Therefore, integrating Microsoft Project with third-party tools becomes essential for seamless collaboration and data synchronization across the project lifecycle.

8.3.1. Third-party Tool Integration

Integrating Microsoft Project with third-party tools extends its functionality and enables project managers to leverage the strengths of different platforms. Whether it's Agile development, resource management, or issue tracking, there are numerous tools available in the market that can complement Microsoft Project's capabilities. Let's explore some common integrations and how they enhance project management workflows.

1. Agile Project Management Tools

Agile methodologies, characterized by iterative development and adaptive planning, have become increasingly popular in software development and beyond. Tools like Jira, Trello, and Asana provide features tailored to Agile teams, such as user stories, sprints, and Kanban boards. Integrating Microsoft Project with these tools allows project managers to incorporate Agile practices into their traditional project management approach.

Benefits of Integration:

- Seamless Data Synchronization: Integration ensures that project tasks, timelines, and resource allocations remain synchronized between Microsoft Project and the Agile tool.

This enables real-time visibility into project progress for stakeholders across both platforms.

- Flexibility in Methodologies: Teams can leverage Agile methodologies within Microsoft Project, benefiting from its robust scheduling and resource management capabilities while adhering to Agile principles. This hybrid approach caters to diverse project requirements and team preferences.

- Enhanced Collaboration: By bridging the gap between Agile teams and other project stakeholders, integration fosters collaboration and transparency. Project managers can track Agile progress within the context of the overall project plan, facilitating informed decision-making.

2. Resource Management Platforms

Effective resource management is crucial for project success, ensuring that the right resources are allocated to tasks at the right time. Resource management platforms like ResourceGuru and Float provide features for scheduling, capacity planning, and resource allocation. Integrating these tools with Microsoft Project enables seamless coordination between project planning and resource management efforts.

Benefits of Integration:

- Optimized Resource Utilization: Integration allows project managers to access real-time resource availability and allocations from within Microsoft Project. This facilitates informed decision-making during project planning and scheduling, minimizing resource conflicts and bottlenecks.

- Streamlined Workflows: By centralizing project plans and resource data, integration streamlines workflows and reduces manual effort. Project managers can allocate resources directly from within Microsoft Project, eliminating the need for duplicate data entry and ensuring data accuracy.

- Improved Forecasting: Integrated resource management data enhances forecasting capabilities within Microsoft Project, enabling proactive resource planning and allocation.

Project managers can anticipate resource requirements based on project timelines and adjust plans accordingly to mitigate risks.

3. Issue Tracking Systems

Identifying and resolving issues in a timely manner is essential for project success. Issue tracking systems like Atlassian's Jira and Microsoft's own Azure DevOps provide features for logging, prioritizing, and tracking project issues. Integrating these systems with Microsoft Project enables seamless coordination between project planning and issue resolution activities.

Benefits of Integration:

- End-to-End Visibility: Integration allows project managers to track issues identified in external systems within the context of the overall project plan in Microsoft Project. This provides stakeholders with a comprehensive view of project progress and potential roadblocks, facilitating proactive decision-making.

- Efficient Issue Resolution: Integrated issue tracking data enables project managers to prioritize and assign tasks directly within Microsoft Project, streamlining the issue resolution process. Teams can collaborate more effectively on issue resolution activities, ensuring timely resolution and minimizing project delays.

- Improved Traceability: By linking project tasks to related issues in external tracking systems, integration enhances traceability and accountability throughout the project lifecycle. Project managers can easily trace the impact of issues on project tasks and adjust plans accordingly to mitigate risks.

Conclusion

Integrating Microsoft Project with third-party project management tools enhances collaboration, improves data synchronization, and streamlines workflows across the project lifecycle. Whether it's Agile project management, resource allocation, or issue tracking, integration enables project managers to leverage the strengths of different platforms while maintaining a centralized view of project progress. By embracing interoperability, organizations can optimize their project management processes and drive successful project outcomes.

8.3.2. Syncing with Agile and Kanban Tools

In today's fast-paced project management landscape, Agile and Kanban methodologies have gained significant traction for their adaptability and efficiency in handling complex projects. Microsoft Project acknowledges the importance of integrating with these methodologies to provide project managers with a comprehensive toolkit. Syncing Microsoft Project with Agile and Kanban tools streamlines workflows, enhances collaboration, and ensures seamless communication across teams following different project management methodologies.

Understanding Agile and Kanban Methodologies

Before delving into the integration process, let's briefly revisit Agile and Kanban methodologies to grasp their fundamental principles:

Agile Methodology: Agile is an iterative approach to project management that focuses on delivering high-quality products or services incrementally. It emphasizes adaptability to change, customer collaboration, and continuous improvement. Agile methodologies, such as Scrum and Extreme Programming (XP), break down projects into smaller tasks or user stories, which are completed within short time frames known as sprints.

Kanban Methodology: Kanban, originating from Japanese manufacturing practices, is a visual framework for managing work as it moves through a process. Unlike Agile, Kanban doesn't prescribe specific roles or time frames. Instead, it emphasizes visualizing workflow, limiting work in progress (WIP), and continuously improving the process. Work items are represented as cards on a Kanban board, which move through various stages from inception to completion.

Benefits of Syncing Microsoft Project with Agile and Kanban Tools

Integrating Microsoft Project with Agile and Kanban tools offers several benefits:

1. Improved Visibility: By syncing Microsoft Project with Agile and Kanban tools, project managers gain enhanced visibility into project progress, resource allocation, and task dependencies. They can track work items across different methodologies from a centralized dashboard, fostering transparency and informed decision-making.

2. Enhanced Collaboration: Integration facilitates seamless collaboration between teams following different project management methodologies. Team members can access and update project data in real-time, irrespective of their preferred methodology, fostering cross-functional collaboration and synergy.

3. Increased Flexibility: Syncing Microsoft Project with Agile and Kanban tools enables project managers to leverage the flexibility and adaptability of these methodologies while benefiting from the comprehensive planning and scheduling features of Microsoft Project. It allows for dynamic adjustment to changing requirements and priorities without compromising on project governance.

4. Streamlined Workflow: Integration streamlines the workflow by eliminating silos and redundant data entry. Changes made in one system automatically reflect in others, reducing manual effort and minimizing the risk of errors or discrepancies. This seamless data flow accelerates project delivery and improves overall efficiency.

Integration Options for Agile and Kanban Tools

Microsoft Project offers various integration options to sync with popular Agile and Kanban tools, including but not limited to:

1. Azure DevOps (formerly Visual Studio Team Services): Azure DevOps is a comprehensive suite of Agile tools that facilitates collaboration, continuous integration, and delivery. Integration with Microsoft Project allows for seamless synchronization of project plans, tasks, and timelines with Azure DevOps work items, epics, and backlogs.

2. Jira: Jira is a widely used Agile project management tool that enables teams to plan, track, and release software efficiently. Integration with Microsoft Project enables bidirectional synchronization of project data, enabling stakeholders to visualize Jira issues, epics, and sprints within Microsoft Project and vice versa.

3. Trello: Trello is a popular Kanban-style project management tool known for its simplicity and flexibility. Integration with Microsoft Project enables project managers to map Trello boards, cards, and lists to Microsoft Project tasks, providing a unified view of project progress and status.

4. LeanKit: LeanKit is a Kanban software that helps teams visualize work, optimize processes, and improve productivity. Integration with Microsoft Project enables seamless synchronization of LeanKit boards, lanes, and cards with Microsoft Project tasks, facilitating cross-methodology collaboration and alignment.

Best Practices for Syncing Microsoft Project with Agile and Kanban Tools

To ensure successful integration and maximize the benefits of syncing Microsoft Project with Agile and Kanban tools, consider the following best practices:

1. Define Clear Workflows: Establish clear workflows and mapping strategies to align Microsoft Project tasks with Agile user stories or Kanban cards. Define how tasks, epics, sprints, and releases in Agile tools correspond to phases, milestones, and deliverables in Microsoft Project.

2. Maintain Data Consistency: Ensure data consistency and integrity across integrated systems by establishing rules for data synchronization, including field mappings, data validation, and conflict resolution mechanisms. Regularly audit and reconcile discrepancies to prevent data inconsistencies.

3. Provide Training and Support: Offer comprehensive training and support to users on how to leverage the integrated environment effectively. Provide resources, tutorials, and documentation to help users navigate seamlessly between Microsoft Project and Agile/Kanban tools.

4. Encourage Collaboration: Foster a culture of collaboration and communication among team members across different methodologies. Encourage cross-functional teams to share insights, updates, and feedback within the integrated environment to drive alignment and synergy.

5. Iterate and Improve: Continuously iterate and improve the integration process based on feedback, lessons learned, and evolving project requirements. Solicit input from stakeholders and end-users to identify pain points, bottlenecks, and areas for enhancement, and incorporate them into future iterations.

Conclusion

Syncing Microsoft Project with Agile and Kanban tools empowers project managers to harness the strengths of diverse methodologies while leveraging the robust planning and scheduling capabilities of Microsoft Project. By fostering collaboration, enhancing visibility, and streamlining workflows, integration enables organizations to deliver projects more efficiently and effectively in today's dynamic business environment. Embrace the power of integration to unlock new possibilities and propel your projects to success.

Conclusion

In conclusion, mastering Microsoft Project is an essential skill for project managers seeking to streamline their project planning, execution, and monitoring processes. Throughout this comprehensive guide, we have delved into the core features and functionalities of Microsoft Project, exploring its capabilities in detail.

We began by understanding the importance of project management software in today's dynamic business environment and the specific benefits that Microsoft Project offers. From its intuitive interface to its robust scheduling engine, Microsoft Project provides project managers with the tools they need to effectively plan, execute, and track their projects from start to finish.

Next, we explored the fundamental concepts of project management, including project scope, scheduling, resource allocation, and risk management, and discussed how Microsoft Project facilitates each of these processes. By leveraging features such as task dependencies, Gantt charts, resource leveling, and built-in reporting tools, project managers can create detailed project plans and ensure that tasks are completed on time and within budget.

We then delved into more advanced topics, such as managing multiple projects, collaborating with team members, and integrating Microsoft Project with other tools and systems. Whether working on a single project or overseeing a portfolio of initiatives, Microsoft Project provides the flexibility and scalability needed to meet the unique requirements of any project environment.

Throughout our exploration, we have highlighted best practices and tips for maximizing the effectiveness of Microsoft Project, from setting up project templates to optimizing resource utilization and resolving scheduling conflicts. By following these guidelines, project managers can harness the full power of Microsoft Project to drive project success and deliver value to their organizations.

However, mastering Microsoft Project is not just about mastering the software itself; it also requires developing strong project management skills and practices. Effective communication, stakeholder engagement, risk mitigation, and decision-making are essential components of successful project management, and Microsoft Project serves as a valuable tool in supporting these activities.

As technology continues to evolve and new project management methodologies emerge, the role of Microsoft Project in the project management landscape will likely continue to evolve as well. From agile project management to hybrid methodologies, Microsoft Project must adapt to meet the changing needs of project managers and organizations.

In conclusion, mastering Microsoft Project is an ongoing journey that requires dedication, practice, and continuous learning. By embracing the principles and techniques outlined in this guide and leveraging the capabilities of Microsoft Project to their fullest extent, project managers can become more effective leaders and drive greater project success in their organizations.

Thank you for joining us on this journey through the world of Microsoft Project. We hope that this guide has provided you with valuable insights and practical knowledge that you can apply to your own projects. Here's to your success in mastering Microsoft Project and achieving your project management goals!